Jules Bonavolonta

Former Special Agent

and Brian Duffy

THE
GOOD GUYS

How We Turned the FBI 'Round—and Finally Broke the Mob

SIMON & SCHUSTER
New York   London   Toronto   Sydney   Tokyo   Singapore

SIMON & SCHUSTER
Rockefeller Center
1230 Avenue of the Americas
New York, NY 10020

Designed by Irving Perkins Associates, Inc.

Manufactured in the United States of America

10 9 8 7 6 5 4 3 2 1

Library of Congress Cataloging-in-Publication Data
Bonavolonta, Jules.
   The good guys : how we turned the FBI 'round—and finally broke
the mob / Jules Bonavolonta and Brian Duffy.
       p.   cm.
   1. Bonavolonta, Jules.   2. United States. Federal Bureau of
Investigation—Officials and employees—Biography.   3. Organized crime
investigation—New York (N.Y.)   4. Mafia—New York (N.Y.)—
History—20th century.   I. Duffy, Brian.   II. Title.
HV7911.B645A3   1996
363.2'092—dc20   95-31357
[B]
ISBN 0-684-81015-8

For Linda, whose unselfish love
through so many obstacles
allowed me to do what had to be done.
I'll love you always.

Acknowledgments

THIS book could not have been written without the unselfish help of so many friends. Many of them are quoted in the text, but many others, who were not quoted, were no less helpful. While it would be impossible to mention them all, it would be negligent to ignore some.

It goes without saying that no book would be possible without the nurturing support of my parents—Ralph and Mary Bonavolonta—whose love and guidance carried me through many tumultuous and, at times, perilous years.

While the cooperation of so many friends and colleagues from the FBI and Justice Department was invaluable, and the list is too numerous to mention in its entirety, several must be mentioned for the significance of their input. My deepest gratitude for their assistance, recollections, humor, and support through "the decade" goes out to Jim Kallstrom, Jim Kossler, Joe Pistone, Barbara Jones, Bruce Mouw, Lou Schiliro, Brian Taylor, Pat Marshall, Sean McWeeney, Neil Welch, Joe Valiquette, Bill Doran, Mike Chertoff, and Laura Ward.

For all those to whom I spoke and unfortunately have no room to mention—you know who you are—please accept my sincere apologies.

To Bob Blakey—thanks for your vision, patience, and stubbornness. Without you, none of this would have been possible. I hope we did you proud.

To my editor, Michael Korda—thank you for your perseverance, involvement, and enthusiasm in the face of overwhelming personal concerns. We both know how easy it would have been to take this book off the table. You are a true "stand-up" guy.

And finally, to Linda, Maria, and Joe, who have always been, and who always will be, a constant source of pride and strength for me. They were always there, especially during the toughest times, ensuring that I kept everything in proper perspective and my priorities in order. I love you all.

Prologue

THE phone rang once. I rolled out of the warm bed and caught the receiver before I hit the floor. I had the maneuver down cold, but I guess I should have: I got lots of calls at three or four in the morning.

"Yeah?" I looked at my watch: two-thirty. Not so bad.

"Hey, I hope I'm not interrupting anything."

"Wiseass." No matter the hour, it was always good to hear from Pistone. I tried to make myself comfortable against the side of the bed and kept my voice low so that I didn't wake Linda.

Joe Pistone led a complicated life. For one thing, he had two names. There was the one his parents gave him, little Joey. Then there was the one the FBI gave him, Donnie Brasco. Donnie Brasco was a punk and a liar whose résumé, if he'd had one, would have described him as a so-so jewel thief.

Donnie was scum. But he was also one of my best friends.

Or I should say Joe Pistone was.

Anyway, because I never knew who might be listening in or whether some bright guy on the other end might have a gun in Joe's ear when he phoned home in the middle of the night, I made sure always to call him Donnie. It was a good habit.

He never slipped up, and neither did I. As a result, Pistone had had quite an amazing run. Not only had no one tried to kill him yet, but the mopes and wise guys Pistone was running with had come to look on him like a brother, one of their own.

An amazing thing.

For the record, as they say, Joe Pistone was the most successful undercover agent the FBI had ever had—bar none. At the time of his phone call to me, Joe had been working undercover against the Italian Mafia for more than six years.

That's six years of living a crazy double life, six years living alongside some of the most violent criminals on earth. And some of the sleaziest, too, if you want to know the truth. It was a hell of a strain, but Pistone never said a word. He was one of the toughest guys I have ever known, and I've known a few. I was damned proud of him.

But I was also worried.

Nine days before his call, on May 5, 1981, three major players in New York's complicated organized-crime scene had been murdered. "Whacked," to use the wise guys' term. Alphonse Indelicato, Dominick Trinchera, and Philip Giaccone were capos in the Bonanno family. A rival branch of the Bonannos had pulled the hit: shotguns and rifles, several dozen rounds. The wise guys had used a chain saw to cut up fat Trinchera's bloated corpse.

Some family.

Personally, I didn't give a shit. The world would be a little better off for the loss of those assholes.

What I was worried about was Joe. He had gotten himself inside the Bonannos, right at the top of the family. But now the Bonannos had gone to battle stations.

I was following the war closely. And I was scared to death Pistone would be drafted. That's why it was so good to hear his voice. "What's up, Donnie?" I asked.

"I got a call from Lefty today."

Benjamin "Lefty Guns" Ruggiero was another human being whose absence from the planet would have made it a nicer place to live. Lefty was high up in the Bonannos, very close to Dominick "Sonny Black" Napolitano. Sonny Black was the acting boss of the Bonannos.

"What did Lefty say?" I heard my wife stir under the covers, and I cupped my hand tighter around the phone.

"He told me that Bruno's down in Florida. He says I should try to find him."

This was definitely not good news. When the three Bonanno capos had gotten themselves murdered the week before, the shooters had missed a fourth Bonanno, Anthony Bruno Indelicato. I had a good guess what was coming next. "So what are you supposed to do when you find our friend Bruno, Donnie?"

Pistone sighed. "I'm supposed to find him, whack him, and leave his body right in the street where I do him."

I thought about the implications of this for a moment. Special Agent Joseph Pistone, working undercover for the Federal Bureau of Investigation, had just been given a contract to carry out a Mafia hit. This was a definite first. It was also, if you think about it a minute, a hell of a thing.

I tried to imagine Pistone on the other end of the line, beat after a long day and night with the wise guys, looking over his shoulder in some crummy pay phone.

When I didn't say anything for a few seconds, Pistone asked the obvious question. "So, uh, what do you want me to do?"

"Do?" I looked over at Linda, and she was sleeping soundly again. I was thinking a thousand thoughts, but first I had to think about Joe, take his temperature, make sure he was okay. "That's easy, Donnie. First, you find Bruno, then you whack him, then you leave his body in the street. Just like they told you."

There was maybe half a minute of silence before Pistone found his voice. "What did you say?"

"Forget about it." I laughed. "I'm just trying to add a little humor to your life, okay?"

Wherever the hell he was, Pistone laughed, too.

We talked a few more minutes before he finally hung up. By then I knew I'd never get back to sleep. Joe was in a tight spot, and there was a lot to do in the next twenty-four hours. For both of us, though, this was a once-in-a-lifetime shot.

As everyone knows, the FBI had this reputation: the most powerful law enforcement agency in the world. I suppose it was true, but it was also bullshit, in some ways at least. Sure, we got our bank robbers, our pimps and gamblers. But against the truly organized criminals, the syndicates that controlled the construction gangs, the restaurants, the docks—the guys who added a fat percentage to the cost of living for most, if not all, Americans —we had screwed up big time. It wasn't that the FBI had missed its shots at the top guys; it had never *taken* them.

Now—maybe—it could be different.

With Pistone and a few like-minded brothers and sisters in arms, I had fought the Mafia to something approaching a draw in New York, which was where the battle against the mob would ultimately be won or lost. But I had fought another war, too— against the FBI itself. I had angered good friends and trusted colleagues. I had made myself more than a few powerful enemies.

I had made my family suffer, too, and God knows I wasn't proud of that.

Now, possibly, some of those debts might be redeemed.

As I waited for the dawn, I roamed the house from room to room. It was a good home. Linda was really happy, finally. Maria and Joey, too. They were two great kids.

I was blessed that way.

For years, though, I had thrown myself at the job first. Linda and the kids had gotten the backseat.

The next few weeks, I knew, would be more of the same; after that, though, it would be better. It had to be.

The sun was nearly up when I went back over the conversation with Pistone for the last time.

With your closest friends you never wonder, you know? You can tell it, the nervousness, the exhilaration, whatever. It's almost like communicating without words. That's the way it was with me and Pistone, anyway. Both of us knew that the next few days would be crazy. While Joe would be pretending to look for Bruno so he could whack him and leave him in the street, a bunch of other guys would be looking for Joe so they could whack him and leave him in the street. The only difference between Joe and the other guys was that the other guys wouldn't be faking it. So if it's a cliché, perhaps you'll forgive me, but my friend's life was on the line, and I had to do whatever it took to make sure he didn't get killed. Still, when we hung up the phone, two Italian-American nobodies from nowhere, we were laughing.

We were laughing pretty hard actually.

Sometimes it really does help to laugh; sometimes, if you don't, you can make yourself pretty seriously crazy.

PART ONE

PART ONE

1

WHAT I remember very early—not my first memories but probably the most unsettling—was the arguments. I was maybe seven at the time, and my job was to help out at the store. That's what we called the tailor shop my father was finally able to open in Newark, New Jersey, which is where I was born.

His full name is Ralph Louis Bonavolonta. He's eighty-two now, still going strong, thank God. Still makes all my suits, too, in fact. Beautiful stuff.

When he got to the United States, my father was a sixteen-year-old kid, all by himself. Didn't speak a word of English. He landed in New York on November 3, 1929, just a few days after the stock market crash. Perfect timing, right? He still tells the story: "One of the first things I start hearing about is people jumping out of windows, breadlines. I'm saying to myself, How the hell am I going to make any money? I thought this was the land of golden opportunity."

Eventually, he did open the tailor shop, and that's when the arguments I was talking about started. I didn't know what the hell was going on, but guys would come in and talk to him, and then he would say something to my mother in Italian, and he would be all upset and bothered. It upset me to see them like that, my parents, but when I got a little older, my father told me what these guys were up to.

What they were up to was extortion.

That's what all the screaming between him and these guys was about. There was a lot of cursing, but my father never paid a dime. He didn't have the money, and that was the truth. I knew because after school I had to come in and run the shop.

My father had three jobs, and he'd leave for the second one at three-thirty, when I arrived. I would take care of any customers who came in, and sometimes I'd have to go into the cash box then. I tell you, if he had five dollars in there, it was a lot of money. Looking back, I wonder how the hell we paid the rent.

Anyway, my first exposure to the Mafia was when these guys came in demanding money. As I got older, my father told me more about some of the stuff he had seen back in Italy. He was from a little town just north of Naples, and he'd tell me how these guys there were so powerful and some of the things they would do, the beatings they would give people.

I heard more from my family. In Newark on Sundays, my father and my uncles would sit for hours while the women cooked inside. The food was great—pastas, meats, sauces. Anyway, while the women cooked, the men talked, and the talk always turned sooner or later to the Mafia. This guy was mafioso, these mafiosi controlled this, these other guys controlled that, some other mafiosi controlled a politician.

My father would spit when he heard the stories. He hated the Mafia; me, I was fascinated.

"Where are the cops?" I asked.

"What cops? They own the cops."

Years later, in high school and college, I read about a lot of great Italians. People like da Vinci, Michelangelo, Marconi, Verdi, Mayor Fiorello La Guardia, Joe DiMaggio. These people were my parents' heroes. For a lot of Americans, though, Italians were scum—criminals and murderers.

And that's what we had to put up with.

In high school I worked for a while as a delivery boy, traveling back and forth between Newark and Manhattan. The guy I worked for asked me once what I wanted to do when I grew up.

"Haven't given it much thought," I said. "Maybe I can play ball for the Yankees."

The guy laughed. "Don't worry about it, kid," he said. "A guy like you can always get a job with the mob."

Asshole, I thought.

College finally gave me a way out. Or I guess I should say the military did, really. Which is kind of strange when I think about it now, since when I went in, the shit in Vietnam was just about to really begin hitting the fan.

But I wanted to go in. I really did.

I was one of only three members of my graduating class at Seton Hall University to be awarded a regular army commission, which meant I went in as a second lieutenant platoon leader with the opportunity to make the army a career.

So they ship me right out from graduation down to Fort Campbell, Kentucky, where I hook up with the 101st Airborne. And here I come, a twenty-one-year-old, wet-behind-the-ears kid, and I'm going to lead a platoon of ass-kicking army paratroopers. And me, I'm a nonjumper—a virgin, so to speak. So the question occurs to you: How the hell am I going to *do* this? Luckily, the platoon sergeant—he had thirty years in—grabbed me, pulled me aside, and showed me the ropes.

Things worked out all right after that.

Vietnam, as everyone now knows, was for shit. And I saw just about the shittiest part of it. It shaped me probably more than anything else in my life—influenced the way I thought about life and the way I would approach things later on in the FBI.

Before Vietnam, though, was Germany, and that was definitely the best thing that happened, because that's where I met Linda, something I very nearly screwed up.

After about a year and a half with the 101st, I had moved on to Special Forces, the Green Berets. They had sent me to Germany then, where I was assigned to the Tenth Special Forces Group. We were in a place called Bad Tölz, a beautiful little town just south of Munich. I was what we called an A-Team leader, training the other guys in unconventional warfare. Since I had picked up a black belt in karate—I had been fascinated with martial arts since I was about seventeen and had trained almost religiously through high school and college—in addition to being an A-Team leader, my superiors also had me teaching martial arts and hand-to-hand combat at night.

It was a lot of fun, but in the back of our minds, some of us knew that the training might come in handy one day soon. We were hearing the stories coming out of Vietnam, and we were certainly reading stuff in the newspapers. From everything we were picking up, it sounded messy. Extremely messy.

I was ambitious, though; maybe some would say stupid. But there was a war going on, and I was determined to go, Linda or no Linda. She was a ski instructor, and after an unbelievably bumpy start, we had started going out. It wasn't too long after that Linda and I realized we really loved each other. I wanted to discuss the subject of marriage, but I was never very good at that kind of thing. Besides—and this is where some people would call me headstrong or whatever—I wanted to be totally focused on what I was doing when I got to Vietnam. That meant, for me at least, not thinking about a wife back home.

"Why do you have to go to Vietnam?" Linda asked me one day not too long before I left. "It's a stupid war, anyway."

I said I was being transferred. "There's nothing I can do."

A few days after I left, one of the assholes who tried to hit on her told Linda the truth: I had asked for the transfer to Vietnam. I had volunteered to go.

In Vietnam, I was lucky for a million and one reasons. One of the biggest, though, was that with all the shit going on around me, I didn't have a hell of a lot of time to wonder what Linda thought about my stupid lie.

2

ON the morning of October 21, 1968, I signed in at the FBI Academy in Quantico, Virginia, one of thirty-five men assigned to new agent class six. That's NAC-6, in FBI-speak.

I couldn't believe my good fortune. Linda had waited for me, after all, and we had just been married. Now I had been accepted as a special agent of the FBI. Though I had always planned on a life in the military, this seemed like a dream come true.

It also—hindsight is a wonderful thing, isn't it?—seemed like the thing I was really meant to do. I remember that when a friend first broached the idea of leaving Special Forces for the Bureau, I said, "Yeah, it could be interesting. It would give me a chance to bust some of these Mafia hoods who are giving my people such a bad name."

That's about as much of an idea as I had as I signed onto the NAC-6 class, but it was enough, I suppose, to start me drifting toward the area of organized-crime investigations. Even I knew back then that the FBI was asleep at the switch when it came to fighting organized crime. For years, Hoover had denied there even was any organized crime. Then local police in upstate New York raided a big meeting of Mafia bosses in Apalachin, New York, and Hoover had been forced to change his tune.

That was in 1957, but eleven years later, from everything I could tell, things in the FBI had not changed much.

There were some bright spots, though. For me, probably the best part of the training at Quantico was a course taught by a veteran FBI agent named Jim Flynn.

Flynn had been the handler for Joe Valachi, the first Mafia hood ever to turn against the Cosa Nostra. The Valachi story appealed to me immensely. From what I could see, it looked like the Bureau was trying to do just what I had done in Vietnam—infiltrate the ranks of the enemy, get behind their lines, find out how they operated, then neutralize them.

After Flynn finished teaching his first day of class with me and my NAC-6 colleagues, I walked up and asked him about Valachi. I was fascinated. What kind of guy was he?

Flynn told some good stories. Valachi was lonely, Flynn replied, a killer—and a real dumb-ass. "Really, he just wanted to talk to someone. We would sit in the jail cell and eat cheese and drink some wine and just talk for hours."

What about working undercover, I asked. Was the Bureau out there now trying to recruit more Valachis?

Flynn was a hell of a nice guy, but his answer wasn't very encouraging. In fact, it wasn't much of an answer at all.

I finished up the NAC-6 class thirteen weeks later fired with enthusiasm but also with a small bloom of doubt flowering in my chest. Please, I prayed, don't let this be like Vietnam.

As Linda and I packed up the U-Haul outside our little rented place near the FBI Academy in Quantico, Virginia, I tried to push the doubts out of my mind. I would be getting my first office assignment in a matter of days. Two kids, we were ready to go anywhere the FBI sent us.

Talk about faith.

3

SO they sent us to Atlanta.

One of Hoover's many rules was that new agents always—always—got their first office assignment real far from where they were born and raised. Linda and I knew the deal going in, so fine, we would put up with wherever they sent us; then we're out of there in a quick twelve months.

By then we'd be a shoo-in for New York.

That's where I wanted to go, of course. At Quantico, I had put it down as my O.P.—office of preference. More FBI-speak.

I knew even before I signed in for my first day at the NAC-6 class that New York was where I wanted to be. It wasn't just that I would be close to my family, though that was important, of course. New York was the only place for doing any kind of serious work on organized crime, and that was what I wanted to do. I had made that decision probably the very same moment I decided to join the FBI.

As a special agent, you can do lots of different things in the Bureau. You can chase spies, bust terrorists, do the white-collar stuff; none of that was for me.

For me, the only thing that made any sense at all was working against the Mafia—against the kind of leeches that had preyed on my father as a sixteen-year-old immigrant to America. There were probably better ways of making a career for yourself within the FBI, I guess, but I felt the same way about that as I felt about the stupid Pentagon brass who had done such a great job directing us in Vietnam: I wanted to do what mattered to me, personally. Screw the bureaucratic bullshit.

So we would wait for New York, Linda and I.

It would only take two goddamned years to get there.

In the meantime, our first child, Maria, was born. The date was November 4, 1969, and as luck would have it, I was out making an arrest at the time. I had been detailed to a really important beat—arresting scumbag deserters from the big U.S. Army base at Fort Benning, Georgia.

But the job came first, right?

So on the morning of November 4, I left the house before dawn to arrest another patriot. Linda went into labor a few minutes later. Remember, my beautiful German wife knew no one where we were living; it was Columbus, Georgia, at the time. We had moved four times since getting married, and now Linda was about to give birth to our first child—alone.

Linda drove herself to the hospital, and the docs and nurses hauled her straight from the driver's seat of our beat-up car to a waiting bed in the delivery room. Maria was born forty-five minutes later.

I got there sometime after that.

As far as the family was concerned, it was not exactly a hell of a beginning; I hoped to do better in New York.

Good luck.

By nearly every measure, August 24, 1970, was an extraordinarily lousy day. It was hot and humid, and the streets of New York stunk more than usual, like an overheated sewer.

I could not have been happier.

I had gotten up early for my first day on the job in the FBI's New York field office and kissed Linda and Maria good-bye. Then I left our little apartment in West Orange, New Jersey, and took the train to Hoboken, where I switched to the PATH line to Thirty-third Street in Manhattan. From there I grabbed the BMT subway north to Fifty-ninth Street, where I transferred to the IRT and continued another nine blocks to Sixty-eighth Street.

Door to door, two hours and five minutes.

Not too bad, I figured.

For New York, anyway.

John Malone was the A-DIC in New York at the time. That's what we called the assistant director in charge. At the time, the FBI office in New York was the only one in the country that had an assistant director running the place. That's because the office was so big. And the reason it was so big was because there was so much goddamned crime in the city.

Makes sense, right?

Anyway, I'm ushered into this big corner office, and Malone stands up to greet me. He's a big, handsome guy with a shock of silver hair. Looked more like a banker than a cop, but then a lot of the FBI brass had that look about them.

"Agent Bonavolonta," Malone says, "you're going to be assigned to the Organized Crime Division."

"Yes, sir, thank you, sir." You could have knocked me over with a feather—an exaggeration, but not by much. I mean, the O.C. Division was where I wanted to be, but the Bureau could have put me anywhere they damn well pleased and there wasn't a thing I could have done about it.

"It's a good operation down there, Bonavolonta. They've got some very good stats, and I have every confidence you'll contribute smartly to that number."

"Yes, sir, I'll do my best. Thank you, sir."

Someone escorted me out of the big office a few minutes after that, and I went to find my desk.

After two years in, I was smart enough to know I wasn't going to change the FBI but just dumb enough to give it a shot, anyway. After I left John Malone's office, I was told to report to Dick Baker. He was the special agent in charge of the Criminal Division in the New York office.

In the FBI, SACs are like bishops in the church, which makes a guy like Malone something of a cardinal, I suppose. A SAC like Baker, anyway, wielded enormous power. He had the final say-so on every criminal investigation run by the FBI in New York. That included the white-collar stuff on Wall Street, public corruption at city hall, the works. Dick Baker was a terrific guy, as I would come to find out. But if you screwed up, he was also a guy who would be all over you like a bad suit.

It was with these thoughts in mind, or something very much like them, that I went to find Baker and introduce myself.

If John Malone looked more like a banker than a cop, Dick Baker looked more like a college professor than anything else. He was a tall guy with salt and pepper hair, and as busy as he must have been, he invited me in, and we just started to talk.

At one point, Baker asked me why I was so interested in working organized-crime cases, and I remember giving him a long speech about the wise guys who came into my father's tailor shop near our little house in Newark, the wise guys demanding protection money, my father protesting like mad. With some cops, and even with some FBI agents, there's this kind of quasi-mystical thing between cops and crooks, the hunters and the hunted. Some guys even talk about psychological bonds between the two, about how the criminal actually needs the cop and the cop the criminal, each to legitimize the existence of the other, ratify his importance in the human pecking order, whatever.

As far as I was concerned, that was a load of shit. Criminals were criminals, and the hoods of the Cosa Nostra, in my opinion at least, were the worst of the lot.

Anyway, somewhere along the line, as I was explaining my theory of Mafia scumbags to Mr. Dick Baker, I guess I forgot my vow to keep my big mouth shut, mind my words, and create a good first impression. So there I was, sitting in Baker's office, telling him how I thought the Bureau could really be doing a much better job fighting organized crime. The current effort, I remember saying, could be run a whole lot better. It was at some point during this brilliant soliloquy that the guy who would be my squad supervisor walked into Baker's office.

So much for first impressions.

"Ed Kavanaugh," Baker said, "meet Jules Bonavolonta."

"Pleased to meet you, Mr. Kavanaugh." I shook hands with the supervisory special agent, and we all sat down.

"Ed," Baker said, leaning back in his comfortable chair, "Jules and I have just been discussing the state of the Bureau's efforts against the wise guys."

"Interesting," Kavanaugh said.

"And Jules has been telling me that he believes the best way to get at the wise guys is from within."

Kavanaugh studied me with interest. "And just how would you do that, Jules?"

I considered my words carefully. Here I am less than an hour into my new job and I'm telling my boss and *his* boss how to do their jobs. "Well," I said, trying for a deferential tone, "I think if we put our guy on the street and let him stay there until he was accepted by the wise guys, then eventually maybe he could get inside and begin working his way up the ladder."

"That's very interesting," Baker said. "What type of person would we want to put on the street, Jules?"

"I'd say it would have to be someone right from this area." I didn't want to sound like a cowboy, but I had thought about this a lot. If they were going to give me the chance to say my piece on day one of my new job, fuck it, I was going to make my points clearly and precisely. "I think we would want to have someone out there who knows how to handle himself with these people. A guy who knows how to keep his mouth shut when he's supposed to and who will be very patient while he waits for the right opportunity to present itself."

Kavanaugh interrupted with a question. "Just how long would this person have to wait for his opportunity, Jules?"

"As long as it takes, Mr. Kavanaugh." In for a dime, in for a dollar, I figured. I looked at Baker and Kavanaugh and plunged ahead. "I don't want to make this sound easier than I think it is. It could take quite a long time for someone to become accepted among the wise guys if he's not known by them."

"But after he's accepted," Baker said, "then we've got someone on the inside, right?"

"Exactly."

"And is this something you would like to do, Jules?"

"I think I would like to give it a try, yes, sir."

Baker stretched out his long legs and studied the ceiling. "Let me ask you a question, Jules."

"Sir?"

"Suppose you do get inside one of the families and you're asked to kill one member by another member. What do you do?"

"Well, sir, I would hope to avoid that type of situation, obviously." Suddenly, I felt like I was back in Vietnam again, picking my way through a Vietcong minefield. The wrong answer here, and *kapow!*—forget about any undercover work for Special Agent Jules J. Bonavolonta. "If such a situation did occur, however, sir, we would have to figure out some way to avoid carrying out the request while still sustaining our operation. Of course, it's always possible that we would just have to terminate the operation at that point. But the main thing is that such a situation should be avoided at all costs."

"Absolutely." Baker studied the ceiling some more.

I fidgeted. For once I hadn't said what I really thought; that would have sealed my fate for good. But I was convinced that if we ever did get an agent so far inside one of the families that he was given a murder contract, it would be an enormous breakthrough. Shit, give me that problem any day.

"You seem to be fascinated with the undercover technique, Jules."

"I've thought about it a lot, Mr. Baker. I could be wrong, but it seems to me it could be the best way to go if we really want to take these Mafia families apart at the seams. It's just the way I feel, but as I say, I could be wrong."

Baker sat forward in his chair, indicating, I guessed, that the interview was over. "Well, thanks very much, Jules. It's been fascinating meeting you and talking to you, and I'm sure we'll be seeing a lot of each other."

"Yes, sir, thank you, sir."

Baker got slowly to his feet and cast an uncertain glance at me and an unreadable look at Kavanaugh. "He's all yours, Ed."

I was off to one hell of a fine start in New York.

4

WHAT I was coming to see about the FBI was that it was a lot like the old good-news, bad-news jokes. The bad news in this case was that the Bureau was an awful, hierarchical bureaucracy that was about as comfortable with the concept of change as a nun was with the idea of polygamy. The good news, though, was that the FBI had recruited some of the finest people in the world, at least in my opinion. There were the bums and losers you find in any organization, of course. As for me, maybe I was just lucky, but the people I got to work with were men and women of enormous pride and integrity.

Many would become friends for life.

The system, though, was another story. Numbers, numbers, numbers—the Bureau was crazy for numbers. I had been in for just two years, and if I had learned anything at all, it was that the Federal Bureau of Investigation was run by numbers freaks. Some days, I thought it ought to be called the Federal Bureau of Accountancy. How many investigations, how many arrests— more, more, more! It didn't matter if 95 percent of the arrests were shitty or if the punk you had busted the night before was back on the street the next day. As long as the numbers kept piling up, you were golden.

So after my illuminating chat with Dick Baker and Ed Kavanaugh, I got my gun and went to look for my desk down on the sixth floor, prepared to make the FBI's arrest numbers grow. Since they were going to put me on a gambling squad, numbers would be no problem, I thought. I have never been much of a fisherman, but whatever kind of crummy fish it is that are always biting and you just throw the things back, you don't even want 'em on the hook. That's what our gambling cases were like.

Real crap.

We called them IGB cases. That stands for illegal gambling business, and more than just about any other kind of cases, they made the brass smile. You could go into a place one night and make maybe a dozen, or even two dozen, arrests.

Watch those numbers jump!

The focus on gambling was what Hoover and his minions called an "intensification" program. The idea was simple. The FBI would concentrate its investigative resources on gamblers in the hope that it could cut off, or at the very least constrict, the supply of gambling money pouring into the Cosa Nostra. Gambling was believed to be the principal source of revenue for the five Cosa Nostra families in New York.

The trouble was, Hoover's theory had a big hole in it, and it was this: For every gambler we busted, two, maybe three, more would show up to take his place. And very few of the gamblers ever seemed to do any real jail time.

I remember one freezing cold night in the dead of winter, in January or February. We had just brought down a pretty big gambling case, and the arraignment took place close to midnight. Preparations for the raid on the gambling place had begun at about four in the morning, so it had been a long day. The arraignment was handled by a young Assistant U.S. Attorney named Rudy Giuliani, a guy I would work with many more times in the years to come. Anyway, we're walking out of the handsome federal courthouse in Lower Manhattan, and one of the mopes I had just busted comes up to us.

"Hey, Jules."

I looked up from talking with Giuliani, and I couldn't believe it. The son of a bitch had already made bail and was back on the street again. I could see that behind the guy there were two vans filled with other wise guys. So there was going to be a party tonight. But before this one guy climbs into the van, he has to show off a little for his pals.

"Hey, Jules."

We kept walking, Giuliani and I. But the wise guy—I don't even remember his name anymore—comes up and tries to hand me a twenty-dollar bill. "You did a real good job tonight, Jules. But it's awfully cold out here; you're going to freeze your butt off. Why don't you go buy yourself a hat?"

I stepped away from Giuliani and grabbed the guy by his lapels. "Listen, shithead, you know what you can get for trying to bribe a federal officer?"

"What bribe? I just wanted to tell you what a good job you did, that's all."

Behind me, I heard the other wise guys hooting and cackling. I let go of the asshole's coat and gave him a shove. "Get the fuck out of here," I said.

Then Giuliani and I were on our way again.

That's the kind of cases we were making under the system designed by Hoover. And the cases never ended. We had gamblers coming out our assholes. All types, too. We had whites, blacks, Hispanics, males, females, maybe even a few transvestites, for all I know. There were real old guys, geriatrics, cripples, the Geritol set. You wouldn't believe some of the people we were arresting; if it gambled, though, we busted it.

That was the game.

Here was the real problem with the Hoover system, though: We were getting only the chumps, the mopes, the guys dealing the cards and rolling the dice.

But who owned the places? Who ran them?

We never had time to try to figure that out.

Just to explain, there was a reason for the obsession with numbers. The way Hoover had set up the FBI, there was an inspection system that worked like this: Every eighteen months, a team of guys from Headquarters in Washington would show up in a field office and turn the place inside out. You would have to account for the paper clips and how often you put new tires on the cars. But the main thing the inspectors looked for when they came through an office in the field was case numbers. Indictments, arrests, convictions—did Office A have more this year than last? No? Then a big black mark goes in some poor guy's book, and there's no promotion, no bonus that year. In Hoover's FBI, a black mark like that could torpedo a career.

The system, in other words, was run by and for bean counters. And that was just one of its problems.

Another was that there were too many guys running around trying to think up bright ideas to impress the brass. Somewhere after my first anniversary in New York, for instance, one of the bright lights in Washington came up with the idea of creating an elite FBI emergency arrest team. We didn't call it a SWAT team back then, but that's what it was.

Headquarters, in any event, thought this was an absolute stroke of genius, and they gave the go-ahead.

Then they made me the team leader.

It was an experiment, and if it worked, I was told, Headquarters would establish some more teams just like ours. So they sent a bunch of us, mostly combat veterans, down to the FBI Academy in Quantico, and the next thing I knew, I was back to where I had started out—in the NAC-6 class—more than three years earlier. We trained hard, took quite a few lumps, and broke a few limbs in the process. We did all the hairy stuff you've probably seen in the movies—the martial arts, special-weapons training, demolitions, rappelling from helicopters.

Back in New York, because there were just two teams, mine and one other, we always had to be on alert. I didn't mind that, but it didn't take too long before I got to have a bad feeling about the operation. The idea was that I and the other guys had to be ready at all hours to go in and knock down doors, kick ass, take names, and all the rest of it.

That was fine. But Headquarters made no bones about one thing: They would always be calling the shots. Always.

This was a surefire way to get someone hurt or killed, I knew. It was also, as Yogi Berra said in quite another context, like déjà vu all over again. In Vietnam, Lyndon Johnson had once boasted that the U.S. Air Force couldn't bomb a Vietcong outhouse without his say-so. Look what happened there. I had seen more than enough of that bullshit in Vietnam, and I wasn't about to go through it again with the FBI. So I finally told Headquarters that I had had enough of amateur hour. They would have to get some other poor devil to run their SWAT teams.

I opened up Bonavolonta's School of Death.

At least that's what the FBI agents who showed up called it. A bunch of the guys in New York had been asking for a martial-arts training school, and we finally decided to set one up in a place not far from the office. We'd work out over the lunch hour or after work, and because of my background—Special Forces and a karate black belt—it pretty much fell to me to handle the instruction.

Most of the guys really enjoyed it, and some got really good. The brass in New York were definitely not thrilled with the idea, though. I guess too many guys were winding up in the hospital or having to take time off, medical leave. Anyway, that lasted for a while before they finally asked me to shut the place down, and then the School of Death was no more.

And that was fine, too, because a bunch of tough new agents were coming into New York, and despite all the bullshit about making numbers and keeping up with our crummy gambling cases, a few of us were beginning to see how we might be able to finally make some serious inroads against the mob.

We had begun experimenting with undercover work, for one thing. A few months before, Dick Baker, the special agent in charge, had given me the chance to try out my theory about putting someone on the street to see if he could hook up with a few wise guys and eventually get inside one of the five families.

Naturally, the someone I had in mind was me.

What happened was, Bob Flaherty, one of our agents working off the O.C. squad targeting the Carlo Gambino family, had developed a pretty good informant. The informant was a woman in her early twenties, streetwise, a looker even if she was maybe a little crude. The important thing, though, was that she hung out with a bunch of gamblers at a couple of places in Lower Manhattan and the gamblers were very tight with the Colombos.

For whatever reason, the woman—I'll call her Lisa because

she's still around and I don't want to cause her any more trouble
—was willing to make some introductions to her gambler
friends. Flaherty the Irishman obviously stood no chance of
passing himself off as one of the wise guys.

So I volunteered for the part.

I didn't need a lot of rehearsal.

Lisa and I had hit it off right away, and we began hanging at
these places downtown. After just a few weeks, we were seeing
the gamblers just about every day, and pretty soon they came to
look at me as just another guy.

What I was finding at that point, though, was that it was easier
dealing with the wise guys than it was with the Bureau. I look
back on it now and laugh, but at the time, I couldn't believe it.
The Bureau had no concept of undercover work—none.

I'll give you an example. Before I was to go to my very first
meeting with Lisa and her gambler friends, I'm brought into
Dick Baker's office, and he walks me down the hall to another
place where I'm supposed to pick up my money. I'm hanging
with gamblers, so I've got to have money, right? And on a young
FBI agent's salary with a wife, a kid, and one more on the way,
I'm sure as hell not going to dip into my own pocket.

That's what I thought, anyway.

So Baker and I show up to collect my walking-around money,
and this guy behind the desk counts out four twenties, one ten,
one five, four singles, and a buck in change. A hundred stinking
dollars, I couldn't believe it!

"Here you go, Jules, good luck."

"Yes, sir, thank you, Mr. Baker."

Somehow I managed to wait until I got out of earshot of
Baker's office before I finally blew my cool. I was with Flaherty,
a good buddy. He had served in the Eighty-second Airborne
Division, so we had a lot in common.

"What the fuck am I supposed to do with this, Bob?" I waved
the hundred bucks under Flaherty's nose.

"Hey, Jules, you're lucky. It's more than most guys get. What
you've got to do now is figure out how to make it last."

"Jesus Christ."

I didn't know beans about playing the horses, but the Bureau had put the arm on some professional handicappers, so Flaherty and I called in a few chits. We got a line on a couple of horses running that afternoon at Aqueduct, and just to be on the safe side, I hit the bank before we went to meet Lisa, and I got another hundred bucks of my own.

So this was the FBI's idea of undercover work, I thought.

It didn't even rise to the level of chickenshit.

Fortunately, my two ponies came through that afternoon, Lisa's wise-guy friends made a few hundred bucks on my tips, and we were, if you'll forgive the pun, off to the races.

Only things are never as simple as they seem.

After I had been hanging with Lisa and the wise guys for several months, I got a call one night. It was another one of those two-in-the-morning deals, and Linda, pregnant with our second child, answered it, listened for a second, then handed the receiver to me.

It was Flaherty.

"You don't sound too good, Bob. What's up?"

"You going in to collect tomorrow like usual, Jules?"

"Yeah, why?" Our handicappers at the track had been doing pretty well, and as a result, I had a pretty good streak going. Since I was a regular with the wise guys by now, we had gotten into a kind of routine. The assholes would bet my tips, then I'd come around and pick up my winnings the next day.

Flaherty knew exactly how we had been working it. "I hate to tell you this, Jules, but your new pals from downtown did a bit of a number on Lisa tonight."

"What do you mean?"

"She's in the hospital, Jules."

"Those motherfuckers!" I couldn't believe it.

"Calm down, she's going to be okay."

I heard Flaherty's words, but it was like I couldn't process them. "She's a good kid, Bob. Tell me what happened."

Flaherty explained that the wise guys had begun asking Lisa

about me and my background, how she knew me and the rest of it. When she couldn't tell them, they started working her over.

"Son of a bitch."

"What they also told her, Jules"—Flaherty made his voice flat and hard—"is that when you show up to collect your winnings today, they're going to break your legs."

I was furious now. "I'll tell you what, Bob. Let's meet in the office first thing in the morning."

"Okay."

"We'll grab a few guys we know can handle themselves."

"Yeah?" Flaherty must have been dog-tired, but I detected a definite note of interest on the other end of the line.

"Then we'll go down there, and I'll go in to collect, just like always. You guys wait outside and watch."

From under the covers, Linda was giving me that look again, like I was halfway out of my mind.

I lowered my voice. "Don't worry about the guys I'm collecting from, Bob. I can handle them. But if you see more guys start to show up and you see me going under, then you guys come on in, and we'll bust the whole goddamned place to pieces. After that, we'll just have a talk with these scumbags about why they shouldn't go beating up on a nice young kid like Lisa."

"Sure, Jules, sure thing." Flaherty was chuckling now.

I took a deep breath. "What's the matter?"

"I think you're fucking nuts, Jules, that's what. I'm with you a hundred percent, you know that. But you know there's no way the office will ever go for this. No fucking way."

And that's exactly what Dick Baker told me the next day.

Only with the expletive, as they say, deleted.

5

SOME of the new agents I mentioned started coming into the New York office in dribs and drabs. In the space of just two years, though—1971 and 1973—the core of the crew that would eventually make it all happen had basically come together. The physicists call this kind of thing synergy, I think. I'll just stick with luck.

None of us new agents knew that at the time, of course, but we had this vision, and each guy's was different from the next. But the thing was, we did have a vision.

Unlike most of the higher-ups we worked for.

One of the very first to arrive was Jim Kallstrom. God bless Jimmy and the fucking horse he rode in on. I'll explain what I mean a little later, but the main thing is that Kallstrom would be with us for the whole goddamned ride. If it weren't for Jimmy, in fact, we might all still be riding out there; the horse I'm not so sure about.

But to start at the beginning:

When we first met in New York in 1971, Kallstrom and I had a lot more in common than either of us knew. Like me, Jimmy had definitely not been born with a silver spoon in his mouth. His father was a car salesman and a weekend musician. His mother was a nurse. Somehow we both managed to get to, then get out of, college. Then we both joined the service.

Kallstrom went to the marines.

In Vietnam, the life expectancy of a Marine Corps second lieutenant, which was the grade Jimmy went in at, wasn't real long. At one point either right before or after he went in, in January 1966, second lieutenants in the Marine Corps were averaging about thirty days on the ground. Jimmy beat the odds, but as I would find out later, he had a hell of a head for numbers.

Kallstrom wound up in I-Corps (the northernmost province of South Vietnam, stretched to the DMZ), where I was. We were both there at the same time, but for all either of us knew, we might just as well have been on different planets.

Typical Vietnam experience.

In New York, we compared notes.

"No plan, no vision," Kallstrom said. Jimmy had been at the siege of Khe Sanh, and anyone who knows anything about Vietnam knows how bad that was. But for both of us, I think, it was the day-to-day stuff, which never got any publicity, that stayed with us. In one corner of the particular hell that was I-Corps, for instance, Kallstrom lost 80 percent of his company in just one day. Today nobody remembers the place. It was called Hill 881. Jimmy lost four out of five men there. That was the Vietnam we remembered. "I believed in the war," Kallstrom said. "But the way it was run—it was just unbelievably piss-poor."

In New York, Jimmy, like me, was already seeing some eerie parallels between Vietnam and the Bureau.

All of us, the agents working the ten O.C. squads there, were stuck in this big bullpen area, each guy assigned to a little cubicle with a desk and a phone. Kallstrom was in the squad next to mine, and we became friends right off the bat. You could see that Kallstrom had that extra something in a way a lot of the other guys just didn't.

Like doing things his way, for instance.

The way it was set up back then, each agent had about a hundred cases he was supposed to handle. If you worked hard and kept at it, you could get the record checks done and all that stuff. But you couldn't put a full-court press on any one case. And you weren't supposed to, either.

But one day not long after Kallstrom shows up, he and I are talking, and he tells me he's working on a case: Paul Castellano. I couldn't believe it. Big Paul was a major capo in the Gambino family, which was the strongest of the five Cosa Nostra families in New York. Because of his family connections, his smarts, and —to be honest—competition that wasn't all that bright, Paul Castellano was on a fast track to become New York's boss of bosses. So I'm thinking, How does a two-bit young FBI agent like Kallstrom come to be running a case on Castellano?

But that's why Kallstrom was so good.

He had done some work on it, a lot of it on his own time, and he had this theory that Big Paul, his top aide, Tom Bilotti, and a few others among the Gambinos were screwing around with the cheese industry in New York. Paulie's big thing was that none of the families should be messing around with drugs, but that was a bunch of bullshit. Some of our guys believed it, but not Kallstrom. He got a wiretap, one of the first ever on the Gambinos. Then he started following cheese trucks around New York. By which I mean he literally tailed the trucks around the city in his car to see where they were going.

It sounds crazy now, maybe, but that's the kind of thing you had to do if you were going to make good cases, and the entire structure of the FBI was set up to keep you from doing it. Like me, it was making Kallstrom crazy. I ran into him in the hall one day, and he grabbed me. "Hey, Jules, you know what I think? I think we got the same fucking guys running this war here that we had running the other one over there."

He might have been frustrated, but Kallstrom stuck with it.

And before he was done, he connected up Big Paulie and his guys with the Mafia in Italy. Kallstrom found out—and remember, this is the early seventies—that Paulie's guys were opening up pizza parlors up and down the East Coast, and he had solid evidence that the pizza places and the cheese businesses were being used as part of a pipeline for drugs and illegal aliens.

Of course, while Kallstrom was doing all this work on Castellano, he was letting the other ninety-nine cases on his desk collect dust. And that was a definite no-no. Plus, to really go after the case he wanted to make on Paulie and the Gambinos, Kallstrom would have needed a team of at least a half-dozen agents for heavy surveillance. That would have taken several months, and we both knew that was never going to happen.

So Jimmy got pulled back into the numbers game, and it would take another fifteen years before we would go after the Pizza Connection case and nail the Gambinos to the wall.

But that was life in the FBI.

The good-news part of it that I mentioned earlier, though, is that more guys like Kallstrom were reporting for duty.

Guys like Sean McWeeney and Joe Pistone, for instance.

McWeeney was a tall, good-looking Irishman, a little older than I. After four years in the navy, he had joined the Bureau and gotten into some O.C. work in Oklahoma and Rhode Island, where he helped make a hell of a good case against a big-time wise guy named Ray Patriarca. After that, the brass brought Sean into New York and made him a supervisor of the O.C. squad working on the Joe Colombo family. "Crazy Joey" Gallo, a renegade member of the Colombo family, had just gotten whacked at Umberto's Clam House, and that had started an all-out gang war in the city, Joey Gallo's guys on one side, the Colombos on the other. The Colombo team was led by two homicidal maniacs, Alphonse and Carmine Persico. Carmine was such a nice guy that he had earned the nickname "Snake" somewhere early on in his bloodstained career. The name became him.

After the Gallo hit at Umberto's Clam House, people were getting shot left and right, including—probably the most notorious screwup—four innocent Jewish businessmen in the Neapolitan Noodle House way downtown. Politically, this was a major-league disaster, and John Lindsay, who was the mayor at the time, declared war on the Mafia.

So Sean and I got our orders. Then we went to war.

Because we lived near each other way out in New Jersey, we began carpooling to the office. Sean would pick me up around five-thirty, five forty-five, and we'd ride in to Manhattan in this piece-of-shit Volkswagen of his. Things were pretty hairy at the time because, besides Lindsay calling for his war on the mob,

the Italian-American Civil Rights League was also beginning
to get its back up about the FBI targeting all these Italian
wise guys. So we'd have these pickets all the time outside our
office, and they'd chant the names of all the Italian agents
working O.C.

Of course, they had gotten my name. So we'd have to drive
past the picketers in Sean's crummy Volkswagen, and he would
say, "Hey, Jules, they're singing your song again."

"Just drive," I'd say. "Would you, please?"

One of the best things that happened, one of the most promising, was that someone somewhere among the higher-ups got it
into his head one day to create an informant-development
squad. It may not sound like much now, but it was a big deal at
the time. The idea was for a team of agents to do nothing but
cull through intelligence files, arrest and surveillance records,
wiretap transcripts, and whatever else they could lay their hands
on, then try to determine which of the wise guys' many friends
and associates might be amenable to the idea of feeding a few
leads to Uncle Sam.

Talk about revolutionary.

The agents on the informant squad would be making no arrests, so naturally that would mean a lot of heartburn for the
bean counters. But the stars must have been in the right align-
ment or something, because somehow Headquarters let the idea
go through, and Sean and I got put on the squad.

So what we did was start with this thing called a 92–2300 File.
Don't ask me why, but that's what the Bureau called it. It was a
fat file filled with information on organized-crime families from
nearly every FBI office in the country. All those crummy gambling arrests I was always complaining about? Every time a wise
guy was involved, the case agent would have to write up a report,
and since New York was basically the American capital of the
Cosa Nostra, copies would all be forwarded to the New York
office. Where, of course, nobody looked at them.

After we got the go-ahead from Headquarters, Sean and I
began poring over the 92–2300 File. Plus, we also had all the

paper generated by the arrests made by the New York office. It was about the only time I felt good about all those rotten gambling cases. By themselves, they were mostly a lot of crap. But in among the crap were quite a few good leads.

Following them up, though, was another thing.

A lot of it was meeting with guys at two or three in the morning. These fucking wise guys, I told Sean one night, driving out to see yet another mope sometime after midnight, have got to be insomniacs or something.

Maybe they were, but we went to see them, anyway.

We'd go see this one guy, Rudy Pippollo, at his house—never before two in the morning. Then he would sit there smoking these god-awful twisty little cigars that stunk like you wouldn't believe and complain that the FBI was too soft on "the god-damned niggers and Puerto Ricans." The guy was a slob. And he'd blow smoke in our faces, Sean's and mine, literally.

But we'd go see the guy, anyway. Night after night—and he never gives us a thing. Nothing. But he's not throwing us out, either, so we keep going back to see him, and he keeps blowing the fucking cigar smoke up our noses.

Finally, we get a break. One day the phone rings, and it's Pippollo on the line, and he's crazy. Incoherent almost. It turns out his sixteen-year-old daughter has disappeared, run off with some screwball boyfriend, who knew?

McWeeney took the call.

"Sean, you've got to help me find her. My wife is going nuts. She can't eat; she can't sleep."

"Rudy, the FBI doesn't chase runaway kids, for God's sake."

"Please, Sean, you've got to help. You find my daughter, I'll give you anything you want. Anything."

McWeeney put his hand over the receiver and winked at me. "It's Mr. Pippollo, Giulio. He says he'll give us anything we want if we find his daughter. Whaddya think?"

"I think we ought to go find his fucking daughter."

Sean nodded, got back on the phone, and told Rudy we'd get right on the case, no problem. I think we turned up the daughter in Ohio somewhere. Old Rudy tried to welch on the deal then, but Sean and I kept on him like stink on shit, and he finally did give us some pretty good information.

Not great, but better than what we had. Which is the only way to think about the game we were playing.

Sooner rather than later, however, the bean counters at Headquarters caught up with us, and that was the end of the informant-development squad. It was a stupid decision to kill the thing. But even so, while guys like McWeeney and Kallstrom and I chafed at the system, we also saw our ranks growing.

Joe Pistone's arrival gave all of us a lift.

Me probably most of all.

Pistone and I had both grown up in Italian families, not far from each other, actually, in New Jersey, though we didn't meet until he turned up in New York. It was only a while after that, too, that we really got to know each other.

At the time Pistone arrived, New York was experiencing an enormous number of truck hijackings, sometimes five or six a day. And we're talking about a million dollars a load sometimes —a lot of money. They were taking the rigs off the docks, stopping drivers at red lights. It was crazy.

So the Bureau forms a truck-hijacking squad and assigns Pistone as one of the lead agents. A good idea. But the squad is not run out of the Organized Crime Division—not such a good idea. I mean, it's very clear to anyone who spends even a few minutes looking at these hijacking cases: Organized crime is behind the missing trucks, no two ways about it; maybe not every single goddamned hijacking, okay, but a lot of them.

Anyway, the Bureau doesn't make the connection, but Pistone, being a smart guy, does.

So he comes to see me.

Pistone had heard about some of my undercover work. Dick Baker had allowed me to work several other undercover gigs after they pulled the plug on the assignment with Lisa and the gamblers. After just a few months in New York, Pistone had begun to do some of his own undercover work off the hijacking squad. At the time Pistone came in to talk, I remember, I had one of our other agents, a real tough kid, working undercover against some other wise guys, and I was supposed to meet him late that night, about one in the morning.

"You mind if I come along, Jules?"

Are you kidding? I thought. "Sure thing, Joe, why not?"

With the exception of Kallstrom, McWeeney, and a few other buddies like Tom Vinton, not too many agents were interested in this undercover business, much less going out on a meet with me at some ungodly hour of the morning. Pistone, though, wants to come sit in some bar with me and my agent and talk undercover work, techniques, et cetera. So that's exactly what we do.

I still remember it now. It was a place over on the West Side. The guy who owned it is still in business, so I'm not going to mention the name of the place, but I liked it because the guy let me use a back room there to meet people and talk.

Anyway, we show up around one in the morning, and before you know it, Pistone and I are like a couple of long-lost brothers. I think we talked for about four or five hours. About how screwed up the FBI system was, about how the Bureau had no O.C. strategy—about the work, mainly.

I still remember coming out of the place. The sun was just up, and it was shooting big buttery shafts of light down at us through the gaps between the skyscrapers.

That meant one thing.

It was time to start another day.

6

I'M still not sure exactly how it happened, but by the time I got together with Pistone in that bar over on the West Side, someone higher up in the FBI food chain had arranged for me to get promoted.

The Bonavolonta family certainly appreciated the raise that went with my little bump up the ladder. On June 30, 1973, Linda had given birth to our second child, Joe, and the money would come in handy. This time, thank God, I was there at the hospital when Linda delivered. I was happier than I thought I would ever be, but I was also concerned about all the things young fathers always worry about: doctors' bills, clothing, saving for college.

The money wasn't the reason I was so happy about the promotion, though. I still felt the same way about titles and the rest of that bullshit as I did back in the army: I didn't give a damn about it. What I did want, then and later, was simply for the higher-ups running the FBI's organized-crime program to start doing things differently. What I wanted, in a word, was influence. I wanted a say.

Even the best of friends can look at the same set of facts and come to different conclusions. This was exactly what happened with me and Pistone. Like Joe, I loved the undercover work. Between 1970 and 1975, I had spent months working undercover against the Cosa Nostra in New York, and I was convinced it was the only way to go—long-term, strategic investigations that targeted the top people who made the syndicates work.

The problem was that the Bureau was still fundamentally uncomfortable with that kind of approach. Someone like Pistone would curse the higher-ups and just work harder; I wanted to take on the brass and force them to change the way we did business, to change the system.

But everyone knows change never comes easy.

In the FBI, the problem was that guys like Dick Baker were intrigued by the *possibility* of getting an agent inside the Cosa Nostra. Institutionally, however, Hoover's system had them in straitjackets. Supervisors could let me or one of the other agents run for only so long before a problem like the kind we had with Lisa caused everyone to get cold feet. Or before Hoover's bean counters sent word that they were coming in for yet another one of their miserable inspections. The result, then, to no one's surprise, was half-assed undercover work.

So while I shared Pistone's enthusiasm for the approach, I had come to a very different conclusion about what I was going to do to make it work. Interestingly, it was a conclusion that Sean McWeeney and Jimmy Kallstrom had come to for many of the same reasons. The only way to change the FBI, the three of us concluded, was to amass enough clout within the Bureau that people would have to listen to what we said. And clout, in Hoover's FBI, meant one thing and one thing only: rank.

In August 1975, I was promoted to supervisor of the O.C. squad targeting the Lucchese family. It was nearly five years to the day after I stepped onto the train in West Orange for my first day on the job in New York. Now I was responsible for the work of the twenty-five men and women on the squad.

My squad.

All my life, the last thing I had ever wanted was to be in management. Now here I was. Several times that first day I wondered if I wasn't making a very big mistake.

I would have taken any of the five squads working the Cosa Nostra families, but as it worked out, the squad assignments mattered less then than at any time since the FBI's Organized Crime Division had been created. Pistone, for instance, was getting closer to the Lucchese and Bonanno families, but technically he wasn't even working organized crime; on the books, he was still working truck hijackings. Similarly, the situation with my squad and the other four family squads was a lot more fluid than it was when I first broke in. There was a lot more sharing of information.

One reason for this was that there had been a big infusion of new blood into New York since I arrived. A lot of the older guys were leaving or transferring out to places like Phoenix or wherever. And for the first time ever, Hoover had decided to allow new agents right out of Quantico to come directly to New York. The new kids brought in a hell of a lot of enthusiasm.

Before long, they also started making pretty good cases.

One of the best of the new kids was a guy named Louie Freeh. I remember when he first came into the office. Louie was one of those guys who somehow, even as a kid, looks a lot older than he is. A slender, straight-talking young guy with dark spaniel eyes that give his face a kind of preoccupied look, Louie might have looked like an older guy, but for all that, you always knew he was basically still just a kid.

Louie and I were different in more ways than age. Whereas I had grown up thinking mainly about a career in the military, Louie, another nobody from New Jersey, had grown up wanting to be an FBI agent and nothing else.

Louis J. Freeh would go on to become one of the very best special agents the FBI ever produced; eventually, he would wind up running the whole goddamned show, as the director of the FBI. First and always, though, I will remember Louie as a friend, one of those rare people you meet in life and know exactly what's what right off the bat and neither of you ever gives up on it no matter what crazy bumps you may hit down the road.

The Bureau was great that way, like I said—because of the people. And because of the people—because of guys like Louie and Pistone and the rest—slowly but surely we were starting to make changes, to make some progress.

The first evidence of that, or at least the first real evidence I saw, was a labor-racketeering investigation the FBI had begun. It was code-named UNIRAC, a contraction of the words union and racketeering. Not too clever, maybe, but the case itself was a good one. It had started out as two separate investigations of corruption on the docks of Savannah, Georgia, and Miami, Florida. The International Longshoremen's Association was involved in both places, and when we heard about the investigations, some of us in New York decided to take a look at what was happening on the docks where we were.

The man responsible for the decision was Tom Emory. Tom had taken over as the new special agent in charge of the Criminal Investigative Division in New York, and he was a man of enormous integrity and personal rectitude. Coincidentally, Emory was also the guy who had pushed me with the brass as the new head of the Lucchese squad. Emory was a classic product of the Hoover FBI, a no-nonsense, by-the-books guy. Unlike the other guys his age, though, Emory wasn't hard-over against change; indeed, in my case, he went out of his way to encourage it.

"Sure, Jules," he would say when I'd pop my head in his office with yet another one of my little brainstorms. "If you think it'll work, give it a go."

On UNIRAC, Emory's idea was simple. Instead of working the case in the typical FBI way, where we would target the guys paying the bribes and boosting the stuff from the docks, we were going to think bigger. UNIRAC, the way Tom Emory envisioned it, would be nothing less than a balls-out investigation of the entire American shipping industry.

In New York, we threw a bunch of agents at the case, and before you knew it, we had judges signing orders allowing us to install bugs on telephones and secret microphones in homes and offices. There were payoffs being made big-time to the longshoremen's union, we soon found out. The money was to maintain labor peace on the docks, keeping the competing unions from fucking things up and making sure there were no walkouts, slowdowns, pickets, or other kinds of high-priced mayhem.

Labor peace is a noble idea, except that this peace was being secured by fat bribes and ridiculous contract rake-offs, and that happened to be against the law. What made all of this so interesting from my particular perspective was that the Cosa Nostra was right in the middle of the whole thing.

From the wiretaps we knew that an underboss of the Genovese crime family was picking up the payoffs at a place called the Shelton Health Club. The Genovese family guy was a thug, an animal named Mike Clemente. The health club itself was all right; it was in Brooklyn, a place for guys to hang out, work out with the weights, maybe play some handball.

Anyway, it was clear what the FBI had to do. We had to get someone inside the club to watch as the payoffs were being made.

Louie Freeh got the job.

The UNIRAC case was enormously complex. Besides the bugs and the wiretaps and the undercover role Louie was playing in the health club, we had elaborate physical surveillance on a bunch of other wise guys and union brass. Before we were done, New York would bring down somewhere over forty people in UNIRAC. FBI agents in Miami and Savannah would take down quite a few more. Louie's testimony from the witness stand, about how he had watched Clemente and some other scumbags pocket fat envelopes full of cash, nailed the door shut on a lot of them.

Naturally, the Bureau got a lot of great publicity from the case, and that made the brass happy. But not happy enough, I guess. They decided to shut UNIRAC down and close the door.

Tom Emory couldn't believe it. "We were just at the beginning," he said, "not the end!" In New York alone, we had hard leads on the Cosa Nostra and the longshoremen's union at every major port up and down the East Coast; Headquarters wouldn't let us follow a single goddamned one.

Now this, I said to Linda late one night after we put the kids to bed, is some kind of way to fight a war.

7

THE psychologists have a term for this sort of thing—self-delusionary, they call it. We had a lot of guys in the Bureau with that very problem.

The way Hoover's FBI worked—except in the rare and extreme cases where someone either screwed up royally or the Bureau itself ran off the rails—the machinery of transfers and promotions clanked along like the chains of Banquo's ghost. Once you got past a certain level—and again, as I say, unless something really strange happened—the transfers and promotions came along as regular as clockwork.

You could puff yourself up about it if you were so inclined, and as I say, a lot of guys were.

I just tried to look at it for what it was, the system grinding along, the chains rattling now and again at some new rut in the road. By now I knew well enough how the system operated. But it was a shock just the same when my number finally came up. It was in October 1977 when I got the word.

The brass had decided to bring me to Washington.

To really understand FBI Headquarters, there are only a few important things to know, and of them, this is probably the most important: The Bureau is organized into twelve divisions, but only two are actually operational. These are the Criminal Investigative Division and the Foreign Counterintelligence Division. The CID, as its name implies, does all the criminal stuff, everything from mob cases to terrorists blowing up the World Trade Center. The second, the FCI Division, is the spooky part of the Bureau. Those guys chase spies.

Now the other ten divisions—that's an interesting story, and it relates directly to the way FBI Headquarters runs or, as is more often the case, doesn't run. The purpose of these other ten divisions is to support the two operational divisions, and by and large they do a pretty good job. But they're stuffed with way too many people—people pushing paper, poking their noses into other people's business, and all the rest of the crap that makes Washington, as a city, such a fun place. I always wondered how much more good some of those people at Headquarters could do if they were out on the street working cases instead of piloting all those government-issue metal desks in an office.

This was life at FBI Headquarters as I found it. It was a place where a few dedicated men and women worked. But for every one of them, I'd have to say there were probably twenty more timeservers, ticket punchers, and fat-assed desk jockeys sitting around doing not a hell of a lot of anything useful.

The agents in the field knew this, of course, and they accorded Headquarters the appropriate amount of respect. "Puzzle Palace" and "Seat of All Wisdom" were two of the more charitable labels affixed to the collection of geniuses we had toiling away inside the J. Edgar Hoover Building on Pennsylvania Avenue; I won't embarrass you with some of the other names.

Anyway, that's where they put me. The brass had decided I was Washington bound, and there wasn't a goddamned thing I could do about it. As Linda and I packed up the house in New Jersey and tried to explain to Maria and Joe why they had to leave their friends behind, I guess I tried to rationalize things. With the same objective in mind, Pistone and I had gone in two very different directions on the question of undercover work. Whereas I had taken the promotion they had offered and become a supervisory special agent, Joe had gone out and gotten himself a phony driver's license, a phony American Express card, and a crummy flat in Brooklyn where the few neighbors who talked with him knew him as Donnie Brasco, so-so jewel thief and wise guy extraordinaire. Joe was getting so deep into the undercover role that the Bureau was getting nervous about his real family, and we were getting ready to move them out of New York.

On the other hand, with the orders that came through transferring us to Washington, I felt like I was being pulled out of the game altogether. I tried to tell myself it wasn't so, but some days that's exactly what it felt like.

The rationalization I talked about went something like this: Okay, you said you wanted to change the system, Jules, so if that's what you want to do, you're going to have to play their game a little, climb the ladder. Then, when the time comes and you've got the clout and the authority, you can start kicking ass, shaping things the way you want.

That's what I told myself.

After the moving van was loaded, though, and we were on the interstate with the kids headed south to Washington, I started wondering if I hadn't done a real good job of bullshitting myself. We all have that capability, you know.

I was probably better at it than most.

Washington was worse than I imagined.

Of course, I helped make it worse than it would have been, but the only way I could have avoided that was by keeping my mouth shut, and that wasn't about to happen. Besides, if you believed the brass, the reason I had been ordered to Washington was because of my supposed expertise in organized-crime cases.

The problem, or one of them, anyway, was my ideas about New York. At Headquarters, I was actually surprised to find a few people who agreed with my views on the need for long-term, strategic investigations of the Cosa Nostra. There were still more people who thought like I did on the need for more intensive undercover work against the mob. What there wasn't, emphatically, was a single, solitary soul at Headquarters who agreed with my conviction that the war on the Italian Mafia could be won only if the FBI fought it on the streets and in the back rooms of the sleazy social clubs of New York City.

"Who gives a shit about New York?" a Headquarters genius asked me one day. "It's a fucking sewer, anyway."

I was so frustrated at that point that, I didn't even answer the guy. There was no fighting this kind of myopia, I thought.

Here I had staked everything on a particular approach—get inside the Bureau, wait until you have enough clout to act, then force the place to change from within. In a very real way, it was the same thing I had done in Vietnam. But whereas I had enjoyed some success in Vietnam, in Washington I was striking out.

This was my life at Headquarters: Answer this survey, fill out that set of forms, brief the assistant director on Case X because he has to brief the director, who has to brief some idiot committee on Capitol Hill. Forms, forms, forms—I was drowning in forms, filed in triplicate, stamped and sealed, with multicolored onionskin duplicates attached.

How many trees we killed for all that paper I never knew, but that was the least of the tragedies in this thing. We had tough, smart street agents like Jimmy Kallstrom out there making cases on their own time; we had ballsy guys like Pistone out there risking his neck every fucking day.

And at headquarters we had legions of pencil-necked geeks in suits moving tons of paper from one side of the J. Edgar Hoover Building to another and then back again.

It was, if you thought about it, a fucking comedy.

Only I was too sick with disgust to laugh.

"Why not leave?"

Unlike me, Linda was happy in Washington. We had bought a pretty place just across the Potomac in Virginia, and she had the house looking great, and the kids were happy. But being the kind of wife everyone should be lucky enough to have, Linda put all that behind her concern for me. Night after night, after we put the kids to bed, she and I would stay up for hours talking.

"Seriously, Jules. You're still young, and you know a lot of people in New York. Why don't you just forget this place and resign? It might be fun, anyway."

At that I had to smile. I couldn't shake the blues, but I also couldn't forget why I had married this woman. We had lost a bundle on the sale of the house in New Jersey and gone into hock up to our ears to buy the new place in Virginia. Linda knew this better than I because she had to make ends meet at home. Still, she was ready to pick up stakes if it would make me happy.

"We can do it, Jules. Just say the word."

"No, I love you for it, Linda, but we'll stick it out."

I didn't say it then, but I wondered inside whether I really could stick it out. Patience, after all, had never been what anyone would call my strong suit.

8

I have never been much of a believer in miracles, lucky breaks, or phony-baloney happy endings. You make your own luck, I figure, and that's basically that.

But sometimes luck just happens, too, although that wasn't something I had had a lot of experience with.

Despite my promise to Linda to stick it out at Headquarters, the place finally wore me down, and I was ready to call it quits. By early 1979, I had been in Washington for more than a year, and I can honestly say that every day was just worse than the one before it. Not only was I not making a difference, as I had hoped back when I went my way and Pistone went his, but the numbers game was chewing me up and the endless paper flow was burying me in bullshit.

No doubt about it, I had to get out. It was one of the saddest decisions I had ever made in my life, but it was also the only one I felt I had. It was over between me and the Bureau.

I wasn't particularly looking to make a gracious exit, but I wasn't going to be stupid about things, either. With a wife, two young kids, and a mortgage, I couldn't afford to just walk out the door in a huff. I needed time to figure out how to make the jump without missing too many paychecks. Some Special Forces buddies had gone to the CIA, and that was an option, but I was afraid it might mean long periods away from the family. I had some friends in business in New York, so there were possibilities there, too. It was all deeply depressing, contemplating the split, but it had to be done, no doubt about it. So I was basically looking around, putting out feelers and indulging my own dark thoughts about Mr. Hoover's FBI, when the light on my office phone flashed one afternoon.

It was a gloomy spring day, dark with slashing rain, and it matched my mood perfectly. Great, I thought, reaching for the receiver. Probably another survey from some deskbound crime fighter wondering what kind of shoes the wise guys wear or something equally useful. "Hello. Bonavolonta."

"Bonavolonta, Kallstrom here."

"Jimmy, how the hell are you?"

I was so down that not too many people could give me a lift just by the sound of their voice; Jim Kallstrom was one of the few. I guess that's one of the things a true friendship offers.

Kallstrom and I bullshitted about office gossip for a few minutes, topic A being the new A-DIC in New York. Judge William Webster, who had been appointed FBI director by President Jimmy Carter, was slowly but surely putting his stamp on the Bureau and trying to bring it out from the bank of clouds it had been under after Hoover and Watergate. One of Webster's first big moves was to transfer an iconoclastic ballbreaker named Neil Welch from Philadelphia to the top job in New York. As assistant director in charge of the FBI's New York office, Welch would have a free hand to run things pretty much the way he wanted.

Already, Kallstrom said, he was shaking things up. "You wouldn't believe it, Jules. He's got the building in an uproar."

Good, I thought. Just what the fucking place needs.

I had followed the installation of Welch in New York pretty closely, not just because I had so many friends in the office there but because Welch was known throughout the Bureau as a big backer of a more aggressive O.C. program and also as someone who didn't give a rat's ass about Headquarters. To give you an idea about Welch and Headquarters, when he had the top job in Philadelphia, he had ordered one of his supervisors to do something or other one day; I don't remember what it was anymore. The supervisor was evidently a conscientious guy, so he decided to check with Headquarters first before he went ahead and did whatever it was Welch wanted him to do. As luck would have it, Welch walks into the guy's cubicle just as he's talking to one of the desk jockeys in Washington. Welch doesn't say a word, just grabs a pair of scissors that the supervisor has lying on his desk. Then he reaches over and snips the phone cord while the guy watches, his eyes bugging out of his head.

"This," Welch tells the supervisor, holding the dead phone receiver from the severed cord, "is what I think of Headquarters. When *I* tell you to do something, just do it, okay?"

I didn't know him, but Neil Welch definitely seemed like my kind of guy.

Before Philadelphia, Welch had had the top FBI job in Detroit, and just about anyone who knows anything about it will tell you that Detroit at the time Welch got there was not just moribund; it was dead. Nothing was happening. To invigorate the O.C. program there—Welch knew what the mob was up to with the unions and on the factory floors—he set up a special surveillance squad. Screw the bean counters, Welch said. If we're going to make good cases against the mob, we can't do it without first-rate electronic and physical surveillance. Never mind that the surveillance agents would be making no arrests. Welch would answer to Headquarters or to the next team of green-eyeshade inspectors who came through from Washington.

But Welch wasn't happy with just setting up a new squad. He wanted to get the thing out of the FBI office downtown, where any mope with a dime for the pay phone could watch them come and go. So Welch moved the entire surveillance squad—most of them were Vietnam vets, by the way; Welch was definitely partial to guys who had served—out of the FBI office and into another building. It was a secret location, and Headquarters hadn't approved it. Indeed, Welch knew Headquarters would never approve it, so he just didn't tell them. He leased the new space, ordered the surveillance guys not to show their faces in the main FBI office downtown, then arranged his budget numbers for Washington to cover the cost of the secret squad location.

That was the kind of guy Welch was.

On his first day in New York, Welch unveiled the same take-no-prisoners approach. New York was a fucking mess, Welch had told friends in the Bureau; he needed to clean house and fast. Publicly, Welch was only slightly more diplomatic. He was going to rebuild the New York FBI office, Welch told a group of newspaper and television reporters, "brick by brick."

On the other end of the phone from New York, Kallstrom had a brick of his own to drop on my head. "Jules, all that yelling you been doing down there, plus the Vietnam record—it's about to pay off big-time."

"What are you talking—"

"Will you shut up for a minute and listen?"

"Okay, what?"

Kallstrom paused, maybe for dramatic effect, I thought afterward. "Welch wants you up here. He's going to talk to Webster about it, but it's basically a done deal, I think."

For one of the few times in my life I was literally speechless. Like I say, I had never been a particularly lucky guy, yet this was about the biggest stroke of luck I could possibly imagine. To go back to New York and work for a guy like Welch? It was too good to be true.

"Jules, you there or what?"

"I just can't believe it, that's all."

Kallstrom explained what had happened. As he had in Detroit, Welch wanted to set up a special surveillance squad in New York. The new squad would handle not just the physical surveillances but more tricky stuff, too: exotic bugs on phones, hidden mikes in the wise guys' homes and clubs. Welch wanted Kallstrom to run the new squad, but he also wanted to create another new slot—for someone to coordinate the work of all the organized-crime squads working out of the New York office. "I told Welch all about you, Jules, your time with the Green Berets. He liked that. Then I told him you were down at Headquarters, totally disgusted with the operation there. He really liked that, I'll tell you. And then he said, 'Hey, I guess he's my guy.' "

On my end of the line in Washington, I listened silently, feeling every few seconds like I was in a dream. Then suddenly I had this horrible feeling. Kallstrom was a great kidder—he'd been jerking my chain the whole time! "Jimmy, will you cut the bullshit! What the hell do you really want?"

Kallstrom has this very peculiar laugh, which for some reason always reminded me of Santa Claus as he's riding off the rooftop after he's delivered the goodies. I heard the laugh begin to erupt on the other end of the line, and I held the phone away from my ear, an awful sinking feeling in my gut. When the roaring on the other end finally died down, I heard Kallstrom's calm, controlled voice in my ear again. "This is no bullshit, pal. It's real. And you gotta give the man a call right away."

It was for real? I asked Kallstrom.

"No bullshit, pal."

Kallstrom and I chattered on like two excited teenagers after that, until I finally hung up the phone. I figured I'd wait about an hour before calling Welch; I lasted no more than twenty minutes. Nervous as a new bride, I punched in the number for Welch's private line in New York and told the FBI's new ball-busting A-DIC that I wanted to come home.

"Okay," Welch said. "You got it."

That was it—no bullshit, no nothing.

Sometimes, I guess, miracles really do happen.

9

IN the spring of 1979, the five Cosa Nostra families that had divided up the glittery spoils of New York were at the top of their game. Since New York was the undisputed financial capital of the world, it should have come as no surprise that the crime organizations that preyed on its vitals were the best in every sense. Smarter, slicker, more vicious—name the category and the Cosa Nostra in New York swept the field.

This wasn't just the big leagues; it was the big leagues squared. And that's before we get to all the bullshit.

By the way, since there has been so much written about the Mafia, it's probably worth taking a minute to talk about what the wise guys were really like. There are a lot of stories, but I'll give you just one to convey a little of the flavor about how these people lived.

One day long before I got my orders to report from New York to Hoover's Happy Valley Headquarters in Washington—in what, before the miracle phone call from Kallstrom, I had come to think of as the good old days—I was working an undercover gig against the Genovese family. I tell this not as some kind of morality tale, although I think it's pretty clear by now what I think of the people who made their living as members of the Italian Mafia. But it's something I saw with my own eyes, and I figure people can draw their own conclusions.

What happened was this: I had an informant who had begun introducing me around to some Genovese family members, and we were hanging out one night with some of them in a place called Pembles, on Manhattan's East Side. It was a nice enough place, with music and entertainment, and I was standing at the end of the bar with my guy when we heard this loud noise. Everything stopped for a second; then, in the middle of the floor, I see this guy in a suit, and he had knocked over a chair, and now he's yelling at this woman sitting at a table with some other guy. I have no clue what's going on, but the next thing I know, the woman gets up, and she's walking toward the door pretty fast when the guy who's doing the yelling runs up behind her, spins her around, and pops her one in the face—with a closed fist.

I couldn't believe it. I had never seen anyone hit a woman like that before. But the guy doesn't punch her just once; he lays into her two more times as she tries to get up.

I was moving toward the two of them without even thinking when the guy I'm with grabs me hard by the elbow.

"What are you, fucking nuts?"

"He's gonna kill her, that shithead. Let go of me."

"No way!" The informant had my elbow in a steel grip. "You make any kind of move, they make you. Then what happens to me? Think for a minute!"

I stopped, watching. The wise guy in the suit was standing over the woman on the floor, and I thought if he hit her one more time, fuck the undercover role, I'm going to dismantle the son of a bitch. But then he grabbed her purse and got her car keys. By now they were almost at the front door of the place, and the wise guy opened it and threw the keys out into the street. "You whore, you fucking slut! Get the fuck out of here."

The woman was in rough shape, but she must have been a tough customer, because she made it out the door under her own steam. The wise guy returned to his table in the corner where a brassy-looking broad in a dress that left little to the imagination straightened his tie and gave him a kiss.

Around the room, the Pembles regulars returned to their drinks like nothing at all had happened, and me and my guy went back to our beers at the bar.

You should understand that my guy, the informant, was not exactly spending his time introducing me around to the Genovese organized-crime family because he was a public-spirited citizen out to lend a hand to J. Edgar Hoover's Federal Bureau of Investigation. He was a fucking wise guy like all the others, but since the Bureau had the arm on him as a result of another pending criminal matter, he was willing, if not happy, to make the introductions I wanted. The guy's name was Artie, and he would come to a tragic end, but not on account of me. Either Artie's wise guy friends or some drug dealers—to this day no one knows for sure—left his severed head out in a dump in Brooklyn and his body somewhere in Queens. Between the two jurisdictions, you wouldn't believe the paperwork that homicide generated, but that's another story.

The only reason I even mention poor Artie is because of the lesson he gave me that night in Pembles about the wise guys' supposed code of honor. I was dumbstruck by the whole thing with the guy who had used this woman for a punching bag while everyone else in the place acted like they were just there for evening cocktails at the country club.

"Art, what the fuck was that all about?"

"What that was about, Jules . . ." Artie had this dramatic way of talking that I tried to ignore. "What that was about was about a matter of honor."

"Honor!" I couldn't believe it. "The son of a bitch nearly killed that poor woman, you idiot."

Artie the informant shot me a look over his glass of beer like I was suffering from some particularly cruel brain disease. "That woman," Artie said, talking very slowly for the benefit of his mentally deficient friend, "was the guy's fucking wife."

His wife? Now I was totally confused. Then who was the broad climbing all over the wise guy back at his table, and what was the wife doing in here with the other guy?

Artie took the questions one at a time. The brassy woman at the table with the wise guy was his girlfriend, Artie explained. "He's in here with her four or five nights a week." And the wife, well, it turned out that was where the question of honor came in. "See, she knows her husband is out with this other broad every night, so she comes in here with another guy to piss her old man off, make him jealous, whatever. So she's just trying to show him she knows what he's doing and she can do it, too. Dumb broad, she deserved everything she got."

I had been hanging around wise guys long enough to understand that Friday nights were for the girlfriend and Saturdays for the wife, but this seemed a little more complicated. Since I was always game to be enlightened on the subject of wise-guy lore and arcana, I asked what seemed like the obvious follow-up. "So this guy, he can do anything he wants, right, go out and screw whoever he wants?"

"Exactly."

"But the wife, she's got to stay home and be a good girl."

"Fucking-A right."

"And if she decides she's going to go out and do something herself, then this guy, he can just up and kill her."

"Now you got it, my friend. It's only right, see. He's the *guy*. He's her *old man*!"

Like I say, I let other people come to their own conclusions about the wise guys. They want to buy the bullshit, fine. I didn't need any convincing that these guys were total scum.

Questions of morality aside, the five Cosa Nostra families in New York were a big goddamned problem. They were into just about everything. Even if you lived hundreds of miles away from New York, if you bought something that was made in or shipped through the city, you tithed to the mob. If you lived in or near the city, it was worse: You paid through the nose. On everything from a newspaper to a $100 million skyscraper, the mob made sure they got their cut, and it wasn't a small one, either.

What angered me particularly—and I thought about it a lot as I prepared to leave Washington for New York—was that the mob preyed especially heavily on Italians. Still.

Watch one of the *Godfather* movies or read some of the nonsense that has been written by so-called experts about the Italian

Mafia and you come away with all this happy horseshit about codes of honor, unbreakable oaths of silence, and mustachioed old dons donating happily to the church.

Bullshit.

It was true that the Mafia had begun back in Sicily with honorable intentions, but that was back in the eleventh century, for Christ's sake. Sicily was constantly being overrun by one army or another, and the Mafia had begun as a secret society to defend its members and their families from the next band of invading marauders. That, as I say, was way back then, however.

Fast-forward to the end of the nineteenth century and you've got miserable poverty in Sicily—and throughout Italy and the rest of Europe, for that matter—and the United States is looking pretty good. That's why my father came over—for the opportunity to work hard and earn an honest wage.

The wise guys began coming over about then, too, but they had another idea in mind. And when Prohibition went into effect in 1920, well, they might as well have put up billboards all over Sicily with big arrows pointing toward America: Attention thieves, smugglers, and confidence men. This way to the land of crooked deals and fat profits.

Of course, criminal groups from other countries came to the United States, too, but the Italian Mafia was tougher and better organized. And their consciences were less troubled, I think, by the idea of preying on their own kind.

People like my father.

I had a lot of time to think about this as I headed up Interstate 95 from Washington to New York, mainly because I was by myself. It's hard for some people to remember now, I guess, but back in 1979 interest rates were going through the roof, and the housing market was flat on its back. Linda and I couldn't even find browsers for our beautiful house in Virginia. We could scrimp and save and try to cut corners, but you can only go so far, and with the move to New York, we definitely hit the wall.

There was no way to move the family.

That meant I was going alone, and we'd see what we could

work out with the sale of the house down the road. I remember driving away from the place, Linda and the kids in the front yard. Everything was in bloom, and the kids were as handsome as new grass. Maria was nine; Joey, almost six.

What in the name of God did I think I was doing? In my heart of hearts I wasn't sure I knew.

I drove north, a gassy lump in my gut.

One of the things the FBI did have that worked real well was databases. Even before I got to New York to report to Neil Welch, I could tap into all sorts of information about what the five families of the Cosa Nostra were into up there. Not surprisingly, they still had their musclemen out and about in Brooklyn and Queens, extorting money from small Italian shopowners. They still had their shylocks putting money on the streets at extortionate rates of interest. And for the unfortunate people who fell behind on the vigorish, the double-digit weekly interest on the loans that never seemed to reduce the principal, there was still the explicit threat of violence. Some of these unfortunate people, I knew, were men and women of my parents' generation, but that didn't matter to the wise guys, of course. They were as ready as ever to make good on the threats and break a few legs.

Even though the five families maintained that traditional end of the business in the Italian neighborhoods of the city, they had long since moved on to bigger and more lucrative endeavors. Of the five, the Gambino and the Genovese families were the biggest and the most powerful. The Gambinos, for example, had their hooks into the meat and construction industries. They also had New York's Garment District locked up from top to bottom, and through Carlo Gambino's son Tommy, one of the few wise guys who actually *was* a shrewd businessman, the family also controlled most of the city's big unions.

The Genovese family had what some people might consider a tonier trade. While they controlled most, if not all, of what moved on and through the docks of New York and at the city's bustling Fulton Fish Market, they also were very big players in the movie and entertainment businesses. It was good positioning on their part, and it would pay off nicely.

This is not to suggest that the other three families—the Luccheses, the Colombos, and the Bonannos—were pikers. The Luccheses had a lock on a hefty chunk of the cargo traffic moving through John F. Kennedy International Airport. The Colombos basically controlled the entire cement industry in New York and could shut down a construction job within a hundred miles of the city with no more than a nod. The Bonannos were a chaotic and neurotic lot, but that didn't mean they weren't dangerous. They were among the first of the families of the Cosa Nostra to get heavily involved in drugs, heroin especially. As Joe Pistone was observing from a ringside seat inside the family, the Bonannos were inordinately prone to sudden spasms of violence. Maybe because they were so nuts, who knows?

Anyway, these were the wise guys waiting for me when I checked in on my first day on the new job in New York.

I still remember the date. It was June 17, 1979.

10

"WHAT we've got here, is we got a big fucking mess."

I liked guys who didn't mince their words, so this was one more thing to add to my list of pluses on Neil Welch. I hadn't even gotten settled yet, and here we are in Welch's corner office, Kallstrom and I, sitting around his big conference table, and Welch is basically giving us our marching orders. But first he had to lay a little groundwork, elaborating, if you will, on why the flagship office of the Federal Bureau of Investigation was such a goddamned basket case.

"We got a morale problem here, we got an attitude problem, and we got organizational problems like you read about—and that's just for starters." Welch leaned across the polished oak tabletop toward us and gave Jimmy and me what I would come to recognize as his best shit-eating grin. "And that's why you two guys are here—to fix the fucking thing."

"Yes, sir."

"I want you to take a good hard look at the system, then give me some recommendations on how to make the thing work."

"Yes, sir." Kallstrom did the honors this time.

"And remember, you're working for me, so when you tell somebody something, it's like I'm telling them, okay?"

"Okay, boss." It was my turn again for the head-bobbing yes-sir, but I must have looked at Welch kind of funny.

"You got a question, Jules?"

New York was an infinitely better place than Washington, but I knew there were big problems and bigger egos. Working for Welch, for instance, were three special agents in charge, or SACs. That's three Hooverite bishops, each one with an enormous amount of power. After that, under each SAC were still more A-SACs, assistant special agents in charge, and they had a hell of a lot of clout, too. Way more, by the books, anyway, than either Kallstrom and I would have as mere coordinators in the O.C. system. How were we supposed to deal with them?

"Boss . . ." I didn't know quite how to say it, but I sure as hell knew what I wanted to say.

"Spit it out, Jules."

For me the worst questions are the ones you never ask; the way I see it, you're almost always better off opening your mouth. "Boss, not to be too blunt about it, but what are we supposed to do with all those SACs and A-SACs crawling around out there? I mean, you got enough of them to field a full ball team with a decent bench."

Welch smiled for the first time that morning. "You guys leave that part of it to me, okay? Just tell me how to straighten the mess out. I'll handle the personnel."

Kallstrom did the yessirs for both of us again, and a minute or two after that, we were on our way out of Welch's inner sanctum. The new A-DIC had talked about rebuilding the FBI's New York office brick by brick. Before you can do that, though, you've got to start in with the jackhammers.

That was where Kallstrom and I came in, I figured.

By the end of the first week on the job, I had the photographs of Linda and the kids on the metal desk in my little cubicle, and that was about as much decorating as I was going to get done. I missed the family enormously. One of the good things about the new job, though, was that it had me so busy I didn't have time to really think about how much I missed them.

Welch had set us a huge task, but there was some reason for encouragement. Because as screwed up as New York's organizational structure was, there was a core of good people, both men and women, and that would give Kallstrom and me a base to build on. Of course, we knew we needed a lot more stalwart souls to join us, and we had already begun putting lines out to see who might be interested. That's why when my phone rang at the end of the first week and it was Tom Emory on the line, I dropped whatever the hell it was I was doing and listened carefully.

Emory was the guy who had given me my first promotion back in 1975, so maybe it sounds a little funny when I say he had an unusually good eye for people; it's the truth, though. At the time of his call, Tom Emory was the new SAC in Newark, and he wanted to pitch a guy my way for New York.

This, by the way, is a perfect example of how the FBI was screwed up royally when it came to the bureaucracy—the bad news—but full of a lot of really good people just the same. Emory, for instance, had nothing at all to gain from pitching me this guy Jim Kossler. I didn't know Kossler, but I had dealt with him on the phone a few times during my eighteen merry months in Washington, and he had seemed like a real sharp guy. As Emory described him, Kossler was more than that—a great street agent, a great supervisor who had helped build one of the FBI's biggest organized-crimes cases in New Jersey. Kossler's problem, as Emory explained it, was that his number had finally come up, and now Hoover's rules required him to get his ticket punched down in the Washington Puzzle Palace; Kossler, being an eminently sane individual, wanted no part of the place.

"If you take him up there with you, Jules, I think we can get him a slide on the transfer to Headquarters." Emory wanted to bring Kossler in as a labor-racketeering coordinator working with me. There was no need for that slot, since I was coordinating all the organized-crime stuff, but to me Emory's word meant everything. Besides, I figured that anyone who felt as strongly about not going to Headquarters as Kossler was going to be aces with me. "You got it, Tom. Tell Kossler to stop by next week and introduce himself when he comes in. We'll go from there."

Three days later, a red-haired guy who looked like he had just stepped off the boat from Galway humming "Danny Boy" stepped into my cubicle and stuck out a big freckled paw. "Jim Kossler, Jules. How the hell you doing?"

It was the beginning of another one of those friendships I was talking about. It was also a key move, like a mid-division NFL team lucking onto a great free-agent deal in the off-season. Kallstrom and I had talked endlessly about putting together a team; with Jim Kossler, we had just gotten a franchise player. Now with Kallstrom and his guys and Kossler and mine, plus a few of the people you have met already and a few more still to come, it was a team that would ultimately break the back of the most powerful crime syndicate in the world even as it turned the FBI, the most powerful law enforcement agency in the goddamned world, squarely on its rock-hard head.

Some days I'm still not sure which was tougher.

Here was the deal in New York: At the time I got back there, we had the one assistant director in charge. That was Welch. But under Welch there were three separate FBI field offices, each one headed by one of the Hooverite bishops I mentioned. We had the office in Manhattan, which made sense. But then we had another office up in Westchester County, up toward Connecticut. And then we had still another out in the borough of Queens, in Rego Park.

Having three different offices would have been fine, I suppose, except that each one was what you might call fussy about its geographic perquisites. You might call it that, anyway; what I called it was fucking paranoid.

Personalities aside, the arrangement was as screwed up as it could possibly be, and the reason for that was—if you put it as a question—do you think Paul Castellano and his scuzzball, drug-dealing pizza parlors really stopped at the Westchester County line? Think they had a whole different operation out in Queens or in Brooklyn, then another one back in Manhattan?

Bullshit.

What I'm saying is that the FBI, in its incomparable brilliance, had established a stupid-assed, monkey-minded bureaucracy that could not have been more conducive to exploitation by the wise guys than if they had set it up themselves.

At one point early on in our little inquiry for Mr. Welch, Kossler and I discovered six separate FBI investigations—not nationwide, mind you; in the New York area alone—into a major capo in the Genovese family named Matthew Ianniello. Ianniello, whose mob nickname was "Matty the Horse," was not exactly cut from the same intellectual cloth as an Edison or an Einstein; a few generations of inbreeding, indeed, had conspired to dilute that particular gene pool to truly unfortunate levels.

Still, whatever his deficiencies in the brainpower department, Matty the Horse had it all over the FBI. Agents from Westchester, Manhattan, and Queens were literally bumping into each other on surveillances of Ianniello. When tempers within the three FBI offices finally boiled over, the agents were ordered to stand down while higher-ups blew smoke at each other in closed-door meetings, fighting over who would take the lead in stalking Matty the Horse. Compared to us, what I'm saying is, Matty Ianniello looked like a positively brilliant guy. Which, if you knew him, is something *really* hard to imagine.

So anyway, we weren't exactly shocked, Kossler and I, to discover that the FBI system was designed by geniuses. Dismantling it, though, was going to be a very big problem.

In the FBI, the biggest problems by definition were always political problems. In New York, the politics of the issue confronting me and Kossler came down to simple arithmetic—how to get rid of two Hooverite bishops in what had traditionally been a three-bishop town? This was just one of the problems we began documenting for our ball-busting new boss, Mr. Welch; it wasn't the only one, though. Not by a long shot.

Looking around, Kallstrom saw even bigger problems than I did. Jimmy was going to be in charge of what Welch was calling "Special Ops." In Detroit, as I said, Welch had moved all the agents doing surveillance work out of the main FBI office downtown and into a secret location that had no identifiable links to the Bureau. In New York, Kallstrom was going to be Welch's overall surveillance honcho, and Welch had even more ambitious plans for Special Ops. If Kallstrom didn't have the toughest job in the FBI, it was right up there.

Kallstrom, who had remained in New York when I went to

Washington, walked me through the system one day. The way we were doing surveillance, he said, was an abortion. Each of the ten O.C. squads in the office had used agents on surveillance on a totally ad hoc basis. These agents had no training, no direction, no plan. They would simply show up at a location, say, at a place where one of the families was running a gambling operation. Then they would hang around and watch who came and went. That was the FBI's idea of conducting surveillance.

It was a joke, and that's putting it charitably. Jim Kallstrom didn't like jokes like that, and he had plans for the FBI's surveillance system.

He was going to nuke it.

I have explained about the FBI's obsession with numbers—arrests, indictments, et cetera. Jimmy and I both agreed that the system was bogus and had to be changed. "We don't need to be doing up here what we did in Vietnam," Kallstrom said, "win a thousand battles and lose the fucking war." The two of us were in complete agreement on the point. The way to go in our war on the mob was long-term, strategic investigations.

From Jimmy's point of view "long-term" and "strategic" meant only one thing: The dipshit squad-based surveillance teams would all have to be destroyed; a whole new system would have to be erected in their place.

If there was one thing that guided Kallstrom's thinking in this area, it was probably his experience working the Paul Castellano investigation a few years earlier, the one involving the crooked cheese businesses and the pizza parlors. This is an important point because it shows how far ahead Kallstrom was in his thinking in this area and, conversely, how the Bureau was still way back in the dark ages. In the Hoover system, surveillance was actually a very simple thing. A suspect would be identified and located. Then a bunch of our guys, in suits and comfortable shoes, would start following him around.

Complicated, right?

The point is, there was nothing wrong with physical surveillance. All kinds of cases—espionage, criminal, whatever—benefit from having agents actually observing criminal activity. Once an arrest is made and a suspect is brought to court, there are few things more damning than having a sworn federal agent on a witness stand testifying to a jury about seeing a guy collect a bag of money, deliver a load of drugs, or whatever.

One of the few things that *is* better than sworn agent testimony, however, is having the bad guy incriminate himself in his own words, then playing those words back to him in front of a judge and jury.

Talk about ruining someone's day.

Now I'm not saying the Bureau under Hoover was a blushing bride when it came to bugging phones, homes, and offices. If you believe half the stuff said and written about the old man, J. Edgar Hoover had had the bedrooms of the entire Congress, the Supreme Court, and Joint Chiefs of Staff wired for sound. The reality, fortunately, was quite different. With ninety-seven U.S. Attorneys' offices around the country and more than half that many FBI offices, in 1979, there were barely more than one hundred wiretaps in place nationwide. That's less than one per office.

The numbers aren't the point, though.

When it came to using electronic surveillance in criminal investigations, the Bureau did it in its typical dumb-ass, myopic fashion. Sure, we got court authorizations to bug phones and place secret microphones in homes and offices. But as soon as we had a bad guy saying he boosted a truckload of TVs or bribed the chairman of the local zoning board, *bam!*—we'd come in, make the arrest, and then the bug would be pulled out.

Kallstrom, as I say, saw this firsthand in the Castellano investigation. With the wire he had on Big Paulie, Kallstrom really needed round-the-clock help, but there was no way he was going to get it. The way Jimmy wanted to do it, you would have agents "on the muffs," listening in on the wire, twenty-four hours a day. You would also have had the physical surveillance of the type Jimmy was doing himself, following the cheese trucks around the city to see where they went.

But that would be just the beginning.

In Kallstrom's vision, the agents working surveillance would be trained professionals, not just guys roped in on an assignment for a few weeks or a few months. Kallstrom wanted the men and women working for him to be experts; nothing less would do. Kallstrom's people would not only be technically proficient in designing and installing secret listening devices; they would be specialists in the area of organized crime, deeply knowledgeable about the five Cosa Nostra families operating in New York.

While I was in Washington, Kallstrom had been assigned the job of beefing up the entire technical support system for the New York office, so he was already pretty well immersed in the whole business of bugs by the time Neil Welch showed up. Welch's decision to put Jimmy in charge of Special Operations now meant that things would start moving a whole lot faster.

As Kallstrom walked me around the office, past the rows and rows of special agents beavering away in their cubicles, he was talking quietly. This squad would have to be dismantled, he said. These people would be moved out of here; we'd have to get some more people to help out over here.

"Hey, Jim," I interrupted.

"Yeah, Jules?"

"Why don't you just drop a fucking bomb on the place, and then we'll start over that way?

"You know," Kallstrom said, "that's not a half-bad idea." He let out one of his big booming Santa Claus laughs after that. A couple of agents poked their heads out of cubicles, staring at us. It was impossible to read their looks.

11

THE Professor and the Wild Man, they called us, Kossler and Bonavolonta—I don't have to tell you which was which. The two of us were not exactly making a lot of friends as we set about doing the bidding of our new boss, Mr. Welch. And Kallstrom, well, Jimmy was just about as popular as we were. Which is to say that quite a few people hated his fucking guts.

Of course, the Bureau being the Bureau, only a few of our brothers and sisters in arms ever actually told us they hated our guts; the rest pretended Kossler, Kallstrom, and I were just a bunch of regular guys. Then, when we were out of sight, they would sit around talking about what prime assholes we were.

Oh, we were having a grand time, all right. Just grand.

For me, the office bullshit was compounded by the personal toll the job was taking. I had several people to whom I was deeply indebted for this. Topping the list was Jimmy Carter, whose basic decency was more than offset, for me at least, by the miserable economy over which he presided. Behind the president was the Ayatollah Khomeini. His adherents called him a holy man; I preferred bloodthirsty lunatic. Either way, by holding a bunch of innocent Americans hostage in Tehran, the bearded cleric was basically holding America hostage. After Khomeini, there were a thousand and one other things conspiring, as I put it in my more self-indulgent moments, against me and Linda and the kids. Such things are probably better left now to the jabberings of the economists and historians, I suppose. The bottom line for the Bonavolonta family, however, was that six months after I had made the move from Washington to New York, our handsome little home in Virginia had about as much chance of selling as I had of being named Queen of the Rose Bowl.

The Bonavolontas, in other words, were still a family living long-distance, and if you have never tried it, believe me, you don't want to. Ever.

Coming home late each night to my dismal little flat, it was easy enough to feel sorry for myself, and I succumbed more than a few times. But for Linda, and especially for the kids, it was worse. With kids, as any parent knows, it's hard to figure how you ever make up for lost time.

God knows I tried, but God knows I failed, too.

There was one weekend when Maria and Joe both had had big things on their plate. Joe was in a T-ball league, and his team, the Rangers, had made the championship finals. The game was set for Saturday afternoon, and that evening, Maria, who had become an accomplished young pianist, was giving her very first recital. I hadn't been able to make it home for the past three or four weekends, but I was determined that I would make it back for the game and the recital, and then the four of us would have a quiet Sunday together before I got back on the road to New York.

That was the plan.

I had bought a crappy secondhand Datsun just for the purpose of making my weekend commute, and I had the thing pointed south on Interstate 95 on a beautiful Saturday morning. I had left myself plenty of time, and I was in good shape that way. More important, I thought, by the time I got out of New Jersey, I had put all the bullshit from the office behind me, and I was thinking of Joey and his game, of Maria and her recital, and of Linda and how much she had done to raise our two kids largely on her own. I owed them all, big-time.

It was somewhere along in Maryland, as I recall it, that the piece-of-shit Datsun suddenly decided to expire and give up the ghost. I definitely remember the phone call home.

We were not wealthy people, and there was no way I could afford to just walk away from my bomb of a car and leave it.

Parts had been ordered, and they would be in first thing Monday. I would have to stay in a motel until then. Once the heap was running again, I'd have to hotfoot it back to New York.

Where, naturally, I would be late for work.

In everyone's life, there are some hellishly long nights. For me, that Saturday night was one of the longest. In the blue light of the droning TV, looking at the four scarred walls of the two-bit truckers' inn, I tried to imagine Joe's big T-ball game, then Maria's recital. As if in a movie, I saw Linda clearly in both scenes, sitting and watching, alone.

I felt like shit.

Compared with other families, of course, we were blessed. For all the pain of the distance between us, we had a strong marriage, Linda and I, and we had been graced with two wonderful children. At times like that, though, when you know you should be there for the family and you're not, there's something inside you that aches like a wound. For me, as long as I lived, I hoped never to feel that ache again.

I would, of course.

The five Cosa Nostra families we had been working on in New York were nothing compared to the FBI brass we were up against. Clearly, many had made it their mission to crucify, or at least neutralize, Neil Welch's crazy crusaders. Kallstrom had clear orders from Welch on setting up the new Special Operations Branch, but he was running into opposition, anyway. Kossler and I—with a more vague mandate to simply "fix" the broken organized-crime program—were running into tougher opposition, and as a result, I was having to spend more and more time fighting a lot of silly-assed internal battles, which meant I had less and less time to make the weekend trips to Washington.

By Christmas of 1979, I had finally managed a few days off, and we had a great holiday, the four of us. It was such a good time that I had stayed through Sunday evening and helped

Linda get the kids off to bed. They had stayed up later than usual; then Linda and I sat up and talked. By one-thirty Monday morning, though, it was time for me to get on the road. I was due at the office in New York in a few hours.

I remember going into Maria's room and kissing her for the last time; she barely stirred. When I went to look in on Joe, he was wide awake. He was also crying. Even when he was younger, just a tiny kid, Joey had run and worked out with me. We were buddies, the two of us; nothing could ever change that. But this business of my being gone all the time *was* trouble.

I've got a big mouth, but there are times when even I don't know what to say. This was definitely one of them. If I could have found my voice, I'm not sure I know what would have come out of me, watching those fat tears run down my son's face.

Joe, however, was a tough kid, and he was not at a loss for words. "Daddy, did you *ask* for this job in New York?"

I glanced at Linda, and she looked away, tears welling in her eyes now. I looked at Joe. "Yeah, champ, I guess I did."

"Why?" Joe riveted his eyes on mine, and I saw that the tears had stopped. My son wanted an answer.

I got down on my knees next to his bed. "Joe, there is only one reason that I would ever leave you and Maria and Mom. And that's because I have something important to do in New York, and I hope you can understand that, okay?"

Joe rubbed a little fist in front of his eyes. A second later, he nodded up and down. "Okay, Dad."

Every father wants to think there's a lot of himself in his son, and there is, usually. With Joe, though, I could see it clearly. As tired as he was, he had stayed up as long as it took to hit me with his question. I knew he couldn't make complete sense of the answer, of course, but still I think he got some of what he wanted. His father was doing something that counted for a lot. Dad wasn't happy being away from home so much of the time, but for now that was the way it had to be.

It's amazing, some of the things we try to rationalize to our-

selves. Was my son fully satisfied with the answer he had received? Was I happy with the answer I had given?

No and no.

Would it have to do, at least for the moment?

Yes, unfortunately.

I kissed Joe good night, got up from the floor next to his bed,
and watched him settle his head on the pillow. At the front door,
I gave Linda a long kiss good-bye.

Outside, it was cold and black, another New Year upon us. In
the Datsun, as I pushed her out onto the highway north to New
York, the tinny heater blew cool air at me.

Served me right, I thought.

"Jimmy, what the hell are we doing here?"

Kossler and I were drinking beer in this college bar way the
hell up in Ithaca, New York, and I would have given him a
hundred dollars if there was a wise guy within two hundred
miles of us. But orders were orders, and the Bureau had sent
the two of us up to Cornell University in the dead of winter, so
there we were.

At the time, our running battle with the FBI brass in Washington was not going particularly well, and to compound things,
Neil Welch had just had a tough operation on his back, and now
he was getting ready to retire. That the long knives had been out
for Welch for some time was no secret. But without Welch's
protection—an assistant director in charge could keep you from
having an incredible load of shit rained down on your head—
we were better than fair game; we were sitting ducks.

So with Welch on his sickbed, his retirement papers being
filled out gleefully by some Puzzle Palace time server in Washington, the orders sending me and Kossler up to the frozen
wastes of Ithaca seemed particularly suspicious.

In fact, as we would find out a little bit later, it was just the
same old FBI bureaucracy grinding along again. But this time,
in what I like to think of as an exquisitely neat twist of fate, the

FBI, in sending us off to Ithaca, would arm me and Kossler with a powerful new tool to subdue the bureaucracy.

Looking back, I figure it was about time we got a break.

The man behind the Ithaca seminar was a genius, pure and simple. G. Robert Blakey had a first name that was an initial, and he wrote and sometimes talked like a lawyer.

Appearances, as they say, can be deceiving.

Long before anyone else even thought of it, Bob Blakey had dreamed up the concept and then the actual language of the Racketeer Influenced and Corrupt Organizations Act. Everyone called it RICO. Congress passed the law in 1970.

Blakey won't say so, but there are some, me included, who believe he coined the name of the RICO law just to mimic the 1930s mob movie *Little Caesar*. (Everyone remembers Edward G. Robinson as the small-town hood Caesar Enrico "Rico" Bandello; most people forget his sidekick, however, the sometime ballroom dancer played by Douglas Fairbanks, Jr.)

Like so many great ideas, the thought behind RICO was breathtakingly simple. Remember all those crummy gambling cases I was always complaining about? Under Blakey's law, you wouldn't target the mopes running the illegal gambling operations; what you would do is use the *fact* of those operations to prove a *pattern* of racketeering activity. Why do this? Because instead of going after the low-level guys at the gaming tables, you would try to connect up all the illegal gaming tables, then go after the organization running the show.

This was exactly what I had been saying all those years, but I didn't know beans from RICO. Somehow in the great bureaucracy of American law enforcement, no one had ever told me or anyone else I knew about Blakey's ingenious law. Now the careful reader will note something interesting here, if not downright peculiar. Congress passes Blakey's law in 1970, right? Here it is ten years later, and Kossler and I—the two guys allegedly in charge of running the organized-crime program in the biggest FBI office in the country—are just getting our first sniff of the thing. What kind of system is that?

Only later would I learn that the Bureau and the Department of Justice were just as much in the dark as I was; at least the people at my level were. But that tells you something about the way Washington works. I'm sure some bright lawyer somewhere in the Department of Justice knew all about Blakey's brilliant law. But without a clear signal from someone higher up in the organizational food chain, that bright lawyer is going to keep his mouth shut, and RICO is going to sit on the books for a decade, as useless as if the law had never been passed.

By my lights, that was a tragedy.

But that didn't mean it was too late to set things right.

To attack the mob the way the FBI was doing, with its insectlike obsession with arrest and indictment numbers, was not just dumb but counterproductive.

Kossler and I knew that, of course. It took Bob Blakey to show us how to make a weapon of that knowledge.

12

FOR my money, the idea of genius has more to do with clarity of vision than anything else. That was definitely the case with Blakey. Hoover might have been embarrassed into admitting there was such a thing as organized crime, but that wasn't the case with others. As early as 1950, Estes Kefauver, an incorruptible Tennessee Democrat, had convened televised hearings on the effect of organized crime on legitimate businesses across the United States. The subject had galvanized the American public. After a while, however, everyone pretty much forgot about it. Everyone but Blakey.

As a line attorney in the Justice Department's Organized Crime Section and later as the top lawyer counseling the U.S. Senate Subcommittee on Criminal Laws and Procedures, Bob Blakey had made himself the nation's preeminent legal expert on the murderous hoods of the Cosa Nostra. A man of angelic mien and ice-hard will, Blakey had also figured out a way to dig at the Mafia's viscera, and this, I think, is where his genius comes in. Because the salient fact about organized crime, as Blakey saw so clearly, was that it was *organized*.

Such a simple concept.

I see it now, of course; sitting in that seminar in Ithaca, though, I was still in the dark. When he started out that first morning, Blakey gave no hint of what he had in store for us. The man is a genius, as I said, but he is also a lawyer. And he got off to a slow, lawyerly start, frog-marching the class through the history of the Cosa Nostra in America, the twenty-four different families that operated across the country, the history of the code of *omertà*, the Mafia code of silence that I had already seen firsthand was a bunch of bullshit.

"Holy Christ, Jim, this is terrible."

"Give it time, Jules. The guy's just getting started."

They didn't call Kossler the Professor for nothing, I thought. Before he had joined the Bureau, Kossler had taught mentally disabled kids—an incredibly tough job. Whereas I was impulsive, an ask-questions-later kind of guy, Kossler was different. He was more patient, more willing to give things time to play out before he made a decision.

So we stuck it out. What else could we do?

Eventually, Blakey found his way to the heart of things and began walking us through the building blocks of RICO, the actual language of the statute and what it meant. The French call this kind of thing *explication de texte.*

That was where Blakey hooked me and Kossler.

It shall be unlawful for any person employed by or associated with any enterprise engaged in, or the activities of which affect, interstate or foreign commerce, to conduct or participate, directly or indirectly, in the conduct of such enterprise's affairs through a pattern of racketeering activity or collection of unlawful debt.

Why are lawyers such lousy writers?

Some of my lawyer friends, when they really get going, rhapsodize about the "majesty of the law." I know what they mean, for I've seen the majesty firsthand, when it helped the Bureau put away some particularly loathsome hood for a real long time. But you look at what most laws actually say—even Blakey's beautiful work of genius—and it's like fighting your way through a thicket of poison commas.

I won't say that the afternoon Blakey finally got into RICO with us was an epiphany, but when he began explaining the concept behind all the dense verbiage, it was like a heavy tarp being pulled off a beautiful piece of sculpture.

"A comprehensive and successful preemptive strike aimed directly at the heart of La Cosa Nostra is the only viable strategy for dealing with this cancer that has existed in American society for more than seventy years," Blakey lectured. "Such an attack can only be implemented through the strategic use of wiretaps and bugs—and RICO."

I shot a look at Kossler. "Holy shit!"

"I *know.*"

"We've got to talk to this guy."

"Right."

Beneath his lawyer's robes, it turned out, Bob Blakey had the soul of a tub-thumping preacher. "Get off the merry-go-round, guys. You've got to get off the damned merry-go-round!"

I had never heard the term used that way, but as soon as it was explained, I saw that it was a perfect metaphor for what we had been doing all those years in the Bureau. The merry-go-round was the stupid-assed gambling cases we worked; it was pulling out bugs and wires as soon as we got the first hard evidence that a crime had been committed; it was Hoover's myopic inspection system. Blakey's merry-go-round was everything I thought was wrong with the FBI, particularly our supposed war against the mob.

Our class eventually ended that first day, and it must have looked to the others in the room as if Kossler and I were hauling poor Blakey in for questioning or something. Bob Blakey is the gentlest of men, slightly built, and I'm afraid Kossler and I descended on him like two linebackers. I forget now whether Jimmy or I asked the first question, but I'll never forget Blakey's answer. It took three days.

The beauty of RICO, Blakey explained, is that it allows you to use the fact of a criminal act—a murder, an act of extortion, whatever—as an *item* of evidence. The idea is as simple as a child's puzzle—connect the dots. Link a murder, an act of extortion here, an illegal drug transaction and some loan-sharking there, and all of a sudden you've got the critical elements of Blakey's inspired vision: a *pattern* of criminal activity. Link the pattern to a particular Cosa Nostra family and you can go after the family legally—under RICO—as a criminal *enterprise.*

Blakey was not a man possessed of a single vision—not by any means. In 1968, two years before he took up his pen and drafted the inspired language of RICO, Blakey had helped author something called the Omnibus Crime Control and Safe Streets Act, which was the centerpiece of Richard Nixon's vaunted war on crime. There was some pretty creative thinking that went into the law, and Blakey's contribution, in my opinion, was by far the most important. He authored Title III of the omnibus crime law. It was under Title III that FBI agents and federal prosecutors could apply to a judge to string a wire or plant a bug in a criminal suspect's home, car, office, whatever.

Title III wasn't ignored in the same way RICO was, but by 1980, when Blakey was giving Kossler and me religion up in Ithaca, Title IIIs—it's a tribute to Blakey, I think, that agents always used the name of his section of the crime bill to refer to bugs and wiretaps—were used only in the rarest of cases. Even when they were employed, though, the FBI used Title IIIs badly. One reason was the Bureau's obsession with numbers. Because agents listening to wiretaps for days on end would not be out on the streets making arrests, the geniuses that ran the FBI didn't believe in using Title IIIs long-term.

Another reason for the relatively scarce use of hidden microphones and telephone bugs—which I don't believe is at all well understood—is that the bar is awfully high when the government applies for permission to invade a citizen's privacy. It may come as a surprise to some, but most federal judges, even the hang-'em-high hard-asses, expect prosecutors and government agents to clear that bar with more than a few inches to spare. The constitutional protections on privacy are extremely rigorous —as they should be. And judges presented with Title III applications want to see a hell of a lot of evidence of criminal activity before they sign off on the installation of a bug or phone tap in someone's home or business. Even the installations of pen registers—which simply record the numbers of outgoing calls from a telephone but make no recording of any conversations— were difficult to obtain. And judges would authorize pen-register applications, like bugs and wiretaps, only for limited periods of time; if you wanted to extend beyond that, the government's lawyers would have to march back into court and make a brand-new application.

This was part of Blakey's vision, too. While he desired tough new tools to use against organized crime, he wanted to make sure that there were sufficient checks and balances on the government agents and lawyers conducting the investigations; what he emphatically did not want was rogue warriors.

Kossler and I understood that. What was new to us—and what we'd have to go back and share immediately with Kallstrom—was how we could combine the more strategic use of Title IIIs with the heavy firepower of RICO. Keep a Title III in long enough and there was no telling how many *items* of evidence we might come up with. Link the resulting *pattern* of evidence to a particular family, then consolidate that evidence with the stuff we were getting from undercover guys like Pistone, and the sky was the limit in terms of what one could do.

Blakey was nothing if not thorough. With his detailed explanation of RICO, he had baked us this wonderful cake, and then he brought along the icing for it, too. If we could document the pattern of criminal activity, link it conclusively to a particular mob family, then convict the family as a criminal enterprise, Blakey explained to Kossler and myself, we could petition a judge to sentence particular members of the family under something called the special-offender law. This was another Blakey brainstorm. Individuals shown to have taken a leadership role in a criminal enterprise could be sentenced by judges under the provisions of the special-offender law to longer prison terms than your ordinary rope-a-dope criminals.

Kossler and I looked at each other wordlessly.

The guy was a fucking genius.

I'm not sure, but on our final day in Ithaca, I think Kossler's feet and mine were barely touching the ground. Since the first afternoon of the seminar, we had spent nearly every waking hour with Blakey, and I think he was genuinely touched by our enthusiasm. He had given this same seminar in Washington, at the FBI Academy at Quantico—all over the place; everywhere he went, he got the cold shoulder. At the U.S. Attorney's office in Manhattan, poor Blakey was practically thrown out of the place when he tried to deliver his lecture on RICO.

The way Blakey explained it, usually the response was more tepid. Prosecutors and agents simply wrote the guy off as some kind of daffy academic, and he was sent gently on his way. What could a goddamned college professor know about organized crime, anyway? Never mind that Blakey had written the laws about which he lectured; he was a prophet without honor among the brass of the FBI and the Department of Justice.

It was a long drive back to Manhattan from Ithaca, but Kossler and I could barely pull ourselves away. It's funny, the people you meet, the ones from whom you draw inspiration and the ones who just kind of take up space. I could see why Blakey had gotten stiffed by agents and prosecutors for so long. He was courtly, soft-spoken; he didn't look like a tough, streetwise government agent or a hard-bitten prosecutor.

And yet, in the ways that really counted, Bob Blakey was tougher by far than all the blue-suited desk jockeys in Washington whose only real interest was in the next step up the career ladder, the next bump up the pay scale.

As I got into the car for the drive home, I shook Blakey's hand again warmly. "Thanks a million, Bob. You've really completed the picture for us."

"Don't thank me yet, Jules. You've got the tools, and you know how to use them. But to do what you guys want to do is not going to be easy—not at all."

"We're going to give it our best shot, Bob. I promise you."

"I know you will. And I'm here if you ever need help—anytime, anyplace."

Kossler and I climbed into the car, and Blakey gave us a final good-bye salute, beaming, I thought, at his two improbable new acolytes. As we were pulling out of the parking lot, Kossler rolled down the car window for a final farewell, and Blakey gave us a few final words of inspiration. "I dream," he said, "of an indictment of every boss."

Kossler and I headed back down the highway to New York, smiling like a couple of genuine idiots.

13

THE Bonanno family into which Joe Pistone had managed to insert himself posing as the jewel thief Donnie Brasco didn't have a whole lot in common with your basic American family.

After a ten-year stretch in a federal penitentiary, a pint-sized psychopath named Carmine Galante had elbowed his way to the top of the Bonannos, on his way, he thought, to the higher reaches of the entire Cosa Nostra structure in the United States. The boss of bosses of the Cosa Nostra at the time was Carlo Gambino, and he obliged Galante by dying of old age. Given Galante's well-known predilection for violence, this was generally considered merciful for the ailing Gambino and his loved ones. New York police had evidence implicating Galante in more than eighty murders, and no one who knew him thought Galante would scruple much over one more hit if old man Gambino didn't step aside.

Long before Kossler and I took our trip up to Ithaca to attend Bob Blakey's seminar on RICO, I knew that a considerable reservoir of ill will toward Galante was developing among the four other Cosa Nostra families in New York. Galante had pretty much cornered the city's lucrative heroin market, and the other four families were not at all pleased by this development. There was plenty of reason, therefore, for the wise guys' professed unhappiness with Mr. Galante.

What goes around eventually comes around, as they say, and Carmine Galante was about to see that for himself. I had become Joe Pistone's control agent by then, and he had been keeping me up-to-date on the activities of the Bonannos. From my other organized-crime squads, I was also getting an earful about the situation developing with Galante. Unlike weathermen who can rely on barometers, Ouija boards, and whatever other gizmos they use to try and predict the next low-pressure front moving in, in the FBI we had no way at all to predict what was going to happen next with the gentlemen of the Cosa Nostra.

My gut said trouble, however, and on a brutally hot July afternoon in 1979 my gut was proved right. Galante had stopped off for lunch at his favorite place, the Joe & Mary Italian-American Restaurant on a grimy stretch of Knickerbocker Avenue in Brooklyn. The place was owned by a close friend of Galante's, and the restaurateur had set up the don's favorite table out on the back patio. Galante was having his usual—fish, salad, and red wine. What he hadn't ordered on the side was the three guys in ski masks with the shotguns and pistols.

Behind the desk in his office fifteen years later, Joe Pistone would hang a blowup of the police photo from Joe & Mary's. In the photograph, little Carmine Galante lays sprawled on the flagstones, a hole in his left eye, his twisty cigar still burning between his lips. A friend of the don's, Leonardo Coppola, is similarly arrayed on the ground, only without the cigar and without most of the top of his head.

It was the opening shot in the beginning of what would be a long war, but before Pistone would have the leisure to worry about decorating his office with gruesome photos of mob hits, he would have to worry about staying alive. We had already moved Joe's family hundreds of miles away from New York, and Pistone was getting to see them only every six weeks or so. Nobody wanted to pull Joe in from the cold yet, though—and he would have killed me personally if I had tried—because he was getting closer and closer to the top of the Bonanno family.

In the wake of the Galante hit, the Bonannos were under heavy pressure not just from the other families; they were split among themselves, too. Philip "Rusty" Rastelli was the new boss, but he was in jail. Several Bonanno captains figured that was reason enough to give Rusty his walking papers.

Rastelli had other ideas.

He also had friends. Principal among them was a powerful Bonanno captain named Dominick "Sonny Black" Napolitano. Sonny Black was big into the numbers rackets and check-kiting scams. He was also a peculiar kind of guy. He did a lot of his business, for example, while he tended his pigeons in a coop on the roof of his apartment building in the Williamsburg section of Brooklyn—not the most businesslike environment. Pistone comes into the picture because he had gotten very close to Sonny Black through one of his deputies, a back-stabbing slime-ball named Benjamin "Lefty Guns" Ruggiero. Lefty Guns was such a stand-up guy that he had once murdered his own son-in-law for skimming a measly few bucks in illegal heroin profits.

It was, as I mentioned, not a nice family.

Besides their peculiar ethical compass, the wise guys in the Bonanno clan were interesting for another reason, and since there has been so much bullshit written about the Mafia, this is probably worth mentioning. As Pistone can tell you, no one can teach an agent how to work undercover; he or she either has it or they don't. What I mean is, if the moves, the banter, and the kibitzing don't come to a person naturally, the chances of that person operating successfully as an undercover agent are pretty much nil. Most people, I think, understand this. What is less well understood is that the truly great undercover agents—and Pistone, as I said, is a legend, in a class all by himself—find ways to make their targets *need* them.

This was the case with Lefty.

Pistone had met Lefty Guns at a social club on Madison Street in Little Italy. Actually, Joe's first contact there was an ugly sociopath, a guy named Tony Mirra. Tony, as Joe described him, was a "stone killer," the only guy around whom Pistone felt he always had to be on his toes. Lefty was less edgy than Tony Mirra and a much better target—a happy combination. So Pistone kept his distance from Tony Mirra and set his sights on Lefty Guns. As it happened, Lefty was running a bookmaking operation for a wise guy named Nicky Marangello, a pathetic little guy who went by the nickname "Glasses" on account of his unattractive eyewear.

Glasses Marangello was the underboss of the Bonannos.

The thing about Lefty was that he wasn't real bright. You read some of the stuff that has been written about the Mafia and you think these guys are geniuses—they're into this kind of exotic financial swindle and that. Let me tell you, anytime the mob gets its hooks into the fancy financial stuff, it's almost always because they've threatened or forced their way in.

Geniuses these guys are not.

And Lefty especially.

Pistone, of course, didn't exactly need this pointed out. Once, he and Lefty had to go out to Chicago to do a little business, and the two of them were standing at the edge of Lake Michigan. Lefty had only rarely been out of New York, and he had no idea of geography—none. Lefty was full of surprises, as Pistone was finding out, but when he told Joe how the Atlantic Ocean sure looked nice that day, Pistone just about lost it.

"Lefty," Joe said. "We're in Chicago. This is Lake Michigan, pal."

"It's the fucking Atlantic, whaddya nuts?"

Pistone figured it was better not to argue, but you can see it didn't take a person of genius to discover that Lefty was anything but. Anyway, once Pistone got a little closer to him, he saw that Lefty was clearly overwhelmed by the bookmaking business he was running for Nicky Glasses. Joe, being the helpful kind of guy he was, offered to give Lefty a hand.

In addition to not being too bright as a rule, wise guys also tend to be extremely lazy. Lefty was no exception, and so within a few weeks of Pistone's offer to help Lefty out, Joe is basically running Nicky Glasses's whole bookmaking show, taking the bets, keeping the ledgers, collecting the debts.

Lefty and Joe, needless to say, became fast friends.

And the friendship paid off—bigger than any of us could have imagined. After Carmine Galante got whacked at Joe & Mary's and Phil Rastelli became the boss of the Bonannos, Sonny Black Napolitano became the strongest capo in the family. Actually, since Rastelli was still cooling his heels in jail, Sonny Black was the acting boss of the family, and Lefty Guns was his right-hand man. And helpful Joe Pistone, well, he got put on Sonny Black's personal crew—right next to the boss.

More important than the nice people my friend Pistone got to hang out with while he was working was that when Kossler and I got back from Ithaca, thanks to Joe we already had one critical element of a long-term strategy against the Cosa Nostra in place. Joe was tight with the Bonannos, inside; he was their guy. To this day, it still amazes me why none of the bright lights in Washington decided to pull the plug on the Pistone operation. Certainly, Headquarters didn't share our view on the importance of long-term, strategic investigations of the Mafia.

As I think about it now, it must have been simply that the whole thing with Pistone was so unusual. The FBI had never had an agent so far inside a criminal operation, and I guess none of the brass at Headquarters could figure out a reason to pull Pistone out. The whole thing was so strange that for all the years Joe had been undercover, the FBI's books still had him assigned to the New York truck-hijacking squad, with me as his control. It was a totally unique operation, something none of the geniuses knew quite what to make of.

So, lucky for us, they left me and Pistone alone.

Having Joe in was just one piece of the puzzle, though; we still had to put the others together.

Jim Kallstrom was maybe the biggest piece. Back in New York, Jimmy was going great guns putting his Special Operations Branch together. When Kossler and I filled him in on our week with Blakey, he got just as fired up as we had. No one needed to tell Kallstrom how to string a wire and run it right, so using Title IIIs the way Blakey had talked about was nothing new to him. But thinking about the strategy Blakey had outlined —about using a bug to go after not just Paul Castellano personally but against the entire Gambino family that he ran—*was* new.

Laid over Kallstrom's newly enhanced Special Ops team and the Pistone situation, Blakey's RICO theory made the other pieces of the puzzle suddenly fit. But as Blakey had said before

Kossler and I climbed into the car for the drive back to New York, implementing his theory would not be easy. To go after a Mafia family, you had to pick your targets carefully. To be more precise, the targets you picked, if they were worth a damn at all, would have to lead you to other targets.

That was the ticket, and Kossler and I weren't back from Ithaca more than a few days before we had all our O.C. squads poring over old cases, arrest records, and intelligence reports to see if we could get a line on just one *strategic* target—one wise guy who could lead us into the operations of an entire family. The targets had to be out there. With the shiny new lenses Bob Blakey had fixed on our eyes now, I figured it was just a matter of time before we found them.

Pistone's situation was another matter. Things with the Bonannos were still much too fluid to make any kind of decision on how to proceed. The split within the family also complicated things enormously. As one of Sonny Black's crew, Pistone would be a natural target for the other side of the family that wanted Sonny Black dead. We'd have to watch that carefully.

Watch and—once again—wait.

It was while I was doing all this watching and waiting and worrying that I got a phone call from Headquarters.

I was being summoned back to Washington.

14

THE J. Edgar Hoover Building on Pennsylvania Avenue looks like it was designed by Franz Kafka on a bad day, which is fitting, I think, given the large number of bizarre, improbable, and hopelessly confused spirits that inhabit the Headquarters of the Federal Bureau of Investigation at any given time.

I had come damned close to quitting the Bureau because of my frustrations with Headquarters on my last go-round there. This time, though, there were three big things that persuaded me to accept the transfer. The first, of course, was the family. We had been separated for fifteen months, and as much as the distance and the long absences tore at me, the arrangement was much more unfair to Linda and the kids. Returning to Washington, despite the legions of imbeciles I would have to deal with there, was worth it for the family alone.

It was time to put them first. For once.

The new job was worth it, too, as it turned out. I would be the number-two guy in the Organized Crime Section, and the number-one guy was none other than my old car-pool buddy and partner on the New York informant squad, Sean McWeeney. Sean had made his bones in organized-crime work, it was his first love, and he was damned good at it. For that reason, the FBI, in its infinite wisdom, had dispatched Sean after his tour in New York, where he was one of the few people we had who was trying to make really good cases, to Portland, Oregon. Now everyone knows, of course, that Portland is an absolute hotbed of Italian Mafia activity—that it is owned lock, stock, and barrel by the mob.

Bullshit.

There might have been a wise guy or two in Portland, I suppose, but I'll give even money those were just guys changing planes en route to Las Vegas or Chicago. Anyway, some genius somewhere must have remembered Sean out in Portland when it came time to fill the top slot in the O.C. Section in Washington, and God love him, McWeeney got the job. For as long as I'd known him, I had felt that I'd go through any door anywhere with Sean McWeeney. So coming back to work with him at Headquarters was another big plus—a thrill, really.

The last thing about coming back may sound strange, so I'll try to explain. It actually hit me one day just before I got the call from Headquarters asking me to come to Washington. Kallstrom, Kossler, and I were coming back from lunch. It was a beautiful spring day, but I was in a black mood.

Kallstrom noticed it first. "What's eating you, Jules?"

"I've been thinking, that's all."

"Well, don't hurt yourself, okay?"

"Guys." I looked at Kallstrom, then Kossler. It was hard to imagine better friends and colleagues, but then those are the very people you're bound to share the truth with, the way I see it. "Guys, what we're doing, it's just not going to work."

"What the hell are you talking about?"

Kallstrom and Kossler were both on me at once, and like three klutzes, we stopped in the middle of the sidewalk, the stream of pedestrians breaking like a wave around us. Kallstrom and Kossler were used to my rantings, but as soon as I started talking, they could tell I was serious.

The three of us had been working our asses off for the past year, and we should have been proud, I said. We had begun putting together a terrific team of agents and supervisors, and Kallstrom was making great progress with the new Special Operations Branch. At the same time, though, we had lost our rabbi, Neil Welch. Worse, we had made more enemies in New York and Washington than the three of us could begin to count.

The truth of the matter was, we were outnumbered. And though we had some clout, it wasn't nearly enough.

I didn't explain this next bit, but it was a big part of what was driving my thinking. None of us were quitters—Kallstrom, Kossler, or me. We would fight the good fight no matter what the odds. But things were different for them. Kallstrom could point to a clear mandate on Special Ops that *forced* people to get the hell out of his way. As for Kossler, he believed every bit as much as I did in the mission, but he hadn't had to give up his family, as I had, to take it on. That's why some days, I guess, I worried more than my two friends about just where the hell our little adventure was leading us. I wasn't a brooder by nature, but given the sacrifices my family and I were making, I would have had to be crazy not to take a good hard look every once in a while at just what it was we were doing.

Which is exactly what I had done.

And which was why I was so damned depressed.

The conclusion I had come to, which I explained to the two Jims, was that the three of us could continue breaking our asses to put our plan and Blakey's beautiful RICO law to work. But without the benediction of the brass down at Headquarters, our ideas about long-term, strategic investigations of the Italian Mafia would never become a matter of policy. Without Headquarters behind us, I told Kossler and Kallstrom, "we and our brilliant fucking plan are doomed."

They both thought I was being way too pessimistic, I know. But as we stood there jawing at each other in the middle of the sidewalk, Kallstrom and Kossler both saw where I was coming from, even if they didn't agree with me a hundred percent.

So often in life, the really good people are gulled by delusion, I think. It's human nature, and the thought process goes something like this: "If we just keep working hard, keep doing our jobs the best way we know how, then good things will happen—because we will have earned them."

Most people want to believe this, just like they want to believe the best of others and of themselves. Despite what some people say, it's harder going through life a cynic, without faith. But the way I saw it, it was also dumb to go through life without taking a sounding every so often, without making the tough assessments. For most of us, it's hard to stand up straight and try to look around the next bend in life's road. So we rely on faith instead and keep right on working.

That's what Kallstrom, Kossler, and I had been guilty of. Just keep at it, keep the faith, we told ourselves. Sooner or later we're bound to prevail.

Only we weren't. I saw that clearly.

Kallstrom asked the obvious question. "So what do we do?"

"I don't know." I hated putting a damper on things like this, but I had too much at stake. "The way I see it, Jim, the only way this thing works is for one of us to be down at Headquarters running interference. The only way is if we can control things from both ends."

Kallstrom and Kossler looked at me. Both said nothing.

I remember the moment perfectly even now. It was that rarest of days in Manhattan, a beautiful bell-clear sky, the light hard as crystal. Around us, people in shirtsleeves were smiling. A young couple sat holding hands.

I shook my head; I had no answers. A second later, the three of us broke from our huddle on the sidewalk and trudged back to the office, Kallstrom and Kossler looking as glum as I had ever seen them. I'm not exaggerating when I say the mood was funereal.

Exactly three days later, my office phone rang, and I got the invitation to come back to Headquarters. Even today, the timing still seems kind of eerie.

There's a reason Congress, the president, the Supreme Court, and just about everyone else who can leaves Washington in August. It's the same reason—the brutal heat and the oppressive humidity—that foreign diplomats classified the city as a hardship post until not too long ago.

August, in any case, was when I showed up at FBI Headquarters. McWeeney and I wasted no time getting to work.

"Look, it's simple, Sean. Success breeds success. They'll never fight you if you make the brass look good, even if they hate your guts while you're doing it."

McWeeney smiled. "It's a big goddamned building, Jules."

"Yeah, and we're the only two in it who know what's got to be done and how to make it happen."

"So what are you saying?"

"You know."

"Yeah," McWeeney said. "New York."

Too many people go through life scared. Scared of taking responsibility, scared someone may take responsibility away from them, scared the fucking sky will fall on their heads, who knows? Sean McWeeney was, decidedly, one of the unscared.

Sometimes friends who work together, men and women alike, get themselves crosswise on an issue and things are never the same again. That could have happened with me and Sean, I guess, but it never did; indeed, surrounded by so many pale ghosts at Headquarters, we became better friends than ever.

But it could have happened the other way, too.

The reason is, we both knew that whatever we wanted to do with the Bureau's organized-crime program, we had to do it first in New York. The heads of the five most powerful Cosa Nostra families were in New York, as were most of the members of the Mafia Commission. The Cosa Nostra had a lock on the city as it did in no other place in the United States. So it wasn't that McWeeney and I were head over heels for New York, although that's what some idiots said; to truly revamp the Bureau's O.C. program, the only way to go was to start the revolution there.

It was the only way that made sense.

Sean and I both knew the city well, having worked there together in the early 1970s. And over the years, while Sean was in Portland and at Headquarters, we had stayed in touch. With what we had going in New York now, though—with Kallstrom's Special Ops Branch, Kossler preaching the Blakey religion to the squads, and me running Pistone deep inside the crazy Bonannos—it was clear to both of us that I had the better fix on the New York end of things now; Sean, on the other hand, had responsibility for the organized-crime program nationwide, and the thing was in worse than a shambles. It needed a good swift kick in the ass.

So Sean, as I say, being one of the unscared, simply told me to run things in New York by myself while he set about cleaning house and putting the fear of God in people elsewhere. "Go for it, Giulio, all the way. New York is your show."

This, I should point out, was a meeting of the minds arrived at before lunch on my first day on the job. Heading out into the steambath heat of Pennsylvania Avenue just after noon, I felt lighter than air. Headquarters was going to be a hell of a lot different this time around, I thought, than last.

I'm not much on lists. The things I want to get done I just keep in my head until they get done, and then I replace them with something else. In Washington that first week, I had two things rattling around in my brain. One was to get rid of the two Hooverite bishops I mentioned up in New York. It wouldn't happen overnight, but since Sean told me to run the show, I put the machinery in motion immediately, and it was basically a done deal.

The second thing was to find a test case.

Before I left New York, Kossler and I had badgered the ten squads there to go back over the mountains of intelligence we had on the five Cosa Nostra families. For all that work, we still didn't have the target we needed who could help us develop a case on one of the families. In Washington, I was burning up the phone lines to Kossler to check on what the squads were turning up, but none of it looked really promising.

It was like looking for the proverbial needle in the haystack, and there was plenty of grumbling. For all the changes Kossler and I had made, there were still people who thought of us as the Professor and the Wild Man, who thought Bob Blakey's RICO religion was a crock of shit, and who basically wished the two of us would step in front of a crosstown bus hand in hand or at the very least leave them the hell alone.

We weren't about to, of course, and now, with Kossler in charge in New York and me running the show from Washington, it was like their worst nightmare come true. I might have felt sorry for some of these people, but I had laid down a marker with McWeeney, and I had to make good on it.

"Success breeds success," I had said.

I needed a success.

15

LIFE works in funny ways sometimes.

On one of my last days in New York, before I made the move to Headquarters, I got an AirTel, which is what the FBI called overnight cables. This one was from the Newark field office, which claimed to have a source who could wire us up with the Bonannos. This was not as improbable as, say, being handed a lottery ticket with the winning number on it, but it was damned close. It was also too good not to check out.

I had put Jim Moody on the case, figuring if anyone could sort out the bullshit and gun smoke in short order, it was probably him. Moody was a big guy, six three, maybe 240 pounds. An American Indian, Moody had served two tours in Vietnam as a pilot with the 197th Armed Helicopter Company. Then and after, Moody was both fearless and lucky, a combination that's hard to beat in any line of work. In his two tours in Vietnam, Moody had been shot down six times; each time his wingman had darted in and plucked him from harm's way.

Moody's assignment from me was to check out the guy from Newark. His name was Vinnie DePenta, and Moody played him like a harp. It was a beautiful thing to behold.

Vinnie DePenta was what you might call a wise-guy wannabe, which in some respects is worse than an actual wise guy, since you have to put up with all of the same bullshit, only from a guy who's not really too interesting. DePenta, in any case, shared two of the essential wise-guy character traits in that he was both lazy and stupid.

At first, DePenta seemed like just another smoke blower. We got lots of guys who worked themselves into a jam, then tried to work their way out by claiming they could wire us up with the mob. Most of these guys turned out to be full of shit, of course, and DePenta at first looked like just one more guy to add to the list. The first time, Moody met with Vinnie out at a motel in New Jersey, just off the Garden State Parkway. Our man, naturally, showed up in full wise-guy regalia. If I haven't mentioned it already, I should point out that the wise guys were some sharp dressers. DePenta, for his meeting with Moody, for instance, arrived in a kind of tan suit with a little greenish gold shine to it, as if it were growing mold or something. The suit is enough of an eye grabber, but DePenta accessorizes it nicely. He's got the shirt, tie, shoes, and socks—all the exact same color and pattern as the suit. So he looks like something that's just crawled out of a petri dish, this greenish glow on him.

DePenta is a short, pudgy guy, maybe a foot shorter than Moody. But he can talk—boy, can he talk! Vinnie has been helping the Bureau out for some time now, he tells Moody, and he has been getting just pure chickenshit for pay. Vinnie is furthermore wired right up to the top of the Bonanno family, he says, and if Jim Moody wants any help from him on those guys, he is going to have to put up some big dough. Some major dough.

"Is that right?" Moody says. "So who do you know, Vinnie?"

DePenta knows everyone in the Bonannos, he says. He's tight with Alphonse "Sonny Red" Indelicato, he is tight with Dominick "Big Trin" Trinchera, and he is also tight with Phil "Philly Lucky" Giaccone. And that's just for starters, DePenta says. Sonny Red has been after him personally, in fact, DePenta tells Moody, to open up a little business somewhere in the city so that the Bonannos could use it to launder money and have a new place for the wise guys to hang out.

"No kidding," Moody says. He lets DePenta run his gums a few more minutes before he finally interrupts.

"Can I tell you something, Vinnie?"

"Yeah, what?" DePenta was wearing a path in the motel carpet, walking up and down in his tan-and-green shoes.

"I think you're full of shit, that's what."

DePenta went nuts, screaming at Moody that he was another fucking FBI idiot, but Moody just chuckled. The only reason DePenta was even meeting with the Bureau was because he had gotten himself in a fix with his good friend Sonny Red Indelicato. This is where the stupidity thing I mentioned comes in. What happened was, DePenta, the wise-guy wannabe, had borrowed money from Sonny Red at the usual shylock interest rate. Then he had put some of the money on the street at higher rates, trying to run his own loan-shark operation. The first problem little Vinnie had was that he wasn't smart enough to know who to lend to, so he had quite a few bad debts. Vinnie's second problem compounded the first because he also wasn't tough enough to collect on the debts he was owed. Problem three was the biggest problem on Vinnie's list, for when he had borrowed the cash from Sonny Red, he told him he was going to put all of it on the street as working capital; in fact, what he had done was bet a lot of Sonny Red's cash on the ponies. DePenta was as good a gambler as he was a shylock, so he had lost everything he had gambled, and now he didn't have the money to pay back Sonny Red.

Vinnie DePenta, in other words, was in some deep shit.

When I told Moody to go meet with DePenta that first time, of course, we knew most, if not all, of this. That's why we figured DePenta was just another smoke blower.

Where the little fella surprised us was later on, after Moody insulted him. Vinnie was about as close to Sonny Red and Philly Lucky as the man in the moon, Moody said. "If you're so tight with these guys, Vinnie, prove it."

"Whaddya mean?"

"It's simple, Vinnie." Moody told DePenta that if he wanted to make any money from the Bureau as an informant and if he was as tight with these capos in the Bonanno family as he said he was, he would have to wear a body recorder, then go talk to Sonny Red, Philly Lucky, and Big Trin and any other Bonannos he could find. Then bring the tape back and play it for him.

DePenta stopped making figure eights in the motel carpet and looked at Moody. "Sure, okay, why not?"

Moody smiled. He gave Vinnie the recorder, showed him how it worked, and told him to meet him back at the motel the following night. Exactly twenty-four hours later, DePenta is back, and he's preening like a peacock. We rolled the tape, and to our everlasting surprise, Vinnie DePenta and Sonny Red Indelicato are chattering away like jaybirds, a bunch of long-lost buddies.

"You fucking guys, you didn't trust me, huh?"

"That's great work, Vinnie, really."

"Well, I tell you what, Moody. You want me to fucking work for you, I'm going to need money, a lot of it. An apartment, too. And I'm gonna need a car, and no piece of junk, either."

"Anything else, Vinnie?"

"That's it, but I'm telling you guys, my chickenshit days with the FBI are over."

"Vinnie, Vinnie, Vinnie." Patiently, Moody explained that the Bureau couldn't spring for the kind of dough DePenta evidently had in mind. Just wasn't possible. "We'll pay you what's fair, Vinnie. That's the best we can do."

"Fair, my ass."

"We'll do it just like before. Same deal, cash on delivery. You make good on this thing with the Bonannos and then we can see about putting you on a salary somewhere down the line."

The names Vinnie DePenta called Jim Moody made even me blush, but Jim just stood there smiling patiently in the crummy motel room, the lights of the traffic shooting by outside. "If that's the way it's gonna be, I'm fucking history, Moody. I'm out of here, and you and the FBI can go fuck yourselves."

I forget now exactly how Moody phrased it, but he indicated to Vinnie, I think, that he seemed, regrettably, to have arrived at his decision in haste and that maybe he should reconsider.

"Whaddya mean?"

"Sit down, Vinnie."

DePenta sat like a stuffed doll on the bed. "So—what?"

"Vinnie"—Moody held the tiny tape cassette in his big hand and waved it vaguely in DePenta's direction—"this tape, you see, it kind of complicates things now."

"Whaddya mean, complicates?" DePenta's eyes flashed from Moody to the tape and back again.

Moody explained that now that the Bureau had the tape, with Sonny Red talking about loan-sharking and referring to all sorts of other suspicious and no doubt criminal activity, we would probably have to call Sonny Red before a grand jury and ask him some questions. As FBI agents, Moody continued, it was our sworn duty to uphold the laws of the United States, and here, with the tape, we had evidence that some of those laws were being broken. "You see, Vinnie, we really have no choice."

"You're gonna play the fucking tape?" DePenta was rubbing his hands together like he was drying them without a towel.

"Well, actually, we would have to ask Sonny Red some questions first, Vinnie." Moody had his hands folded in front of him like a Sunday school teacher, and he looked like he was genuinely sorry for DePenta. "If Sonny Red didn't answer our questions, of course, Vinnie—or worse, if he lied—then, then, Vinnie, we'd have no choice but to play the tape for him."

Vinnie DePenta was no genius, as I said, but the implications of Moody's little speech were clear even to him. As soon as we played the tape for Sonny Red, he would know that DePenta had worn a wire to record the conversation. Sonny Red might wind up doing time. But Vinnie DePenta, well, he was, as he had just told Moody a few minutes earlier without quite understanding it, basically history.

"You fucked me," Vinnie DePenta said.

I wouldn't have phrased it quite that way, I don't think. The way I saw it, with Vinnie DePenta able to put us in tight with the Bonannos, we finally had that test case we had been looking for for so long. Of course, we already had Joe Pistone next to Sonny Black Napolitano, the acting boss of the Bonannos. But with DePenta now, we would be wired up with the other side of the family. Between my old friend Joe and our new friend Vinnie, we could start documenting a pattern of criminal activity and go after the Bonannos as a criminal enterprise.

Finally, Bob Blakey's brilliant idea seemed within grasp.

By the time I got down to Washington, Moody's reports on Vinnie DePenta's tape-recorded conversations with the Bonannos were heaped in a tidy pile on my desk.

16

ON a quick visit to New York, I grabbed Jim Kossler, and the two of us decided to get the hell out of the office and get a bite to eat at a lunch spot we liked over on Thomas Street, just west of Broadway. The place was nothing special, but it was close enough to the office so that we could be back in no time if something came up.

Lunch was what we needed, not so much to feed our faces but just to sit and talk. Kossler and I had Vinnie DePenta on the brain. What we didn't have, though, was a plan we were happy with to use the little guy against the Bonannos. It was less than two blocks to the restaurant, and Kossler and I walked in silence, chewing it over until we were inside.

"So, Jim, you figure out yet what we want to do here?"

We weren't even in our seats and the waiter was already filling water glasses and shoving menus at us. The place didn't charge much, so they counted on turning over the tables fast.

"Well, we got the money all sorted out. For starters."

We took a look at the menus, and the waiter walked away.

"Yeah, that sounds good on the money."

Kossler and I had decided to set DePenta up in a little business he wanted to call D&M. Basically, what it would be was an import business that we hoped would attract the attention of the Bonanno family or, for that matter, any of the other New York families. DePenta was going to be the bait.

"He's not thrilled about any of this, of course."

"Yeah, but fuck him. What choice does he have? Besides, we're helping keep the guy alive. And he's making a few bucks on the side—more than a few bucks, in fact."

I had approved New York's request for a thousand dollars a week for DePenta. The way the deal was set up, five hundred would go directly to Vinnie so he could make his vig payments to Sonny Red Indelicato. The other five we would put in an escrow account for DePenta's own use later on. DePenta had told Jim Moody in no uncertain terms that he wanted nothing to do with the federal Witness Protection Program once his little off-Broadway production for us was finally shut down. So while he was running D&M and trying to lure wise guys into the business, DePenta had five hundred dollars a week coming in, the money earning interest for him in one of the big banks downtown.

"Vinnie will be all right, I think, Jules. The tough thing, though, the thing I'm not too sure about, is what the hell we do exactly with D&M."

"You mean the imports."

"Right."

The waiter came back, and Jimmy ordered the lasagna, and I got the stuffed shells.

"We've got to be goddamned careful here, you know."

"I know, I know."

"We start a fucking war between the families because of D&M and we'll both be out there looking for work."

Kossler nodded, grabbing a seeded roll from the bread basket. "Well, look, we don't want to touch tomato sauce, right?"

"Everybody's into tomato sauce."

"And no olive oil."

"The Colombos will go batshit."

"The same for cheese and the Gambinos."

"Yeah, I know, I know. So?"

"So, we're still thinking is what."

I nodded and chewed on a breadstick.

The objective we had with D&M was simple. We knew from Pistone's undercover work that the Bonannos were using a variety of food products imported from Italy to smuggle heroin into the United States. By setting DePenta up at D&M, we hoped and assumed that Sonny Red Indelicato would come calling so that he could have his people in Italy piggyback on D&M shipments to the States. Our idea was for D&M to legitimately buy and import *something* from Italy and then retail whatever it was back here. To that extent, it would be a legitimate business. Our real goal, though, was to get the wise guys into D&M and make a case against them by monitoring what they did. What we didn't want was for D&M to start any kind of conflict between or among the families that were already in the Italian import business.

Kossler finished his seeded role and reached for another. "You got any bright ideas, Jules, I'm all ears."

I broke my breadstick in two and ate half. "Shit, Jimmy, what do I know?"

A minute later, the waiter returned with our meals, and Kossler speared a square of lasagna with his fork and held it between us like a trophy. "Hey, Jules?"

I turned one of my shells on its side and scraped tomato sauce off the top. "Yeah, what?"

"Pasta, Jules." Kossler was smiling like he had just been anointed with holy oil. "Pasta, Jules, that's fucking what."

I looked at my stuffed shells; then I looked at Kossler and the little square of lasagna dangling from his fork. Then I looked at my shells again.

We decided to put Vinnie DePenta into pasta.

With stakes this high, you don't screw around.

Not only was I spending a big chunk of the taxpayers' money setting Vinnie DePenta up in D&M; more important, I had promised Sean McWeeney a success in New York. Most important of all, though, at least the way I was looking at it, was that the validity of everything I had been preaching for the past few years would be judged by this one case. If this had been a test in school, it would have been pass or fail. Only, if I failed, I figured I could fold up my tent and go home. In the FBI, careers were made—and unmade—by things a hell of a lot smaller than this. That's why I went looking for a lawyer.

I actually didn't have to look very far, because I knew exactly who I wanted. Barbara Jones was not only one of my favorite prosecutors; she was one of my favorite people of all time. A five-foot, four-inch blond dynamo who would steamroll her way from one end of hell to the other if that's what it took to make her case, Barbara Jones was definitely someone you want on your side and not on the other guy's.

Barbara and I had met a few years earlier, and not under the happiest of circumstances, either. She was working a case I had one of my agents assigned to, and the guy came back to the office one day and told me the prosecutor wanted him to wire up this little old lady with a tape recorder. I knew the case; I tried to keep up with all my agents' cases. The lady in question was an elderly Italian woman, courtly and dignified. She had been receiving threatening phone calls having to do with some no-account nephew of hers or some dumb thing. My agent says Barbara Jones wants this poor woman to start taping the calls.

"Bullshit," I said. "Who is this Barbara Jones?"

It didn't take me long to find out, and then we had some fur flying between the two of us before Barbara finally agreed that the woman wouldn't tape a goddamned thing. Barbara didn't back down easily, though, and I admired her for it. Out of that start grew a friendship I would cherish for the rest of my life.

The reason for getting Barbara on board was simple. With the setup we had engineered for DePenta at D&M, I was confident we were going to have a winner, but the investigation would be only half the battle, and it wouldn't be worth a damn if we couldn't make the case stand up in court. Kossler and I had Blakey's RICO lessons down cold, and any time we had any doubts on something, Jim would get on the phone to Bob and run whatever it was past him. On the Title IIIs, Jim Kallstrom had made himself not just a technical wizard when it came to bugs and mikes; he had made a careful study of the law, too, and we didn't have any reason to expect problems introducing tapes and the rest of it when we got a case we could take to court.

So we were three geniuses—Kallstrom, Kossler, and I.

But we weren't going to be trying our case before a judge and jury. A Justice Department lawyer would be doing that, and for our test case, I wanted nothing but the best.

To me, that meant Barbara Jones.

In Washington, the Bureau had given me a big office on the third floor of the J. Edgar Hoover Building with a window looking out on the bustle of Pennsylvania Avenue. It was more office than I needed, or wanted. Some guys hang all sorts of things on their walls—their perfect-attendance certificates from third grade, their merit plaques from Kiwanis. I wasn't against that; I had just never given any thought to what my office looked like. If it had a desk and a phone, hey, I was a happy guy.

Back in the office the day after I talked with Kossler, I called Jim Kallstrom in New York. Jimmy knew Barbara as well as I did and felt the same way about her. I would have talked to Barbara myself about joining us in the hunt on D&M, but this was something I thought needed to be pitched person to person, and I couldn't break away from the bullshit at Headquarters for another trip to New York. So I asked Kallstrom to talk to Barbara about handling D&M for us.

Jimmy said he would call right away.

"This is a fucking ungodly hour, Kallstrom."

"And a pleasant good morning to you, Barbara."

The coffee shop on Lafayette Street was just behind the federal courthouse on St. Andrew's Plaza. The place was run by an imperious Greek whose empire consisted of six small tables. At barely seven in the morning, less than twenty-four hours after my call to Kallstrom, he and Barbara Jones were the Greek man's only customers. They had the place to themselves.

Kallstrom signaled for a cup of coffee for Barbara, and she borrowed his copy of the *Times* and scanned the front page, ignoring the remains of a powdered doughnut on a plate.

"This better be good, Jim."

"It is, don't worry."

The Greek delivered black coffee in a thick mug, and Kallstrom explained his plans for the installation at D&M.

"Who's this character DePenta?"

"A nobody. But he's our nobody." Kallstrom then explained about the recruitment of Vinnie DePenta by Jim Moody.

"And D&M?"

"The way Jules and Kossler got it set up, they're in the pasta game. Our game is we wait and see who comes calling."

"Meaning the Bonannos."

"Them first, but whoever else is interested."

"And get it all on tape." Barbara Jones took a sip of scalding coffee and winced.

"Only if you'll help us with the applications."

"So you need a lawyer."

"No, Barbara." Kallstrom put his coffee down. "We need you."

Barbara blew slowly on the steaming coffee mug, then shoved Kallstrom's copy of the *Times* back across the table to him. "I'm in," she said. "Let's get started."

The next step was to get D&M wired for sight and sound.

In the Bureau, as I mentioned, we called this part of the job Special Operations. Neil Welch had cut Kallstrom out of the rest of the FBI herd to develop Special Ops a few years before, and Kallstrom had just run with the thing since then. By the time he was ready to tackle D&M, Kallstrom had five Special Ops and surveillance squads—about sixty agents in all. Two of the best were John Kravec and Joe Cantamesa.

After leaving Barbara in St. Andrew's Plaza, Kallstrom walked back over to 26 Federal, took the elevator to the twenty-fourth floor, and asked his secretary to find Kravec and Cantamesa and have them come to his office.

John and Joe were there in five minutes, smelling trouble.

"This is going to be an easy one, guys, I promise."

"Sure, boss. Like all the other easy ones."

John Kravec was a tall, thoughtful man who was also a born pessimist, a guy who looked at life through his ever-present spectacles and immediately had about a hundred and one doubts and questions about whoever or whatever was staring back at him. Over the years, Kravec's innate pessimism had served him well in Special Ops because in Special Ops no job was *ever* as easy as it seemed. Fortunately, Kravec was also a technical whiz. Before tracking wise guys for the FBI in New York, John had tracked guided missiles for NASA in the Caribbean. So when he ran into a problem on an installation, Kravec could almost always be relied on to jury-rig a solution. What he couldn't be relied on was to take Kallstrom's don't-worry, be-happy attitude lying down.

"I'm serious, John." Kallstrom crossed his feet on his desk. "This one's an absolute walkover."

"A fucking piece of cake, John." At five ten, Joe Cantamesa was four inches shorter than Kravec, fast on his feet, funny, another technical whiz like Kravec. Joe had done three years in the army, specializing in communications.

"I don't know what I'm going to do with you guys."

"Tell us the deal, boss."

Since the FBI practically owned D&M, Kallstrom explained, Kravec and Cantamesa wouldn't have the usual problems of gaining entry to a locked building in a tough neighborhood. Kallstrom went on to talk about the layout of the place, how it had to be wired upstairs and down, for both audio and video.

Kravec and Cantamesa listened, taking notes. Neither of them said it, of course, but the D&M job *did* sound easier than the black bag jobs Kallstrom usually saddled them with.

Late one afternoon a few days after meeting with Kallstrom, after Barbara Jones got our applications approved for the Title IIIs at D&M, Kravec and Cantamesa showed up outside the place with agents Kenny Doyle and Howard Forbes in an undercover van. The four agents were dressed in coveralls, carrying toolboxes, and they looked for all the world like guys ready to rip out walls and do a number on the plumbing. Inside, the agents fanned out. Upstairs, Kravec had Forbes and Doyle wire Vinnie DePenta's office with mikes and cameras. That was no problem.

In the conference room down the hall from DePenta's office, Kravec and Cantamesa took special care. We had arranged to put a wet bar and a small cooking range in the room, wanting the wise guys to feel perfectly at home. The hope was that Sonny Red and his thugs would drop by to talk business with DePenta, then maybe repair to the conference room, have a glass of wine, a little sauce and pasta, and maybe then start to bullshit about the fabulous money to be made in the heroin trade.

In the conference room, Kravec, Cantamesa, Doyle, and Forbes arranged and rearranged the microphones and cameras as if they were rare flowers. By the time they were done, it was nearly dawn, and they had fixed it so that anyone sitting or standing just about anywhere in the long room would be recorded on audiotape and video camera with virtually no distortion.

Before they left, Kravec and Cantamesa wired the downstairs, where the shipments of pasta would come in and then be sent out to local retailers. Finally, there were the weatherproofed cameras for outside the building. These would pick up license-plate numbers and the like. The way Kravec and Cantamesa had it rigged, the whole system would transmit instantaneously back to 26 Federal so that we could watch and listen to our hearts' content as Vinnie DePenta and his playmates discussed the vagaries of the pasta business and whatever else crossed their busy little minds.

Finally, D&M was ready to open for business.

As it turned out, Sonny Red Indelicato disappointed us and failed to turn up at D&M. I'll explain why in a minute. What did happen was that DePenta wound up getting lots of visits from a gentleman named Frankie Falanga. Frankie's nickname was "the Beast," a sobriquet he had acquired during his years as an enforcer for the Colombo crime family. One of Frankie the Beast's favorite tools in that line of work was a baseball bat, a Louisville Slugger, actually. Jimmy Kallstrom's little mikes and cameras recorded a lot of, shall we say, compromising conversations between Vinnie DePenta and Frankie the Beast.

Between the secret bugs and cameras at D&M picking up the chatter between Vinnie DePenta and Falanga and the late-night phone calls from Joe Pistone to me at home, I was getting a constant flow of information from all sides of the crazy Bonanno family, and I definitely did not like what I was hearing. I liked having the information, all right, but not if the price was the health and well-being of my friend Pistone.

Things were getting a little too hairy.

"You fucking worry too much, you know it, pal?" It was Pistone again, in one of his middle-of-the-night phone calls home. It was just a few weeks after the installation at D&M.

"And you think everything's coming up roses, Donnie. I'm just telling you, watch out, all right?"

"Yeah, yeah, I'll watch out."

"Don't say it. Do it."

"I'll do it, I'll do it. Jeez."

"Then I'll talk to you, okay?"

"Yeah, okay. Give me a few days."

This is one reason I was worried about Pistone: One fine spring day early in April 1981, the acting boss of the Bonannos, Sonny Black Napolitano, made the pilgrimage out to Paul Castellano's mansion in Staten Island's exclusive Todt Hill neighborhood. The boss of bosses of the Cosa Nostra, Big Paul wasn't much for going out on the town or hanging out with other wise guys; he had everything he needed at home, including a comely little mistress who, according to the Castellano family books, was actually no more than the godfather's household maid; books, however, as every wise guy knows, lie. Gloria was the boss of bosses' lover. Having become something of a shut-in with his little Gloria, Castellano actually conducted his mob business on his own terms: Anyone who wanted to see him had to go out to the White House, which is what people called his place on the top of the hill in Staten Island. The house occupied the highest point of land in all of New York City.

What Sonny Black wanted to talk to Big Paul about, as it turned out, was business. And being a tiny bit smarter than your average class of wise guy, Sonny Black had come armed with a proposal for the boss of bosses.

What would the Gambino family's position be, Sonny Black asked Castellano, should the Bonanno family go to war?

The don raised an eyebrow. Big Paul didn't like wars.

Sonny Black plunged ahead, anyway. Like a good lawyer, he had not asked a question to which he did not know the answer. Everyone knew Paul Castellano didn't like unpleasantness—unless, of course, there was something in it for him. So before he addressed his question to the don, Sonny Black Napolitano had decided to couple it with the offer of a deal. Should Big Paul agree to support his side in the Bonanno family feud, Sonny Black said, he would personally guarantee the godfather a generous cut of all the revenues generated by the family's narcotics business. The don paused, then nodded in agreement.

Sonny Black nodded back. It had cost, but Sonny Black had gotten exactly what he had come to Staten Island for: The boss of bosses had promised to bless his side in the Mafia war that now was certain to come.

After leaving the hushed confines of the White House, Sonny Black had the less pressing but still important matter of sewing up the support of the "zips." This is what the American Cosa Nostra called the Sicilian wise guys who had begun operating in New York. The Sicilian faction of the Bonanno family had as its leaders two certifiable animals named Salvatore Catalano and Salvatore Feruggia. It remains lost in the mists of wise-guy history precisely what baubles Sonny Black Napolitano dangled in front of the two Sals, but you can be confident, I think, that the terms of the deal were suitably tawdry. Whatever they were, the zips would support Sonny Black; unless, of course, they got a better offer from the other side.

Things were beginning to move quickly now.

On April 23, Joe Pistone met with Lefty Guns Ruggiero, his idiot sidekick. They were in Miami, and it was a beautiful spring day; the awful humidity had not set in yet.

"Things are happening, Donnie."

"What's the deal, what's happening?"

"It's the commission. We just got a job by the commission." Lefty explained that the Mafia Commission had assigned Sonny Black and his crew to do a hush-hush job. Lefty would be out of touch for a while, but once the job was done, he and Sonny Black would give Pistone a call.

"Is everything okay, Lefty?"

"Yeah, yeah, no problem." Lefty paused and looked past Pistone at the swaying palm trees and the washed blue sky.

"You're sure, huh?"

"Yeah, yeah, Donnie, no problem." Lefty looked Pistone straight in the eye now. "Of course, if things get screwed up, your life could be in jeopardy."

Jeopardy was a big word for Lefty, so Joe figured things must be really serious. "You'll call me, huh?"

"Yeah, we'll call, Donnie."

Pistone phoned late that night to give me a fill.

By then, Lefty Guns Ruggiero had disappeared.

17

ONE of the more useful pieces of information Jim Kallstrom's little microphones had picked up for us at Vinnie DePenta's D&M warehouse was that Sonny Red Indelicato did a lot of business out of a dumpy apartment in Little Italy, right on the edge of Chinatown.

This, it turned out, was why he hadn't been showing his face around D&M. Every time Sonny Red wanted to talk to Vinnie DePenta about the money he was owed, about the pasta business, the state of the world, or whatever, Sonny Red summoned the little guy to his place. The address was 117 Elizabeth Street.

If you don't know New York, this is a pretty interesting spot. What I always remember about it is the smell. On each side of Elizabeth, you have Hester and Broome streets, where they have a lot of open-air stalls selling fresh fish. Even if you like fish, and I do, the smell tends to get to you after a while. What was nice about Elizabeth Street, though, was that Mott and Mulberry streets ran parallel to it, and for me there is no sweeter smell in the world than the aroma of those beautiful little mom-and-pop bakeries as their old brick ovens disgorge one kind of Italian pastry after the next.

I never got to know Sonny Red, so I don't know if he liked the fish smell more than the pastry smell, but most days, if the wind was right, he had his choice, which was nice for him. What I did know was that from what Vinnie DePenta was telling us and from what we were hearing on the tapes we were getting from D&M, we definitely needed to get inside the flat at 117 Elizabeth.

It was time for Kallstrom's black-bag agents again. Once again, John Kravec and Joe Cantamesa got the call.

Like most of the people Kallstrom had recruited for Special Ops work, Kravec and Cantamesa had to be not only first-rate technical wizards, although they got plenty of training on that score. But having the sci-fi know-how was worthless if you couldn't figure out a way to get the bugs, mikes, and cameras into wherever it was we needed them. What this meant was that in addition to being extremely smart and sober-minded individuals, Kallstrom's agents also had to have the wit of a stand-up comic and the balls of those big fucking lions they have out in front of the New York Public Library on Fifth Avenue.

Kravec and Cantamesa, happily, fit the bill.

Their first shot at 117 Elizabeth came the first week in May. Posing again as home repairmen, Kravec and Cantamesa wandered into the backyard next to Sonny Red's ground-floor apartment. They had not gone more than a few feet when a window above them flew open and an old Italian woman in widow's black stuck her head out. "I know who you are; you're FBI men." The woman's voice was shrill as a bird's, but from that height it carried. "You're here to tap our phones, I know it!"

Kravec and Cantamesa froze; then Cantamesa shouted back. "That's right, lady, we're FBI guys, all right—absolutely!"

Four floors above them, the lady in black shook her head, then stuck it back inside. Kravec and Cantamesa stepped quickly into the brick apartment building—and ran right into an obscenely fat lady with a very large knife.

"What the hell was that all about?"

Cantamesa laughed. "The old lady upstairs, she thinks we're FBI, here to tap the fucking phones."

"Yeah, sure." The lady with the knife had been chopping vegetables, and there were slivers of pepper on the blade, green, red, and yellow. She waved the knife at Cantamesa's belt buckle and smirked. "If I even thought you two guys were FBI, I'd cut your fucking balls off."

The two agents smiled like a couple of goombahs, and the lady with the knife trudged back to her kitchen. Their anatomy intact, Kravec and Cantamesa went about their business. Sonny

Red's apartment was in the back of the old apartment building, so the way they worked it was, Cantamesa stayed up front as the lookout, while Kravec went inside. Looking for all the world like the guy just sent for by the building superintendent, Kravec slipped up to the door, worked a little of his magic on the lock, then stepped inside.

Kallstrom's guys were not actually there to place a bug but to see where they would stick it when the judge approved our application for 117 Elizabeth. This, by the way—the surreptitious entry of a private residence by law enforcement agents conducting an official investigation—is all perfectly legal.

Just for the record, as they say.

Inside Sonny Red's dingy flat, Kravec worked his way slowly back to the bedroom. All quiet there. Bedrooms tend to be pretty good places for bugs, and *in* a bedroom one of the best places for concealing one of our little electronic wonders is under the bed. So Kravec gets down on all fours and decides to take a look around under Sonny Red's rack. This is not exactly as easy as it sounds, for in addition to being six feet two, John Kravec also goes about 210 pounds. Anyway, he manages to insert himself under Sonny Red's bed and have a look around, and as he's trying to slide himself out, who should walk into the bedroom but Sonny Red himself. Turns out the guy had been in the crapper down the hall.

"Who the fuck are you?" Sonny Red was fussing with his trousers, but he had Kravec fixed with a definite look.

"Easy, mister." Kravec was in what you would have to call an awkward spot. His body was stuck halfway under the bed, and he had to crank his neck a good ways around so that he could look up at Sonny Red. "I'm the exterminator; they sent for me."

"Oh, no problem, just do what you gotta do, then." Sonny Red finished tugging at his trousers and yawned. "Listen, I work nights, and I got to get my sleep, okay?"

"Sure, you bet, mister."

As Kravec watched from his spot on the floor, Sonny Red Indelicato proceeded to disrobe. He removed his shoes and socks first, then his shirt and undershirt, which he tossed in a ball on the floor. Next came his trousers, and then the under-shorts. In the space of a few seconds, the powerful capo of the Joe Bonanno organized-crime family was stark naked.

Then he fell on the bed with Kravec still half under it.

Seconds later, Sonny Red was snoring fitfully, deep, rumbling snorts ruffling his puffy lips.

"Good night, mister," John Kravec said.

Sonny Red Indelicato didn't answer, his face crumpled into a knot of dirty bed linen.

Kravec thought about it a minute. Then he decided that he and Cantamesa should come back some other time to continue their study about where to put the bug at 117 Elizabeth.

This is how wise guys go to war.

Personally, I have nothing at all against sucker punches and other sneaky little tricks when they're employed against an enemy. I had pulled plenty of stunts like that in Vietnam and later, working undercover in New York. So I understand all about it. Still, for some reason, the way Sonny Black Napolitano set up Sonny Red Indelicato—by now I had come to think of the two Sonnys in the Bonanno family as opposite numbers in a grim game of wise-guy checkers—was really kind of piss-poor.

It offended me—almost.

What happened was that Sonny Black, as the acting boss of the Bonannos, had summoned Sonny Red, Philly Lucky Giac-cone, and the fat man, Dominick "Big Trin" Trinchera, to a meeting. Supposedly, the sit-down was going to allow all hands to calm things down so that everyone could get back to concentrating on making money again by peddling the world's most addictive drugs to America's poorest and most disfranchised citizens.

This wasn't the way they thought about what they did, of course; all they thought about was the money.

I was always taught never to speak ill of the dead, but I mean, how dumb do you have to be, really, to show up for the kind of meeting Sonny Black was calling—and especially to show up with no muscle, no protection, no nothing?

Well, our three heroes did just that.

The date was May 5. According to Sonny Black's invitation, the wise guys were going to sit down for a late lunch, break bread, and see about making peace.

To this day we still have no idea about the restaurant where the hit took place. We do know it was out in Brooklyn somewhere. We also know that before Sonny Red, Philly Lucky, and Big Trin even started to tuck into the antipasto, a half-dozen shooters appeared out of nowhere, long irons smoking like something out of a John Wayne movie—autopsies showed later that the weapons used were all shotguns and rifles. The shooting was so crazy that one of Sonny Black's own assassins got shot himself. He turned up at a hospital a few hours later, claiming that an irate motorist had plunked him as he was cruising the neighborhood, trolling for an afternoon hooker.

The restaurant, wherever it was, must have been a mess.

We started piecing things together not long after the hit.

Some of Kallstrom's guys spotted Pistone's friend, Lefty Guns, late in the day on May 5. Lefty was coming out of an apartment with a suitcase, so it looked like he might be going away for a while. The wise guys, however, could never get anything quite right. Lefty had told his wife to send him some clothes for his disappearing act, and being the dutiful wise-guy wife she was, Mrs. Lefty Guns had done just that. But somehow she had managed to send only the jacket to his favorite suit; the pants she forgot. So Lefty decided he had to make a quick trip home, and as luck would have it, when he stopped in to pick up his pants, Joe Pistone called from Florida, and he was able to pump Lefty for a bit of information.

Lefty had told Pistone about the "job" he and Sonny Black had been assigned by the Mafia Commission. Through a series of grunts and other noises unintelligible probably only to Pistone, Lefty Guns conveyed the information that the job had been completed and that, as a consequence, he would be making himself pretty scarce for a while.

"How long you going to be gone, Lefty?"

"It'll be a while yet."

"A while?"

"Yeah. Everything went fine, though."

"That's great. Great news, Lefty."

"Yeah, fucking thing's done, no problem."

Actually, despite having wiped out Sonny Black's principal rivals in the Bonanno family, there were quite a few problems. Lefty Guns, it turned out, was wrong once again.

Though Pistone and the rest of us were still unclear about exactly what had happened and what the "job" was, the ever-helpful wise guys had left us lots of clues. A few weeks later, for instance, some kids playing in a vacant lot out in Queens would discover Sonny Red's badly decomposed body. The wise guys couldn't even bury their dead right.

A mope named Joey Messina had been given the job of disposing of Sonny Red's corpse, and given the alternatives, I'd have to say it was a choice assignment. Because no one could move the fat man Trinchera, Sonny Black's hit men had had to cut up the body with a chain saw. Messina, on the other hand, just had to drag Sonny Red's body outside somewhere and bury him. The only problem was, Messina didn't dig the hole deep enough, and New York's warm spring rains plus countless numbers of stray dogs, cats, and the city's endless legions of rodents had combined to surface Sonny Red's body in a matter of days. The kids saw what looked like a fat stick poking up out of some weeds. In fact, it was Sonny Red's left arm. New York homicide detectives unearthed the rest of the corpse, which was wrapped in a sheet, the legs bound with cord. The medical examiner figured the time of death at approximately three weeks earlier, but we were able to fix it more precisely than that. Sonny Red's corpse still had his expensive self-winding Cartier wristwatch on it, and the thing had stopped ticking on May 7. We summoned a Cartier technician, and the guy told us that without any wrist movement at all—none—the watch would keep functioning for approximately forty hours, forty-five at most. That jibed nicely with the late lunch on May 5. The details are interesting in hindsight. At the time, though, I was more concerned with what was going to happen next. When you're at war—and we were definitely at war now, no question—it always pays to think a little bit ahead.

Two days after the hit on Sonny Red Indelicato, Philly Lucky Giaccone, and the now-dismembered Big Trin Trinchera, John Kravec and Joe Cantamesa were able to place their bug in the apartment at 117 Elizabeth Street.

A judge had reviewed our application for the secret mike and come to the obvious conclusion: Sonny Red Indelicato was definitely not a legitimate businessman. The only hitch with the installation was on the way out, when Cantamesa ran straight into Sonny Red Indelicato's son, Bruno. Bruno Indelicato was perspiring like a pig, he looked more than a little like he was stoked on cocaine, and he had a pistol, which he proceeded to stick directly into poor Joe Cantamesa's ear.

"Who the fuck are you, you son of a bitch?"

Cantamesa, to his everlasting credit, didn't pull a Ralph Cramden, the old *hamana-hamana-hamana* thing; he tried to reason with Bruno, but Bruno's eyes were wild, unfocused.

In fairness, I should point out that Bruno's somewhat agitated mental state was rather understandable. You see, Sonny Black had summoned Bruno to the fateful lunch two days earlier, and Bruno had shown up late. He had gotten stuck in traffic or something, who knows with wise guys?

Anyway, to this day, the general feeling among Kallstrom's guys was that poor Joe Cantamesa would have bought it once and for all that day at 117 Elizabeth were it not for the old lady upstairs who had yelled out the window at him a few days earlier. Joe was busy explaining to Bruno that he was a repairmen and not a hit man dispatched by Sonny Black when the old lady's voice comes trilling down from an upstairs stairwell.

"Leave him alone, you idiot, the guy's a repairman, he was here the other day."

Once the old lady's words registered in Bruno's addled brain, he stuck his pistol back in his pocket, turned Joe Cantamesa free, and went back to his crummy apartment—to worry some more. Even someone as profoundly stupid as Bruno Indelicato knew he had plenty to worry about now. Bruno was on the list of people Sonny Black wanted whacked, and he had to assume that a wise guy would be trying for him sooner than later. A contract, after all, was a contract.

Who knew they would give the goddamned thing to Pistone?

18

BY the time the sun was up, I was already dressed.

Pistone had called at two-thirty with the news that he had been given the contract on Bruno, the terms explained in typically crude wise-guy style: Pistone, as he explained it, was instructed to "find Bruno, whack him, and leave him in the road where I do him." Like I said, there was no way I was going to get any sleep after hearing that news, so I walked the floor for the rest of the night instead. If I were an insomniac, I could have made a career for myself as a marathon walker.

While I walked, going from room to room in the darkened house, I thought about everything I had to do. I made the easy decisions first. We would pull together a team of agents in New York and Florida; that had to happen immediately. If we found Bruno first, Pistone couldn't very well whack him, could he? I made a few quick phone calls and put that in motion, so at first light a crew of our guys would be out scouring the usual wise-guy hangouts looking for Bruno to pick him up.

It would buy us time, if nothing else.

There were plenty of other things to deal with, but it was more logistical bullshit, easy stuff, and I ran through the list a few times, ticking off the items almost unconsciously.

The big thing I saved until last. In many ways, it was the easiest decision, but I knew it would cause no end of trouble: It was time to bring Pistone in from the cold.

I knew that Joe would fight the decision. The longer he had stayed undercover, the more committed he had become to taking down the entire Cosa Nostra. The frustration he felt at being away from his own family for so long he had channeled into a white-hot anger at all of the families of the Cosa Nostra. Between Joe and the Mafia, it wasn't personal, but it was damned close. It was one of the big reasons he was such an incredible agent.

But great agents, like great athletes, don't want to be yanked from the game; when the clock's ticking down and everything's up for grabs, in fact, the great ones want the ball.

That's the way it was with Pistone.

For months Joe had been telling me how he would become a "made" member of the Bonannos by the end of the year. With the contract he had been given on Bruno, that was all but a done deal now, I knew; to become a made guy, you had to witness a murder or, preferably, do one yourself. Pistone wouldn't whack Bruno; that was a given. But the fact of the contract meant he was effectively already a full-fledged wise guy. Once he was actually made, Pistone kept telling me, he would be privy to the innermost councils of the Cosa Nostra. After that, it would be only a matter of time before the Bureau could bring the entire miserable enterprise crashing down on the wise guys' heads.

I knew Joe's argument, and I agreed with it. But I had an argument of my own: I didn't want my friend to end up dead.

In addition to being Joe's friend, I was his control in the Bureau, and that made it my job to look after him, to do what I could to keep him safe. In my judgment, the contract Pistone had been given on Bruno moved things to a whole new level, one where I couldn't do much to guarantee his safety.

To me that meant one thing: It was time to pull him in.

What would make the decision so difficult was, once again, the FBI itself. Thanks to the information Pistone had been feeding us the past few years, we had opened major organized-crime investigations not only in New York but in Milwaukee, Tampa, Newark, and Miami. I doubted that the brass at Headquarters had a clue about the stress Pistone had been under—six years of living a double life. All they knew was that Pistone was helping us make a hell of a lot of big cases, and pulling him out now would be like killing the goose that laid the golden egg.

I understood that argument, but no case was worth an agent's life, and there was no doubt in my mind that Joe Pistone's life was seriously in danger. The reason is, basically, that the wise guys were like a bunch of gossipy old women. They didn't have too much in the way of heavy thoughts rattling around their brainpans, so they mainly passed the time bullshitting each other. This meant that within a few hours after Pistone was given the contract to find and whack Bruno Indelicato, maybe a hundred or more mopes and wise guys knew about it. Of those, the ones who had sided with the unfortunate Sonny Red side of the Bonanno family might now decide to start settling scores by going after Pistone.

So Joe was coming out, I concluded, and that was that.

As soon as I got to Headquarters, I walked straight into McWeeney's office to tell him the news. He chewed on it a minute and then, being the stand-up guy he is, agreed.

"You're absolutely right, Giulio, no question about it." McWeeney has the smile of an altar boy, and he lit it up for me now, his blue eyes twinkling as he leaned back in his chair. "Of course, that doesn't mean they're not going to dump a lot of shit on our heads upstairs."

"I know, Sean, I know."

McWeeney was still smiling, but his eyes had a cloudy look to them, like he had just remembered something sad. "No, Jules," he said, "I mean a *lot* of shit."

Pistone was the first to start dumping the shit.

Before we hung up early that morning, I had asked Joe to make an excuse to his wise-guy friends and jump on a plane. He had agreed without asking why, and that afternoon we were sitting in a tiny hotel room in a place called Crystal City, Virginia, just across the Potomac River from Washington. I had registered under a phony name, and Joe got a cab there from the airport. It was five minutes away.

We started out talking more or less aimlessly about the hit on Sonny Red, Philly Lucky, and the fat man Trinchera, and we were just generally catching up with each other when I popped it on Pistone, the fact that I was pulling him.

The explosion was everything I expected.

"What are you, out of your fucking mind?" Pistone had a temper, and he reminded me of it now, getting to his feet, his dark eyes like embers. "What do you mean you're pulling me?"

"Am I speaking English, Joe? Am I stuttering or something, you don't understand what I'm saying?"

"You're pulling the plug." It was an accusation. Pistone was leaning over me, furious.

I waited a minute, silent. Like Pistone, I score pretty high in the temper department, but I had to keep it in check now.

"You made the decision before I even got here, right?"

"That's right, Joe, now sit down." I waited, but Pistone wasn't about to sit, so I continued. "It's finished, Joe. It's fucking over, that's it."

"Just like that." Pistone's muscular shoulders sagged slightly. "Six years and suddenly it's over? Bullshit!"

"It's too dangerous, Joe—and it's time."

"I'm not going to get killed, Jules. I'm going to be fucking made. *Made!* Do you know where we can go from here?"

"What do you think, I'm stupid?"

"Six years, I don't fucking believe it." Pistone was pacing now, laying the guilt on me. "And then it's over?" Pistone shot me another black look. "Where the fuck do you get off?"

"Hey, Joe."

Pistone didn't answer. He was as hot as I'd ever seen him.

"I'm doing this because I love you, man."

Silence.

"And besides that, it's not your fucking decision." I thought for a second he might take a poke at me, but Pistone just held his ground, glaring. "It's my decision, Joe, and I already made it, so that's it. End of story."

"Just like that.

"That's right."

"Well, let me tell you something, then, Jules, you're making a big fucking mistake, okay?"

"A mistake."

"Yeah, a big one."

"Then it's my mistake, okay, Joe? And that's too goddamn bad, because I already made it, and that's it."

Pistone laughed then, and it broke the tension. Neither of us could stay angry with the other for too long, thank God. We had been so close for so long that we knew each other like brothers, each other's strengths and weaknesses. I'm not ashamed to say that somewhere in both our souls was a large corner office the door to which said: "Macho."

The door didn't open too often.

Just as there are some kinds of feelings I'd probably never admit to, the same was true of Joe, and despite all the stress, the loneliness, and the strain on his family, Pistone would never ask to be pulled in from the undercover role. In the six years he was under, he never complained to me once, but I was close to Joe's wife, Peggy, and I knew how the double life and long absences from home ate him up. Once, Peggy had had a serious car accident and was hurt badly; Joe couldn't get away from the wise guys to get home and see her; not being there then nearly killed him. Joe and Peggy had three beautiful daughters—Colleen, Noreen, and Doreen. In the years he was living the life of Donnie Brasco the jewel thief, Joe missed birthdays, confirmations, and plenty more.

So Joe's life was in danger, and the macho business wouldn't allow him to admit that. Joe and Peggy—God bless them both —had such a strong marriage that there was no danger there, but the macho thing wouldn't allow Joe to place even that ahead of his work against the mob.

For me—as pissed off as Pistone was at me—this was like the reverse of a Hobson's choice: Whether I looked at the thing from a personal or professional standpoint, the answer was the same: Donnie Brasco was history.

It was one thing for me to say it, though, and still another to make the decision stick. Given the shit we would take from Headquarters and from the field offices where Joe had all these investigations hanging fire, the only way we would prevail was if Pistone and I stuck together in the days to come.

The little hotel room was thick with stale air, and every few seconds planes from Washington's National Airport etched themselves against the sky outside our window.

"So?" Pistone's anger had seeped from him like air from a leaky tire, and he collapsed in a chair. "What next?"

"What's next is the sound of shit hitting the fan."

Pistone smiled, his first. "People are going to go fucking crazy, you know that."

"No shit, Joe."

The field offices would go over my head; I had no doubt about that. It was doubtful the field would go to the judge, William Webster, the director of the FBI. But they would definitely go to Dana Caro and Buck Revell. Dana was the Bureau's deputy assistant director and Buck the assistant director, the number-three guy in the Bureau and Dana's boss. Each was a great guy, but if you screwed up or pissed off the wrong people, Dana and Buck could make your life a powerful misery. Together, they could make some folks wish themselves among the deceased.

So we would have them to deal with, but given the stakes, I told Joe I didn't particularly give a shit.

"How're you going to handle it, though?"

It was my turn to pace now. "If we stick together—if they can't play you against me, Joe—we'll be fine. But you know they're going to try and steamroll both of us or drive a wedge between us so they can keep these cases going."

"They've got a lot invested, Jules."

"I know what's on the line. But I don't give a shit what any of them say because there's a life at stake here."

"And you're going to use that."

I stopped pacing and thought once more how much my friendship with Pistone meant to me. "You're goddamned right I am, Joe. Like a fucking club I'm going to use it."

19

ON May 16, the day after I broke the news to Pistone, I grabbed a shuttle to New York and sat down with Jim Kossler. I had called him the day before to tell him about the decision on Pistone, and he wasn't at all happy about it. In his office at the top of 26 Federal, the blue pipe smoke curling to the ceiling, he told me so in no uncertain terms.

"I just think you're wrong, Jules. Dead wrong."

"I hear you, Jimmy, and I appreciate the arguments."

"You wait till he's made, till Pistone's totally on the inside, we could bring down the whole goddamned family."

"We could also get him killed, Jimmy."

Kossler removed his pipe and leaned toward me across his desk. "We all know the risks, Jules. And no one's minimizing them. Something happened to Joe, none of us would ever forgive ourselves. But look at the shot we got here."

"I know, Jimmy. But I just don't think we can risk it."

"Okay." Kossler leaned back and studied a smoke ring. "I can't argue with you on this one, you know that."

"I appreciate it, Jim."

"Besides, you'll get plenty of shit from everyone else."

Truer words, I thought, were never spoken.

Within forty-eight hours of the decision to pull Pistone, Headquarters was buzzing like a hive of angry bees. Besides New York, Tampa, Miami, Milwaukee, and Newark had all put together big, ambitious investigations employing Joe's undercover work. Pulling him now, supervisors and agents in the field argued, would stop all those cases in their tracks.

I couldn't keep up with all of it, but I knew the field offices were deluging the brass with AirTels and telexes on the Bureau's in-house telex. The phone lines were also burning up.

The object of all the complaints, naturally, was me.

Things by this time had begun to get a bit nasty at Headquarters. Sean McWeeney had given me the New York operation to run, and the FBI's institutional distrust of New York had manifested itself, in some quarters at least, into a growing resentment toward me personally. The dam burst five days after I told Pistone he was coming out.

"This *is* the typical New York attitude!"

"You're damn right it is, Dana."

Dana Caro was the deputy assistant director for the Criminal Investigative Division. A ramrod-straight former marine, Dana had a big corner office on the third floor of Headquarters, plaques and commendations covering the walls.

"New York this, New York that—what about the job, Jules?"

"This *is* the job! And you're goddamned straight it's a New York thing. New York is the first step in the strategic plan. Don't you understand that?"

"What do you mean, don't I understand?"

"Sometimes I think no one in this whole damned building understands. Except me and Sean."

"That's bullshit, and you know it." Dana had a way of tensing his upper body when he was angry or upset, and he was mad enough now that his torso was twitching like a tuning fork.

"Bullshit, my ass, Dana. Forget about New York for a minute. Here you've got Pistone, and he's been given a fucking contract on Bruno. You know what that means?"

Caro glared at me, saying nothing.

"That means he's in the middle of it, that's what. That means that if he's supposed to be looking for Bruno, you can bet your ass Bruno and his buddies are looking for Joe."

Dana slashed his hand through the air, indicating, I guessed, that I should shut the fuck up. "We're going to have to sort this out, Jules. But not just here, not now."

"Okay," I said. "Let's talk later, then."
A day later, I was ordered to appear at a full-dress war council.

The meeting was held in Crystal City, in the same hotel where I
had met with Pistone to tell him he was coming in from the
cold. Sean had arranged for a Bureau tech team to sweep the
room for bugs. Coffee and sandwiches had been ordered and
delivered, the hotel staff instructed to keep their distance. It was
probably overkill, but in the halls, the downstairs lobby, and out
in the parking lot, we had plainclothes agents, each of them
armed, watching for wise-guy spies.

My dance card was something to see. Headquarters had invited supervisors and case agents from the field offices in
Tampa, Miami, Milwaukee, New York, and Newark. Jim Kossler
was representing New York, and though he didn't agree with me
on pulling Pistone, we were good friends, and he would never
break ranks. That wasn't the case with the rest of them. Tony
Amoroso was an O.C. supervisor from Miami, and he had flown
up to grab his pound of flesh. Tony had played the role of the
bogus Saudi sheik in the FBI's Abscam investigation of several
crooked congressmen. He had paid his dues, was one tough son
of a bitch, and I expected him to give me no quarter. From
Tampa, another Tony—Tony Daniels—had arrived, loaded for
bear.

Daniels had a legitimate beef. FBI Tampa had opened up a
case it had code-named "Coldwater," and it was a hell of a good
investigation. Tony had set up one of his agents, a guy named
Ed Robb, in a gambling club not far from downtown Tampa, on
Route 19. The place was called King's Court, and Robb, posing
as a wise guy named Tony Rossi, was supposed to be the owner.

The way these things work is, you don't just drop a guy like
Robb in the middle of a city like Tampa and have him pretend
all of a sudden he's a wise guy opening up a club. Santo Trafficante controlled most of the mob's gambling business in Florida, and he could spot a phony a mile away. If Trafficante

spotted Robb, the chances of Ed's ever making it to retirement and collecting the gold watch and the pension weren't too good.

This is where Pistone had come in.

With his close ties to the Bonannos, Joe, posing as Donnie Brasco, had shown up in Tampa and introduced Tony Rossi all around to the wise guys down there. Donnie let it be known that he was Tony's partner from New York, and if there was any trouble with King's Court, he was going to hear about it, find out the reasons behind it, and then deal with the problem.

Pistone, in other words, was key to the Coldwater case.

"Jules, Joe, how you doing?"

"Good, good. How's it going, Tony?" We were in the hall outside the conference room, and I extended my hand, Pistone following suit alongside me.

Behind us, most of the others had already filed into the room. Sean, the ranking guy, would preside, seated at the head of the rectangular table. Kossler was already seated, setting a match to his pipe. Down the table I nodded to a dozen other guys I knew, supervisors and agents with whom I had crossed paths one way or the other over the years.

Pistone grabbed a seat at the far end of the room, and I found a place halfway down the left side of the table. The room was airless and gray, the hotel curtains pulled across the bank of windows, blotting out the bright spring afternoon.

There was a shuffling of chairs, and then Sean brought the meeting to order. "Gentlemen." McWeeney turned his altar boy's smile on the men up and down the table. "We don't need to go into a long discussion about why we're here."

There was some muttering from somewhere down the other side of the table, but I ignored it.

Sean continued: "Certainly no one more than those of us here understands how important Joe Pistone has been to the Bureau's efforts against the Cosa Nostra."

At the end of the table, Pistone sat slumped in his chair, studying his shoes, it looked like.

"The time has come, however, to make a decision." Sean

paused significantly. "And that's why we're all here—to get everyone's point of view on this thing."

There was silence around the room, so Sean laid down the day's pecking order. If there were no objections, Milwaukee, Newark, and Miami would have their say first.

No one objected, and I poured black coffee, struggling to pay attention, as the presentations began. The spiels were pretty much the same: Pulling Pistone out from his undercover role now would be "a disaster." Too much was at stake. If Headquarters gave it just a few more months, the payoff would be enormous.

Sean thanked Tony Amoroso and the others, then turned to Kossler, who passed, giving me a blank look.

"Tony?"

"Thanks, Sean." Like me, Tony Daniels was an Italian American, a hard charger with a short fuse. "I don't think I have to tell anyone here how much the Bureau has got invested in the Coldwater investigation."

I looked around the table but said nothing.

"Everyone knows the great work Tampa has done." It was Sean's job to be the diplomat, and he sat at the head of the long table, nodding like a wise pasha.

"The point is," Daniels said, "you pull Pistone now, you shut us down just when things are beginning to take off."

Jim Kinne was the case agent on Coldwater. He nodded silently next to Tony, hanging on every word but smart enough not to get into the fight with the big dogs.

"Look, Tony, no one is saying this is easy."

"Never mind easy, Sean." Daniels was giving no quarter. "We're ready to go on King's Court, and all of a sudden we're getting the red light here. We're being told to hold our fire."

There was a definite undercurrent in the hotel meeting room, and I wasn't the only one to feel it: Sean and Joe did, too. The way it looked to a lot of people was this: Sean was a nice guy, and Joe was, let's face it, a hero; me, I was the asshole, the guy who made the call that had pissed everyone off.

That was fine with me, I thought, sipping my coffee. I didn't mind being the bad guy as long as my decision wasn't reversed. I had no way of knowing for sure how effective the lobbying against me had been with the higher-ups. My bottom line was that an agent's life was in danger.

Who could argue against that?

After nearly two days of bitching and moaning from my colleagues in the stuffy hotel room, Sean finally gave me the floor. A lot of guys in Sean's position—he was my boss, remember, and he had to work with every one of the people sitting in that room—would have sat me down beforehand and told me to make nice or whatever; not Sean. So I got up and said my piece.

"Joe Pistone," I began, "has been under cover for six years. Six years!" I made a point of engaging the eyes of everyone sitting up and down both sides of the long table. "As some of you have noted so eloquently, Joe has been more successful than any of us could have ever imagined. He has moved with soldiers and capos. He has lived in the same house as a Cosa Nostra boss. He was so good the wise guys now want to make him one of their own."

There was a stirring around the table at this remark, but I ignored it, winking at Joe, who was sitting off by himself now.

"Everyone in this room," I continued, "has plenty of reason to be thankful to Joe for his courage and for his dedication. You have all made great cases from his work."

This was a shot across the bow, and that was precisely the point. There was some uncomfortable shifting of butts in seats.

I continued: "The question on the table now is a simple one: When is enough enough? Some of you say six more months. But while we're sitting in our offices those next few months waiting for Joe to bring us bigger and bigger cases, he's out there with the wise guys, and they're in the middle of a shooting war. So this is what I say: I say Joe comes out—now. Not in six months, but as soon as we can make it happen without blowing everything he has already given us." I surveyed the room and found no one ready to interrupt, so I finished up quickly. "It is very tense out there right now, fellas. One mistake, one slipup, and Joe buys it for good. Who in this room wants that on his conscience?" I paused again. "Who in this room will tell me that any case—anyone—is worth the life of one of our own?"

Sean shot me an invisible wink, and Joe studied his shoes. When I sat down, there was absolute silence. That and a sense of having prevailed—but at a price.

The only part of the war council that was worth a damn in my opinion was the very last part, and it was great.

What we had to do was decide the best way to break the news to Pistone's buddies, Lefty Guns and Sonny Black, that Joe was not a dopey wise guy like them but a special agent of the FBI. There are a million ways to ruin someone's day, but believe me, this has got to be right at the top of the list, walking in on a major Mafia guy and telling him, "By the way, this fella you've been hanging around with the past six years, planning, talking about, and *doing* all those crimes? He's really a cop, asshole."

And you are screwed. Royally.

Aside from the glee we felt in thinking about breaking this particular piece of news, there was an important strategy question that had to be answered before we broke up. Most of the guys thought the best way to handle it was to send a few agents over to see Lefty Guns and just tell him straightaway. Joe and I had discussed this privately, and we definitely disagreed with this view, for reasons I'll explain in a minute.

Since I was already such a popular guy with my colleagues, I figured we would listen to what they had to say, then make some kind of reasonable decision.

I let the other guys talk first.

The argument for telling Lefty Guns first instead of Sonny Black was basically simple: Lefty was such a stupid mope that once he got it through his thick head that his friend Donnie Brasco really was an FBI agent named Joe Pistone, he would immediately go crazy and do something rash for which we could clap his sorry ass behind bars.

This, Joe and I agreed, was old thinking. Hoover thinking.

Think about Blakey's strategic philosophy and it was not hard to turn the argument for telling Lefty Guns first squarely on its head. Sure, Lefty would go crazy and do something stupid, but what does that buy you? It buys you one very stupid wise guy on ice. So what's the alternative?

Tell Sonny Black first.

For all his manifest deficiencies of character, Sonny Black Napolitano was a pretty logical, even clever, guy. He could be excitable, like just about every wise guy I've ever known; as a rule, though, he was calm and collected.

If I didn't have to break any more china in this last war council, I was going to be a pretty happy guy, so the way we played it was this: After all the other guys got done laying out their reasons for breaking the news about Pistone to Lefty Guns first, I asked Joe what he thought we ought to do.

Pistone looked up from his chair for maybe half a second and said, "I think we tell Sonny Black."

There was some more bullshit after that, but Pistone's position carried the day, the interminable meeting finally broke up, and Joe, Sean, and I got down to details. Pistone had a meeting already set up with Sonny Black in a few weeks, toward the end of July. The two of them were supposed to have a sit-down in Florida with Santo Trafficante, the powerful mob boss down there, to discuss some problems they were having with a gambling operation. Joe would have to be at the meeting because Sonny Black essentially had turned over to him the Bonanno family's stake in the Florida gambling operation, so he was running it.

The meeting was set for July 27.

That meant we had just a few weeks to get ready. Pistone would have to make himself scarce between now and then, staying in touch with Lefty Guns and Sonny Black by phone but keeping off the streets as much as possible so that the other side of the Bonanno family couldn't take a shot at him.

As for me, I had to get with Kallstrom, Kossler, and Barbara Jones immediately. The reason for going to Sonny Black first was that we knew that once he was told about Pistone, he would start reaching out to other Bonanno family members and even capos and bosses of other families. He would have to pass the news fast and start issuing instructions, and we wanted to be listening in on those conversations. That meant Jimmy Kossler and Barbara Jones would be pulling quite a few all-nighters putting together applications to install wiretaps and secret microphones in a bunch of different places. Once we got a judge's signature giving us the go-ahead, Jim Kallstrom's Special Operations squads would have to work some more of their black magic to get us into the wise guys' apartments, social clubs, and offices.

There was a lot to do and not a hell of a lot of time.

The wise guys, as I think I mentioned, were not especially well known for their habits of personal hygiene, and Special Agents Jerry Loar, Jim Kinne, and Doug Fencl were reminded of this once again as a very sleepy Sonny Black Napolitano unbolted the door of his crummy apartment and allowed the agents inside. The time was 6:30 A.M; the date, July 28.

Loar, Kinne, and Fencl had a message to deliver.

Fencl, who knew Sonny Black and had tried unsuccessfully to recruit him as an informant for us, spoke for the delegation. "Sonny, you know a guy named Donnie Brasco?"

"Yeah, sure," Sonny Black said cautiously. "Yeah, I know Donnie."

Fencl had brought a photograph with him, and he handed it to Sonny Black. The photo was a group shot. In it, Fencl, Loar, and Kinne were standing alongside Joe Pistone, a.k.a. Donnie Brasco. Pistone, it should be noted, was smiling broadly.

Sonny Black finished scratching his crotch and rubbing the sleep from his eyes. He studied the photo.

"Recognize the fourth guy, Sonny? Take a good look."

Sonny Black said nothing.

Fencl shoved the photo under Sonny Black's nose. "Did you know Donnie Brasco is an FBI agent, Sonny?"

Sonny Black nodded slowly but said nothing.

Fencl asked the question again. "Donnie works with us in the Bureau, Sonny. What do you think about that?"

Sonny Black finally got a word out, one syllable. "So?"

Even today, Fencl and the other guys puzzle over this response. It was like Sonny Black Napolitano either didn't give a shit or maybe just didn't know what else to say.

Fencl studied the photo himself for a second, then looked at Sonny Black. "What do you suppose is going to happen, Sonny, when they find out your friend Donnie Brasco is an agent?"

Sonny Black appeared to ponder the question, but evidently he didn't like the answer, because he said nothing.

Fencl homed in. "You know, Sonny, there might be some trouble on this." He pulled out his FBI business cards and handed one to the acting boss of the Bonanno crime family. "If there's anything I can do to help, you can get me at this number. You can call anytime, Sonny."

Sonny Black accepted the card; then his hand fell to his side, and he looked at Fencl kind of sideways. "Doug, you know there's nothing I can do about this—it's over."

But it wasn't.

Like I said, the wise guys had an amazing ability to bullshit themselves. After Sonny Black showed Doug Fencl and the other agents the door, he hiked up his pajamas and convinced himself somehow that the whole business with Donnie Brasco–Joe Pistone could be salvaged, after all.

A few minutes later, he started making phone calls.

20

DESPITE the fact that it was clearly the right thing to do, pulling Pistone was still a gamble. We needed a big win to show that our brilliant new strategy was working. So far, though, we hadn't put a point on the board, and we had just sat our franchise player on the bench.

With Sonny Black running his gums into Kallstrom's secret microphones, of course, we had the makings of a big case. But already we were hearing ominous rumblings from Headquarters about the number of Title IIIs we had up and the number of agents Kallstrom, Kossler, and I were dragging into our little adventure. Monitoring the bugs and wiretaps was chewing up tons of manpower, and the physical surveillance Kallstrom's guys were into now was adding a whole lot more. At the same time, we also had our thing going with Vinnie DePenta over at D&M—still more man-hours down the drain. The message from Headquarters: Where the hell were the indictments?

Sometimes you can hear the long knives being sharpened.

For me, anyone who doesn't second-guess himself is crazy. On its best days, life is a complicated, challenging business, and even the smartest people operating with the best intentions in the world don't do the right thing all the time.

Nobody bats a thousand.

So while I knew I was right in pulling Joe, I also knew where I stood with some of the brass at Headquarters.

Some days, when the flak was flying fast and furious, Sean McWeeney would look at me, his blue eyes crinkled with fatigue.

He was too honorable a guy to ever say it, but I got the message as plain as day. So far we didn't have the big indictment or the big knockout at trial; how long would the brass upstairs be willing to wait?

So Sean and I worried about this, and when we were finished worrying at work, we packed our troubles and toted them home to worry some more there. We both knew the strategy would work—if it was given time. With the murder of the three Bonanno capos, we also knew we had been handed a terrific opportunity. The price we paid for it was pulling Pistone, but the payback was going to be worth it—we hoped.

It wasn't just that we had Sonny Black Napolitano on the hook now; as acting boss of the Bonannos, he was definitely a big fish. What we got with Sonny Black, though, was not one big fish but the chance to net a whole school of them. When he started dialing for his life on the morning of July 28, Sonny Black basically gave us a road map to the entire Bonanno family's criminal operations. Blakey had preached about going after the Cosa Nostra as a criminal *enterprise*. Through his frantic dialing, Sonny Black was helping us to do just that.

And then we got a bonus.

For all the unflattering things that have been said about Vinnie DePenta, by me and by others, if you were prepared to allow for a little loan-sharking, gambling, and the rest of it, DePenta was an okay guy. What I mean is, he had served his country honorably in the armed forces, and long after he was done cooperating with the Bureau, he just slipped back into the woodwork and never caused any trouble for anyone again.

That was later, though. After the hit on Sonny Red Indelicato and the two other Bonanno capos, Vinnie DePenta came running to us, sure that he was going to be whacked next. He still owed Sonny Red a lot of money, and whoever inherited the debt might not be as understanding about the repayment schedule as Sonny Red had been. So Vinnie's worries were real.

Instead of getting whacked, though, DePenta was paid a visit by Sonny Red's brother, J. B. Indelicato. His brother had just been murdered, but old J.B. didn't spend any time crying on Vinnie DePenta's shoulder; what he had on his mind was money. Kallstrom's hidden microphones picked up the conversation. "Just keep up with the business," J.B. told DePenta. "Now you belong to me."

Such a sentimental soul.

But D&M didn't belong to the Bonannos at all. One of the wise guys I mentioned who was a regular visitor to D&M was a gentleman named Frankie Falanga, whose mob nickname, for a number of very good reasons, was "the Beast."

Frankie the Beast had once worked as Joe Colombo's driver, right up until the time the old man got whacked in the middle of New York's Columbus Circle, thus adding another bit of lore to the colorful history of the place. By the time Frankie the Beast started palling around with Vinnie DePenta at D&M, he had come a long way from his chauffering days. He was tight now with the Colombo family's acting boss, a sad old guy named Tommy DiBella. Being the kind of guy who naturally looked after the family's interests, Frankie the Beast thought the Colombos should have a piece of D&M. Frankie became especially convinced of this after DePenta complained one day about the pressure he was getting from the Indelicato family, particularly from J.B. and J.B.'s worthless but dangerous cokehead nephew Bruno.

I won't tell you that Frankie the Beast had a big heart, but he did know a good thing when he saw one, and Vinnie DePenta's D&M company definitely looked like a good thing. By now, we were bringing pasta into D&M from a couple of different distributors in Italy, so that end of the business was working. What wasn't working was any kind of approach to DePenta from Sonny Red Indelicato, mainly because Sonny Red was no longer drawing breath. The murders of Sonny Red, Philly Lucky, and Big Trin Trinchera had upset everything.

There was no doubt in our minds that Sonny Red's brother, J.B., would be trying to piggyback their heroin shipments onto DePenta's pasta imports once things settled down a bit. Now with Frankie the Beast coming around, it looked like the Colombos might have the very same idea.

Frankie the Beast virtually said as much.

The day DePenta was complaining about J.B. and Bruno Indelicato coming around making threats, Frankie the Beast made his intentions concerning D&M clear—or at least as clear as an ape like Frankie the Beast could make them. Picking up his trademark Louisville Slugger—Frankie the Beast seldom went anywhere without his trusty bat—the Colombo family enforcer told his new friend Vinnie not to worry about a thing. "I'll fucking crack open their skulls with this thing," Frankie the Beast swore, Kallstrom's tapes reeling the words in and trapping them for posterity. "If they fuck with you, they fuck with me. You're with us now, understand?"

So the Colombos *did* want a piece of D&M.

For those of us who had helped set Vinnie DePenta up at D&M, it was heartening to see the little guy so much in demand, but the way Kossler and I saw it, if it came down to Vinnie going with the Bonannos or the Colombos, he was definitely going to go with the Colombos; with everything we had from Pistone and with Sonny Black still confiding his innermost thoughts into our Title IIIs, we didn't need any more help on the Bonannos.

Suddenly, we had two mob families in our gun sights.

The talk between Vinnie DePenta and Frankie the Beast Falanga didn't exactly make for illuminating conversation. I mean, you wouldn't have to worry about it tracking too closely with *Masterpiece Theatre* or anything. As it turned out, Frankie the Beast was something of a student of wise-guy genealogy, for example, and DePenta, who was no slouch at the subject himself, made like he didn't know beans about it. Frankie the Beast thought this was a tragedy, and he spent hours trying to remedy the deplorable gap in DePenta's education. Frankie the Beast explained, for example, how the Colombo family was actually formed by a boss named Joe Profaci way back in 1931 and how it was only after Profaci died and Joe Colombo took over thirty years later that the Colombo family actually got the name Colombo. The tutoring sessions were something to hear.

Maybe the point has been made already that the wise guys weren't exactly geniuses, and I don't mean to overemphasize it. But the Falanga-DePenta colloquy on mob history bears an uncanny resemblance at times to Bud Abbott and Lou Costello discussing the national pastime. In that sense, I think, it's a classic.

Here's a sample:

Frankie the Beast: "Now, everybody's got a family, right? DiBella's got a family, right?"

Vinnie DePenta: "Right."

Frankie: "He's got the Profaci family. And the Bonannos have got this guy. And the other guy has got that guy. Then there's another crew. You get it?"

Vinnie: "I thought DiBella was Colombo."

Frankie: "*That's* Colombo."

Vinnie: "Profaci?

Frankie: "Right."

Vinnie: "Profaci-Colombo are one and the same?"

Frankie: "Profaci's all one, that's all one. It's all one."

DePenta's head was spinning after a few hours of this, so eventually he turned the conversation with Frankie the Beast into what he hoped would be a more profitable avenue. Could the Colombo family really protect him from these crazy Bonannos?

No problem there, Frankie the Beast assured DePenta. "It's a strong family. Don't worry, Vinnie."

DePenta shook his head, dazed. "What a zoo, Frank. All I know is I ain't got nothing to worry about, right?"

Frankie the Beast indicated that this was so and ended the conversation on a philosophical note. "You know what the name of the game is here, right, Vinnie?"

"Yeah, what?"

"Make fucking money, that's what."

Thus spake Frankie the Beast.

• • •

Just as I had had many occasions over the years to thank the good Lord for the stupidity of the wise guys, their basic greediness also created opportunities for us that otherwise would never have existed.

This was the case with our investigation of the Colombos.

After listening to Frankie the Beast unburden himself to our man DePenta in the upstairs conference room at D&M for a few weeks, it became clear to us that we had to get inside Tommy DiBella's house. Once again, the idea was to think strategically. We could have easily strolled into D&M one day and slapped the cuffs on Frankie the Beast and charged him with a variety of felonies that would have put him away for a long time. But to what end? Sure, we would have taken a dangerous animal off the streets and retired his Louisville Slugger to the wise-guy Hall of Fame. But the Colombos would have found themselves a new enforcer the next day, and who knows, it's not likely, but the next guy could turn out to be even a lower form of life than Frankie the Beast. By going after the higher-ups, though, we would be sticking with our strategic plan, which was the only way we would ever take out the entire family.

That meant getting Kallstrom's guys inside DiBella's house out in Staten Island, and that looked like trouble—until the wise guys handed us a solution on a platter.

One day over at D&M, Frankie the Beast was taking a break from educating Vinnie DePenta in wise-guy lore when he noticed one of Kallstrom's carefully concealed video cameras.

Our agents listening in on Kallstrom's mikes were paralyzed for a second; then someone ran to tell Damon Taylor, the supervisor of our Colombo squad. A former Green Beret, Damon was something of a philosopher, intellectually someone more in tune with Jimmy Kossler than me. After Kossler and I began preaching Blakey's RICO religion to the troops, for example, Damon became one of our first converts. For hours after that Damon would sit in Kossler's office exploring some of the more arcane points of RICO theory, the blue smoke from Kossler's pipe wreathing the two of them in a saintly haze.

Kossler and Taylor were in Jim's office when they got the news about Frankie the Beast's discovery at D&M. Obviously, this could have been very bad news indeed; it turned out just the reverse. Once again, Kallstrom's tapes told the story:

"Hey, this looks like a great system you got here, Vinnie." We couldn't believe it. Frankie the Beast thought Kallstrom's video camera was part of a security system DePenta had had installed at D&M. "What did it run you, anyway, Vinnie?"

We didn't actually hear DePenta sigh with relief, but you can pretty much assume it happened. And giving credit where credit was due—the little guy saw the opening Frankie the Beast had left, and he drove right through it like a pro. The "security system," DePenta said, was actually a freebie. A couple of buddies of his had stolen the thing and put it in for him for nothing. *Nada.*

"No shit," Frankie the Beast said. It just so happened that Frankie's boss, Mr. DiBella, was at that very moment looking for a security system for his own house. The one DePenta had, Frankie said, looked like it would be just about perfect.

No problem, Frank, DePenta said. His buddies could boost another security system. just like the one he had. If Mr. DiBella wanted it, it was his—gratis.

DePenta had just said the magic wise-guy word—"free."

The next thing we knew, Frankie the Beast was telling Tommy DiBella that "the macaroni guy"—this is what Frankie called DePenta out of his hearing—would get DiBella wired up with a top-of-the-line security system, no payment necessary.

A few days after that, Jimmy Kossler sat down once again to prepare the papers for the Title III application, while Kallstrom's guys began rigging their electronic gear. It would be one of the rare jobs they had where they could stroll right through the front door of a place and string the FBI cameras and microphones under the wise guys' noses.

Sometimes life is a bitch; everybody knows that.

Sometimes, though, it deals some mighty sweet surprises.

21

SOMETIMES life deals some real low blows, too, the kind that leave you gasping. This is what happened a couple of weeks after our guys paid their early-morning visit on Sonny Black Napolitano to explain about Joe Pistone.

Joe had done his job so well that Sonny Black refused to believe that his trusted associate, his friend the jewel thief Donnie Brasco, was a turncoat. "Donnie's been snatched by the fucking feds," Sonny Black moaned to Lefty Guns Ruggiero in one of the many conversations we recorded. "The feds came over here and tried to make me believe he's an [FBI] agent. . . . Can you believe the balls of these guys?"

I don't think Sonny Black was familiar with the term, but what he was in was your basic state of denial. After telling Doug Fencl that the jig was up, Sonny Black had somehow convinced himself otherwise. First, he thought Donnie Brasco had been kidnapped by the FBI and that we were just playing with his head. Judging from the conversations we picked up on the Title IIIs, this lasted just about a week before Sonny Black finally came to the conclusion that his old friend Donnie Brasco was really Joseph D. Pistone, special agent of the FBI. For a wise guy —even one as powerful as Sonny Black Napolitano, the acting boss of one of the biggest Cosa Nostra families—the shit just doesn't get a whole lot deeper than this.

Neck-deep doesn't even begin to get it.

Because a disaster of these proportions had never befallen the wise guys before, there was really no Mafia protocol for Sonny Black to consult on what to do next. What there was, however —besides the abiding sense of dread that had turned Sonny

Black's bowels into a churning tub of bad marinara sauce—was a general wise-guy rule of thumb that calls for all the bosses to get a fast heads-up on bad news from whoever's responsible for it. Sonny Black made the obligatory phone calls, and the usually voluble Mafia dons responded with a quietude more frightening than the most intemperate wise-guy profanity. Sonny Black, it seemed, suddenly didn't have a lot of friends.

It has been said that desperate times demand desperate measures, and I guess it was no different with the wise guys. But none of us expected what happened next.

The bosses put out a contract on Pistone.

This was no ordinary contract, either. All of the bosses had signed off on it, which meant that mopes from all of the five New York families would be gunning for Pistone, that it was basically open season on my friend Joe. The contract was also open-ended, which meant that the mob would pay off whether Joe was murdered next week or next year or the year after that; the hunting season, in other words, never closed. What was most unusual about the contract on Pistone, though, was the price. Normally, the wise guys were cheapskates when it came to killing people, even people they didn't like a whole lot. A few thousand bucks for a hit, depending on the target, was about average.

The contract on Pistone was for half a million dollars.

McWeeney was in his office when I barged in with the news. "A fucking hair on his head is hurt, Sean, and these assholes aren't going to have room to breathe. All bets are off."

"Easy, Giulio."

"Fuck easy, Sean." I said I was going to put New York on a full-court press until the Pistone contract was lifted.

"Agreed. Do it, Giulio."

Five minutes later, I was on the phone to Kossler, who was already two jumps ahead of me.

"I knew you'd be calling, Jules."

"These fucking assholes. I want the word out!"

"Done already. We've gone to all the bosses, and they're getting the message loud and clear."

"Anything happens to Joe—"

"They know, and we're going to keep reminding them."

I thanked Kossler and breathed a little easier. We didn't have any promises from the wise guys, and even if we did, so what? But we had sent a warning, and that was something.

Besides, we had Pistone safe and sound. Minutes after Joe had left his final meeting with Sonny Black in Florida, a team of agents had bundled him into a car, and he was off. Joe had been reunited with his wife and daughters that same evening. To this day, we still can't talk about where we moved the family, but the night Joe came out, we beefed up the security in and around the house. Heavily armed agents were on duty twenty-four hours a day, but after we got word of the contract, we laid the security on even heavier. It was a pain in the neck for Peggy and the kids, but I know it was made up for in a big way by the fact that Joe was finally home and in from the cold. The Pistones were a family again.

For my money, that was the best thing of all.

But I was still nervous—and pissed off.

Less than twenty-four hours after we got word of the Pistone contract, our agents had talked to every wise guy who counted about getting the thing rescinded. Paulie Castellano, the boss of bosses, got a visit from our guys. So did Tommy DiBella, the acting boss of the Colombos; Anthony "Fat Tony" Salerno, the boss of the Genovese family; and Anthony "Tony Ducks" Corallo, the boss of the Luccheses. Of course, we also made sure we got word to the crazy fucking Bonannos, both to Sonny Black, who was an angry, nervous wreck, and to Phil Rastelli, the Bonanno family boss then finishing up a long stretch in the federal penitentiary.

That was fine as far as it went, I thought. But I didn't trust the wise guys. Several times I double-checked the security arrangements for Joe and Peggy and the kids. I was satisfied, that the wise guys would never find the family. And even if they did, with the firepower we had laid on, the wise guys would need a platoon of big tanks to get anywhere near them. That was reassuring.

And it would have to do, I figured—for now.

• • •

Sonny Black's itchy fingers on the telephone plus Joe Pistone's six years of undercover work were the key ingredients of the indictment that we began drawing up against the Bonanno organized-crime family in the fall of 1981. As we had planned, Barbara Jones was our lawyer on the case. And, in one of the nicest pieces of happenstance I could have possibly imagined, Barbara was joined on the prosecution team by none other than Louis Freeh. Louie had wanted to be an FBI agent all his life, and in a very real sense the Bureau had become his life. During a tour at FBI Headquarters, Louie had met his wife-to-be, Marilyn. She was working at the time as an FBI secretary, and by the time Louie was named FBI director thirteen years later, she would have presented him with four handsome sons. For each, the planets revolved around Louie.

As much as he loved the Bureau, Louie had collected a law degree right after college, and after six years as a special agent, he had decided to try his hand as a prosecutor. By the time we were ready to start bringing down the Bonanno case, Louie was wearing the sober blue suit of an Assistant U.S. Attorney. Barbara and I agreed he would make a terrific addition to our team, and for once, the higher-ups agreed.

So Louie was on board.

By late October, Barbara and Louie had put the finishing touches on our indictment, and Jimmy Kossler and I looked at the thing in wonderment. On the face of it, there was nothing to set this one apart from the scores of indictments filed by federal prosecutors around the country each week. There were the names of the individuals charged, of course. And there was the usual government legalese that gave even the lawyers headaches.

But there was something else, too. Something new.

In Case No. 81-CR.803, the *United States of America v. Napolitano et al.*, the allegations of murder, extortion, drug trafficking, and gambling were not narrowly drawn. They were not a mere means to the end of putting a few hoods behind bars. What the allegations were—remember Blakey?—were the building blocks of a much bigger case. Barbara Jones and Louie Freeh had done their work well, and Kossler and I had conferred with Blakey, our *consigliere*. For the first time since it had been drafted more than a decade before, Bob Blakey's beautiful brainchild, the Racketeer Influenced and Corrupt Organizations Act, was being rolled out as the government's big main gun against an entire organized-crime family.

RICO's revenge, we called it.

Sonny Black's big mouth and Joe Pistone's heroic undercover work had given us enough evidence to arrest a small army of Bonannos; what RICO gave us was the wherewithal to bring down the whole rotten corporate structure *behind* the family. Flying back and forth between Washington and New York, I conferred with McWeeney, Kossler, Jones, and Freeh. Despite the rumblings from Headquarters somewhere high above me, Jimmy Kallstrom's guys were not about to pull any of our Title IIIs or give up on any of our surveillances. We had the wise guys of the Bonanno family fixed like butterflies to a corkboard, and that's exactly where we wanted them—right up until the moment we crossed every last *t* and dotted every last *i* in the indictment.

We knew from one of the Title IIIs that a contract had been put out on Pistone's crazy friend Lefty Guns Ruggiero, and we had to assume that the mob had made similar plans for Sonny Black Napolitano, although we didn't know that for sure. In any case, we weren't about to leave either one of those guys to the Mafia to deal with, so we went out to pick them up.

Lefty we found with no problem.

Kallstrom had ordered a twenty-four-hour surveillance on Lefty's apartment down in Knickerbocker Village, right on the edge of Chinatown. The morning we decided to bring Lefty in, Special Agents Lou Vernazza and Vic Hagan had the surveillance duty, and they were sitting across the street from Lefty's place, maybe forty yards down the block, a one-way street. Vic and Lou had been out on the site for four or five hours, killing time in the undercover car, a big white Lincoln with a green top. The pimpmobile, they called it. Surveillance work can make you crazy with the boredom, the waiting, and the rest of it, but the agents assigned to the stakeout on Lefty were edgy. We had picked Lefty up on one of the Title IIIs after he got the news about Pistone, and among the few coherent statements he had made, Lefty had done a pretty good imitation of Edward G. Robinson snarling that the feds would never take him alive. Specifically, what Lefty said on tape was this: "Any FBI agent comes to bust me, I'm gonna fucking kill him first."

Lefty, like I say, was a dumb son of a bitch, but since we knew he was also a stone killer, we would have been even dumber if we didn't take him at his word. So Kallstrom's guys on the stake-out were taking no chances. Both Hagan and Vernazza had their Bureau-issue sidearms, but Lou also had a shotgun resting across his knees in the passenger seat of the Lincoln pimp-mobile. Hagan and Vernazza weren't expected to arrest Lefty; we had dispatched a more heavily armed arrest team from 26 Federal for that purpose. All Vic and Louie were supposed to do was hang out in the pimpmobile and make sure Lefty didn't disappear before the arrest team got there.

The Bureau has all sorts of rules and regs about making a collar safely. Like so many things in life, though, the stuff in the rule book doesn't always apply. This was the case with Lou Vernazza and Vic Hagan. They didn't know it, but while they were sitting in front of Lefty's, waiting for the arrest team to show, the arrest team, in a brand-new Bureau car, was getting broadsided by some jackass cabdriver who had run a red light a mile away. This is not really an unusual occurrence in the Big Apple, but it doesn't happen to the FBI all that often.

What happens next is this: The arrest team can't leave the scene of the accident, Vernazza and Hagan are getting antsy watching Lefty's front door, and then Lefty pops out and starts walking like a windup toy, moving real fast down the one-way street, going the wrong way.

"What do we do, Lou?"

"Do?" Vernazza released the safety on the shotgun and shouted at Hagan. "Go after the son of a bitch, you idiot!"

"It's a fucking one-way street, Louie."

"Fuck it, will ya? Let's fucking go!"

Hagan eased the Lincoln from the curb, but Lefty was about sixty yards down the street already, moving fast. Vernazza rechecked the shotgun, his right hand on the door lever. When the pimpmobile was within twenty yards of Lefty, Louie jumped out. Vernazza is a hell of a big guy, he goes about 240 pounds— and we used to kid him about his looks: He bears an uncanny resemblance to Luca Brazzi, the sadistic enforcer in the first *Godfather* movie.

"Lefty!"

Lefty Guns looked over his shoulder, and he never said it, probably because he didn't think about it, but I bet his whole miserable life did flash before his eyes. If you saw a 240-pound guy who looked a lot like Luca Brazzi's twin brother running after you with a shotgun, this would be a very understandable reaction, I think.

What Lefty said was this: "I'm not packing, I'm not packing!" Then he threw his hands in the air.

Lou Vernazza threw Lefty against the nearest wall, and Hagan was right behind him. The two agents took a second to catch their breath before Louie read Lefty his Miranda rights and placed the cuffs on him. The arrest team showed up a few minutes later, and they bundled Lefty into a car and hauled him off for booking back at 26 Federal.

In the car on the way downtown, Lefty turned to one of the arrest-team agents and shook his head. "Who the fuck was that big guy with the shotgun, anyway?"

Sonny Black was another story.

We couldn't find the acting boss of the Bonannos anywhere. And his phones had suddenly gone dead—definitely not a good sign. We knew Sonny Black had attended a meeting with Paul Castellano and the bosses of the other families back on August 14. Ominously, that was the same day our Title IIIs on Sonny Black's phones stopped talking to us. At the time, we had no way of knowing for sure, but it didn't take a genius to figure what had happened. By November, we had confirmed it. A guy out walking his dog came across a corpse in a creek. This was out in Staten Island, not too far from Paul Castellano's mansion, in fact. Both hands had been cut off the corpse, and the thing was so badly decomposed that the technicians in the morgue had to go to the dental records to make the ID.

The casket at Sonny Black Napolitano's wake was, needless to say, closed. Some of the important wise guys showed up, anyway.

Some even shed a tear or two.

22

IT'S a funny thing about lawyers. You start making work for them, and they start multiplying like flies. And I mean this as no disrespect, since, as the saying goes, some of my best friends are lawyers. It's just that it happens to be true.

Anyway, with Sonny Black dead and Lefty and a few other big Bonanno capos stewing in a federal lockup following our indictment, Barbara Jones and Louie Freeh were swamped. Bond hearings, depositions, pretrial motions—there was all the usual pretrial bullshit plus an incredible amount of additional pressure.

This was the government's first shot at a RICO case against a Cosa Nostra family, and Barbara and Louie were damned if they were going to blow it. We had Bob Blakey to steer us through the shoals, of course, but textbook theory is one thing and the here and now of the courtroom something else again. No one could predict how a trial judge would rule on RICO-related issues, and you could be sure that the Bonannos' high-priced counsel would try every trick in the book to get the RICO count thrown out. This meant lots of extra preparation for Barbara and Louie. It also meant we would need another lawyer on the team.

Enter Bruce Baird.

Bruce was a tall guy, almost painfully thin. He was courteous, thoughtful, and soft-spoken—a true son of the Midwest. And he was an absolute tiger in court. Months earlier, Bruce had been assigned to work with Barbara Jones and Louie Freeh on the Bonanno case. After the murder of the three Bonanno capos, Barbara and Louie began doing the spadework for a separate investigation of the hit itself, leaving poor Bruce scratching his head about what to do about the undercover shop we had set up with Vinnie DePenta at D&M.

That didn't last long.

After Kossler and I decided to aim the DePenta operation at the Colombo family, Bruce Baird simply shifted his gun sights from the Bonanno family to the Colombos. It was Bruce, in fact, who handled the application for the Title IIIs on Tommy DiBella's house. After that, he would be with us the whole way.

On a bitterly cold day in January 1982, a U.S. District Court judge signed the paperwork Bruce had prepared for the installation at DiBella's place. A few hours later, one of Jimmy Kallstrom's guys, Special Agent Ken Doyle pulled up outside the DiBella residence. Doyle had helped John Kravec and Joe Cantamesa do the wiring job at D&M. He was a pro's pro, and like Kravec, Cantamesa, and the rest of Kallstrom's agents, he could think quick on his feet when he had to.

Outside DiBella's front door, Doyle pressed the bell and waited. A minute later, he was face-to-face with the acting boss of the Colombo crime family.

DiBella was an old guy, in rotten health, and like all the bosses, he had a big, pendulous gut. He also had a pasty complexion, like he hadn't seen the sun in maybe half a century.

"Mr. DiBella?"

"Who wants to know?"

"I'm Vinnie DePenta's friend, the guy with the security system he said you wanted."

DiBella gazed dully at Doyle through rheumy eyes. "DePenta's friend, huh?

"Yeah, that's me."

"Yeah? Well, you look like a fucking FBI agent to me."

"No shit, Mr. DiBella, really?" Doyle laughed. "What does one look like?"

It was the old man's turn to chuckle. "Ah, I'm just busting your balls. Come on in, guy."

Kenny Doyle spent the next few hours trundling back and forth to the car with the various components of Tommy DiBella's "security system." Before the day was out, the thing was up and running, and that evening, we recorded the first of many conversations from Tommy DiBella's little kitchen.

There is this impression, I think, among a lot of people that the Mafia preyed only on other hoods and thugs or on people either stupid or desperate enough to borrow money from mob shylocks. This was a lot of nonsense, of course, and one of the beauties of the case we would build against the Colombos is that it gave us the chance to prove it beyond a shadow of a doubt.

Sometimes simple facts get lost behind big words. In the case of the Mafia, they are words like "labor racketeering," for instance. Ask a lawyer and he or she will explain it this way: "A labor racketeering violation occurs when a criminal group gains control of a labor union to commit illegal acts."

That's good as far as it goes, I guess. But it doesn't really bring the story home, if you know what I mean. Labor racketeering really is something that costs you and me money—sometimes a lot of it. From the tape recordings we were making from Tommy DiBella's place, for instance, we learned that the Colombo family had gained control of Local 66 of the Laborers International Union of North America; the mob basically owned the local, is what it came down to. At this point, a lot of people will probably say something like "Gee, that's terrible, but unless I'm a big developer putting up skyscrapers or football stadiums, you know, it doesn't really affect me."

Which is dead wrong.

The Colombo family, just to give an example, was collecting $800 for every single-family house being built in a nice middle-class suburb of New York. The construction companies putting up the houses paid the money to the Colombos—in exchange for exactly nothing. Or to be more precise, the companies paid the Colombos in order to keep union labor *off* their job sites. They also paid a fat salary to Frankie the Beast Falanga for a no-show job, which further added to the cost of the homes, which would then be purchased by young families and older blue-collar workers fleeing the tumult of the city.

This isn't the same as some thug stealing your purse or demanding your wallet at gunpoint, I'll grant you. But it is a pernicious kind of thing, and in addition to costing a lot of decent, hardworking people a hell of a lot of money, it's the kind of thing that really eats at a society.

Which is just a fancy way of saying the whole deal stunk.

On a miserably hot morning in July 1982, Louis Freeh rose from his chair in a handsome courtroom overlooking St. Andrew's Plaza in Lower Manhattan and began saying nasty things about a dead man before he moved on to the living. The dead man was Sonny Black Napolitano, now memorialized, courtesy of the Federal Bureau of Investigation, in *United States of America v. Napolitano et al.,* Case No. 81-CR.803.

Sonny Black would have liked none of the things Louie had to say that morning as he delivered the government's opening statement in the Bonanno case, but even he would have had to agree that if the actual words were a little harsh, Louie's tone was polite and deferential. After outlining for the jury the highlights of Sonny Black's lengthy criminal career, Louie introduced the jurors to each of the five defendants who had survived the Bonanno family wars to make it into court. Mr. Anthony Rabito, whose nickname for some reason was "Joey," was wearing the red shirt; Louie pointed him out for the jury. Mr. Antonio Tomasulo, who went by the nickname "Boots," was seated alongside Mr. Rabito. Farther down the line, gray-faced in matching brown suits, were Nicholas "Mr. Fish" Santora and John "Boobie" Cerasani. Last but not least, Louie introduced the jurors to Lefty Guns, whose given name, as spelled out in the criminal indictment filed against him, was Benjamin Ruggiero.

Introductions completed, Louie next walked the jury through some wise-guy vocabulary, explaining, for instance, that a "hit" was wise-guy shorthand for murder, that a "score" was just another way of describing a robbery.

Finally, Louie cut to the heart of the matter. "The bread and butter for these defendants came from truck hijackings, armed robbery, narcotics trafficking, and gambling operations," he told the ladies and gentlemen of the jury; the five wise guys listened morosely. "When taken together with the acts of murder charged in this case," Louie continued, "they constitute a pattern of racketeering—a pattern which was committed between 1974 and 1981 in New York, New Jersey, and Florida. This pattern of racketeering"—Louie paused for emphasis here, and even the wise guys looked up from their shoe tops—"forms the basis for the charges in this indictment."

RICO's revenge.

To make the RICO count stick, Barbara and Louie had to get the jurors to focus not so much on each of the criminal acts that they would be describing in the courtroom but to see those acts as a kind of tapestry. "The proof," Louie told the jury, "will come to you in installments, one witness at a time, one piece of evidence at a time. Be assured, however, that as the trial progresses, these pieces will fall into place, and they will paint for you a clear, simple picture of a criminal enterprise known as the Bonanno family of the Cosa Nostra—an enterprise motivated by greed and power."

Strip all the fancy talk and law-book mumbo jumbo away from it and what a trial is really about is telling a story. And at the end of the day, what it all comes down to is a very simple question: Does the jury believe the story or not? In the Bonanno case, Barbara Jones and Louie Freeh were blessed with a lot of compelling evidence. They had the tapes, which they would play for the jury, from the Title IIIs Kallstrom's guys had installed at Sonny Black's place and elsewhere. They had a lot of evidence from our physical surveillance of the defendants, too. But what Barbara and Louie really had going for them in the case against the Bonannos was a world-class storyteller: Joe Pistone.

Before they got to Pistone, though, Barbara and Louie had another witness who would tell some stories on the Bonannos. This was a guy named Raymond Wean, a genuine human slug whose thirty-year criminal career included the hijacking of $50,000 worth of tuna fish. Ray Wean was a bad guy, and the jury would see that right away. But he was our informant—

he had cut a deal so we would go easier on him in another case—and what the hell, Barbara and Louie were going to put him on.

Pistone, though, was the main show.

And he very nearly *didn't* go on.

Despite the warnings we had given to the bosses of the five families in New York, the contract on Pistone's life had not been lifted. Being the kind of guy he is, Pistone barely even thought about the contract. As he was preparing for the Bonanno trial with Barbara and Louie, though, he got news that really threw him. An informant of ours who worked with the FBI office in Buffalo reported—just days before Pistone was set to take the witness stand—that there were rumors on the street about the wise guys trying to get to Pistone through his family: A contract may have been issued for Peggy and the kids.

Joe went nuts. "Those fucking guys, I'll deal with those assholes myself! *I'll* fucking deal with them!"

"Joe. Listen, Joe." It had fallen to Barbara Jones to break the news to Pistone. Barbara and Louie Freeh had been working over the weekend with Pistone to prepare for his testimony Monday morning. The three of them were in Barbara's cluttered office on the ninth floor of the U.S. Attorney's office at 1 St. Andrew's Plaza just across from the federal courthouse.

"No, you listen! These fucking animals, they think they're gonna go after my family now?"

"The Bureau will handle it, Joe."

"Fuck the Bureau."

"Joe, listen to me!"

"No, Barbara."

"Joe, listen! We don't even have to put you on."

"Are you crazy? I didn't spend six years under cover to walk away now, goddammit."

"It's still your decision, Joe." Louie Freeh was a young assistant prosecutor, and he was respectful of Barbara's role as the lead attorney, but Barbara needed support here. "If you say no, Joe, we don't use you. Period."

"No—I mean no, I'm not gonna walk away." Pistone had his hands jammed in the pockets of his suitcoat, and he stared at Barbara and Louie. "I'm going to go on. But the first thing I'm going to do is, I'm going to go see Paul Castellano, and I'm going to talk to him about this so-called contract on Peggy and the girls."

"Joe, Joe."

Pistone ignored Barbara's interruption, staring at Louie, then Barbara, then back to Louie again. "You guys have a problem with that, with me seeing Paulie, Barbara?"

"Let the Bureau handle it, Joe—*that's* all I'm saying. There's no way anyone will get to Peggy and the girls. And if you are going to go on, we've still got a hell of a lot of work to do."

Joe turned away from Barbara and Louie. From her ninth-floor office above St. Andrew's Plaza, Barbara had a spectacular view of the Brooklyn Bridge, and Pistone took his time admiring its silhouette in the dying light. Finally, he turned away. "Those bastards, I don't fucking believe it!"

"Joe?" It was Louie again.

Pistone slumped into a chair. "Let's just do it, okay, guys? Let's get the fucking show on the road."

In court, Barbara Jones is tough as nails, but like the best prosecutors, you don't have to tell Barbara a thing about human nature. She admired Pistone enormously, but maybe more than any of us, she saw how the strain was eating at him. They continued going over Joe's testimony, but Barbara knew as plain as day that Joe was still obsessing about Peggy and the kids.

After about an hour, Barbara called a break, and Pistone went to get coffee. In her office, Barbara and Louie talked about what they ought to do next.

"He blows up in front of the jury like that, Lou, it would be a disaster."

"I know, I know." Louie Freeh knew Joe Pistone as the most disciplined of men, but there was no telling how this kind of mental strain might cause him to act in front of a jury.

"I'm worried for him as much as anything."

"Me, too, Barbara, but Joe's a tough guy. Let's give it another day and see what happens."

Sunday afternoon I was at home watching the Orioles, playing I forget who, when the phone rang and I grabbed it.

Barbara made about twenty-two seconds of small talk before she got down to business. "It's about Joe, Jules."

For a split second my worst fears flashed through my mind. "He's all right, isn't he?"

"Yeah, he's all right." Joe was fine physically, Barbara said; no problem there. "But it's this business with Peggy and the girls."

"It's chewing him up."

"Chewing him up? He wants to go see Paul Castellano!"

"Oh, shit."

"Look, I understand that, okay?"

"It was your family, you'd feel the same way, right?"

"Right. But he's talking about Castellano—about going after the wise guys himself. He can't let it go, Jules."

"Barbara." I rested both elbows on the desk in our family room and cradled my head in my hands. "What are you telling me?"

There was a long pause on the other end of the line. "What I'm saying, Jules—and I want to be very clear about this because you know how I feel about Joe . . ."

"Yeah, I know, I know. Just tell me what you're gonna tell me."

"What I'm saying, Jules, is that I am seriously considering whether to put Joe on tomorrow."

"At all?" I couldn't believe it. Pistone was supposed to be our star witness against the Bonannos.

"I've talked about it with Louie, Jules, and we both feel we could put him on real quickly, then cut it short."

"Wait a second, wait!" I looked at my watch. Shit, it was only three-twenty. I could make the four-thirty shuttle and be at Barbara's office by six-thirty.

"Look, I think it'll be okay, Jules."

"Don't tell me it'll be okay." I paused. "Okay, Barbara?" I had the phone cradled in my ear and was already shoveling notes and other junk into my briefcase. "I'm on my way to the airport, all right? Just don't do anything with Joe until I get there."

There was another silence on Barbara's end of the line. Then: "Hey, Jules?"

"Yeah, what?"

"I think he'll be real glad to see you."

The U.S. Attorney's office was almost deserted by the time I got there, shortly after seven. The guards knew me on sight and waved me through, and I found my way to Barbara's office upstairs on the ninth floor. Pausing at the door, I could hear three muted voices—Joe's, Barbara's, and Louie's. On the face of it, things sounded just fine, the lawyers prepping their big witness for his debut the next day.

I knocked, a sick feeling in my gut.

Barbara opened the outer door, and I stared past her at Joe.

"Jules, what the fuck?"

"How you doing, Joe?"

Pistone looked terrible—nervous, exhausted, played out. But he flew out of his chair, anyway, and we hugged each other like brothers. What can I tell you? This kind of thing makes some people uncomfortable, but we were two hot-tempered Italians, and we knew without saying it how much our friendship meant to each other.

"How you doing, man?"

"Okay, okay."

"He's doing great, Jules."

I looked at Barbara over Joe's shoulder, thankful more than I could say that she had called me.

"So." I held Pistone away from me so I could get a better look at him, then grinned at Barbara and Louie. "Shit, I don't know, I've seen him look a hell of a lot better myself."

"Well, he's doing great."

"Yeah, so you say." I winked at Barbara, then looked at Joe. "What do you say we take a break, huh? Get a little air?"

"Yeah, good. Whatever."

"Okay with you, Barbara?"

"No problem, Jules. We could all use a break."

"Okay." I looked at Joe. "So? Let's go."

Louie decided to tag along, and Barbara turned to some other stuff she had to have ready for the next day.

"We won't be long, Barbara, okay?"

"Jules, it's okay." She looked at me again. "All right?"

"Just a few minutes, Barbara." Pistone was already halfway out the door.

"Joe, take a break. God knows you deserve it."

The three of us—Joe, Louie, and me—left Barbara hunched over her desk and stepped out into the cool marble hallway. The lights were off in the long corridors of the government office building, and from outside, we could hear the last sounds of the late weekend traffic in the distance. We walked without talking for a while, listening to the road noise. Joe knew what he needed, talk or quiet, and I was there for either.

Pistone finally broke the silence. "Jules, I tell you—"

"Joe." I had to interrupt before he got himself worked up again. "Nothing—nothing!—is going to happen to Peggy and the girls. As long as I'm around, you've got anything you want for them. Anything—and they're going to be okay."

"Those assholes." Pistone said it quietly, but I could feel the passion behind it.

"Joe, listen." We paused at the end of a dark hallway, and through a half-closed office door, I could see the last of the summer twilight fading outside. Under the winking streetlights the city looked peaceful and scrubbed clean, almost. "You are the finest undercover agent this agency or any other agency ever has had or ever will have. Now what you've got to do is go in there tomorrow, say your piece, and then get back to Peggy and the kids. Just get this over with, okay?"

Joe nodded. "I know, I know."

"Getting pissed off, what's that gonna solve?"

"Don't *you* give me that shit now! You telling me you wouldn't do the same thing?"

He had me there, but there was no percentage in admitting it. "You've just got to focus on tomorrow, Joe. That's it, okay?"

"I'm there, don't worry." Pistone squeezed my shoulder.

"Yeah, okay."

We walked for another hour or so, and Pistone finally turned to me as we made the last turn before we got back to Barbara's office. "Hey, what the fuck are you doing here, anyway?"

I put my arm around my friend's shoulder. "I just wanted to be with you, man, that's all."

"Ah," Pistone said. "Bullshit."

The next morning, I was sitting in the courtroom when Barbara Jones rose from her seat at the prosecution table and said, "Your Honor, the government calls Special Agent Joseph Pistone."

At the defense table, Lefty Guns had this big shit-eating grin on his face, and when Joe walked into the courtroom and took his seat in the witness box, Lefty flashed his stupid pearly whites at Pistone, as if to say, "Hey, man, we're buddies, right? No way you're going to talk."

But talk Joe did.

And the longer he talked, the more Lefty's face seemed to transform itself into a mask of pure hatred, the lips compressed and bloodless, the eyes as dark and hard as agate.

For nine days Pistone testified.

When he was done, Barbara Jones delivered her summation for the jury. Three days after that, the jury returned with their verdicts. The ladies and gentlemen of the jury convicted Mr. Lefty Guns Ruggiero, Mr. Fish Santora, Mr. Boots Tomasulo, and Mr. Joey Rabito of violations of the Racketeer Influenced and Corrupt Organizations Act and a host of related crimes, including gambling, murder, and extortion. Only John Cerasani was acquitted. The four Bonanno family members would be sentenced to combined prison terms totaling seventy-six years.

Score one for the good guys, I thought.

A big one.

23

THE Colombo family, by the time we really started working them hard, in the fall of 1982, didn't look like it was at full strength. The appearance was deceiving.

The boss of the family was a guy named Carmine Persico, whose nickname, "the Snake," should pretty much speak for itself. Carmine the Snake was temporarily in jail on a parole violation, so Tommy DiBella was running things as the acting boss. But DiBella, as I mentioned, was not a well man, and so the day-to-day affairs of the family business fell to the Colombo's underboss, a flashy dresser named Gennaro Langella, a guy everyone called Gerry Lang. Besides being something of a clothes horse, Gerry Lang was that rarest of rarities among the wise guys: He was a genuinely smart guy. Lang's right-hand man, on the other hand, was emphatically not a smart guy. What Dominick Montemarano lacked in smarts, however, he more than made up for in energy and ambition. Montemarano, whose nickname was "Donny Shacks," was a one-man crime wave.

I mention this because as fortunate as we had been to get inside Tommy DiBella's house with Kallstrom's microphones, it soon became clear that a lot of the action in the Colombo family was taking place elsewhere. We got some good stuff from the Title IIIs at DiBella's; as the family's acting boss, he had to be kept up-to-date on what was going on. But from what we were picking up on our hidden mikes at D&M as well as what we were getting from the heavy physical surveillance we had laid on a few of the Colombo capos, the family's heaviest action had Gerry Lang and Donny Shacks right in the middle of it.

Kossler and I talked about this endlessly between Washington and New York. If we were going to take out the Colombo family structure the way we had just done with the Bonannos, we knew we would need to look a whole lot harder at Gerry Lang and Donnie Shacks.

Which is exactly what we proceeded to do.

The way we worked the Title IIIs was like a daisy chain. From D&M, albeit with a bit of luck and some fast talking by Vinnie DePenta, we got the Title III on Tommy DiBella's place. From what we picked up on Kallstrom's mikes there, we got enough evidence to get another Title III on Donnie Shacks's home telephone. That was back in July, just as Barbara Jones and Louie Freeh were getting ready to try the Bonannos. From what Donnie Shacks had said on the phone from his home, we got still more evidence that persuaded a judge to grant us yet another Title III, this one on Donnie Shacks's social club. The court order was signed in the first week of September, and Jimmy Kallstrom's guys went out to have a look at the place the same day. The target was a bitch, probably our toughest yet.

The place was called the Maniac Club.

Lou Vernazza got the call.

As you already know from the way he made the collar on Lefty Guns, Lou Vernazza, a large, generally fearsome-looking human being who, even if he was just asking the time of day, could make the faint of heart break out in a cold sweat, was handy with a shotgun.

Big people have it rough. Look at a guy like Lou Vernazza and most people think big and tough—period. Not too many people would imagine that the guy's a gourmet cook, a genuinely kind man who's a soft touch for the kids and old ladies.

Of course, Vernazza had a devious mind, too, which is why he was one of Kallstrom's favorite supervisors and why Jimmy decided to ask him to scope out the Maniac Club.

Kallstrom was in his office up on the twenty-sixth floor at 26 Federal when Vernazza came in to get a fill on the job.

"What have you got, boss?"

"A tough one, Lou. A bitch." As usual, Kallstrom had his feet on his desk, his tie loose around his neck.

"This is Montemarano's place, right? The club?"

"Yeah." Damon Taylor's squad had spent dozens of hours on surveillances of the Maniac Club, and Damon had passed on the reports for Kallstrom to digest. Kallstrom had the paperwork on his desk, but he didn't bother to look at it.

"What's the problem with the place?"

Kallstrom kicked his feet off the desk and leaned forward in his chair. "The big problem, Lou, is dogs."

"Dogs, huh?" Vernazza was hunched like a bear in the narrow armchair across from Kallstrom's desk.

"Yeah, two dogs, actually."

"Big ones?"

Kallstrom nodded. "Rottweilers."

"Shit."

"I got an idea, though."

"What's that, boss?" Vernazza tried to keep a straight face. Kallstrom's brainstorms didn't always sit real well with his Special Ops supervisors.

"We got it from Donnie Shacks, actually."

"No shit."

"Yeah, a conversation the other day on the Title III from his house?"

"Yeah?"

"He's bitching about the dogs to Gerry Lang."

"What about?"

" 'Those fucking dogs,' Donnie says. 'They shit in the club one more time, they're fucking outta here.' "

"So?" Vernazza paused.

Kallstrom shrugged his shoulders and laughed. "What I'm saying, Lou, is maybe we figure some way to get the dogs to take a shit inside the club."

Vernazza cackled evilly. "Then Donnie gets rid of the fucking rottweilers for us."

"Exactly." Kallstrom leaned back in his chair and studied the ceiling. "The only thing is, Lou . . ."

Vernazza finished the sentence. ". . . is how we get the dogs to shit inside the fucking club."

"Right."

Vernazza climbed out of the uncomfortable armchair and stretched. "Leave it to me, boss. No problem, okay?"

"Okay, Lou, let me know what you come up with."

"No problem, boss. I'll be in touch." Vernazza moved his considerable bulk through Kallstrom's door and out into the corridor. Kallstrom scratched his head, wondering what the big man would come up with for the dogs.

The centerpiece of the Vernazza plan was meatballs. He briefed the plan to Jimmy the next day, Kallstrom let loose one of his big Santa Claus laughs, then gave his okay.

"Fucking meatballs," Kallstrom said. "I don't believe it."

"Just wait, boss. You'll see."

That afternoon, Vernazza took a few hours off and went home to cook up his meatballs using an old family recipe. Lou followed the recipe to a tee—except for one thing: Mama Vernazza had never been known to spike her meatballs with laxatives, purgatives, or any other kinds of pharmaceutical goodies designed to loosen the bowels and gladden the heart.

That's what Lou did, though. He added some laxatives, quite a lot, in fact, folding the medicinal goo carefully in with the ground meat, the herbs, and the spices that were the mainstays of the Vernazza family's famous meatball recipe. The things came out of the oven brown and savory, and Lou wasted no time hustling them back to the office for that evening's adventure.

It was time to pay a visit to the Maniac Club.

The club was out in Brooklyn, and this is as good a place as any, I suppose, to explain a bit of tradecraft. Normally, the way we would go in on an installation like the Maniac Club was with three teams of agents. There would be the lock guys, the guys with the light fingers who could fiddle just about any lock known to man. Then there were Kallstrom's Special Ops guys. The squad assigned to the Maniac Club job was led by Lou Vernazza. It would be up to Lou's agents to provide protection for the lock guys, who would make the covert entry to the club. Once they had beaten the locks, a team of tech agents on Vernazza's Special Ops squad would hide and string the microphones inside the club and make sure they worked. Finally, we had what we called the "substantive" guys. These were the agents who were actually working a particular investigation. Whereas Kallstrom's guys would hopscotch from case to case as they were needed, the substantive guys were the agents who worked a case from beginning to end. Since the Maniac Club job was part and parcel of our investigation of the Colombo family, Damon Taylor's squad were the substantive guys on that run. It would be up to them to provide surveillance for Vernazza and his squad as well as for the lock guys. If Damon's people saw any sign of trouble, especially in the form of wise guys with weapons, they were to sound the alarm and radio the guys inside the club to get the hell out as fast as possible.

These things, it should come as no surprise, are practiced over and over again, and they are the subject of intense training and retraining at the FBI Academy at Quantico. But there is only so much you can train for, you know? I mean, nobody at Quantico ever taught Lou Vernazza how to bake shit-inducing meatballs for a couple of killer dogs, if you know what I mean.

At 2:30 A.M., we rolled out of 26 Federal with just two teams of agents. Since we weren't planning on actually going into the Maniac Club that night—the objective was just to get the dogs to relieve themselves in the club so that Donnie Shacks would get rid of them for us—we didn't need to deprive the lock guys of a night's sleep. So we had just Vernazza's Special Ops squad and Damon Taylor's Colombo case squad.

"You got the meatballs, Lou?"

Vernazza grabbed for the secure radio mounted on the dash of his Bureau car. "In the trunk, boss. Nice and warm."

Technically, Kallstrom didn't have to go on the installation at the Maniac Club, but the Colombo case was shaping up as a big one, and he wanted to make sure everything went right.

At that time of night, it was only a twenty-minute drive from

Lower Manhattan out to the Maniac Club, but it took another ten minutes or so for Damon's squad in their unmarked cars and undercover vans, to get into position.

The car-to-car radios crackled quietly; Kallstrom checked with Damon and his team and then with Vernazza and his guys. All the agents were in position.

"Okay, Louie," Kallstrom said into his radio. "Showtime."

"Ten-four, boss."

Slouched in the front seat of his unmarked car just down the street from the Maniac Club, Kallstrom had a pretty good view of the proceedings. He watched as Vernazza emerged from his car just across from the Maniac Club, then saw him unlock the trunk and reach inside for the pan filled with meatballs. In the glow of the streetlights, the aluminum foil covering the meatballs shined like a precious metal. Using his side-view mirror, Kallstrom watched Vernazza tiptoe Pink Panther–like across the black asphalt. Even with his windows rolled up, Jimmy could hear the two rottweilers erupt a second later.

In the side-view mirror, Kallstrom could see the two attack dogs baring their teeth and throwing themselves against the metal cyclone fence. Vernazza seemed totally unperturbed. Carefully, as Kallstrom watched, Louie peeled back the double sheet of aluminum foil. Then, like a softball pitcher in a just-for-fun Fourth of July game, he started lobbing the meatballs one by one, underhand, over the fence to the two dogs.

Within seconds, the barking stopped.

Kallstrom checked his watch. It took Vernazza less than three minutes to dispose of his meatballs.

From their various perches around the perimeter of the Maniac Club, Damon's agents and Vernazza's agents waited, and those who could watched. The two dogs galloped up and down their fenced run, sniffing the ground, searching for any last undiscovered morsel of meatball. What the dogs didn't do, however, was approach the black fiberglass doggie door that had been cut into the side entrance of the Maniac Club.

In his car, Kallstrom checked his watch again. Fully ten min-

utes had gone by. "What the fuck is going on? Louie, somebody
—what the fuck is *happening?*"

Vernazza's voice came back over the radio. "Nothing, boss.
Nothing yet, anyway."

One of Damon's agents nearby made a crack. "The fucking
rottweilers, it looks like they're smiling."

"Shit," Louie said.

"No," Damon's agent shot back. "*No* shit—that's the problem."

Feeling antsy, Kallstrom got out to stretch his legs. He had
more than two dozen agents in less than a square block. The
chance of being seen doing something suspicious was a risk we
lived with on every operation. But if the rottweilers weren't
going to play ball tonight and go in and take a dump inside the
club, they had to get the hell out of there and come back with
another plan. He gave it another five minutes, then radioed Vernazza and Damon Taylor. "Abort, guys. We'll try again in a day
or two."

Two nights later, Lou Vernazza was back with another batch of
meatballs. This time, Kallstrom had ordered the team of lock
agents to accompany Vernazza's and Damon Taylor's squads.
One way or the other, they were going inside the damn club.

Vernazza had explained about the meatballs the day before.

"Thorazine?" Kallstrom had asked Vernazza.

"Enough to knock out a herd of elephants, boss."

"It's gonna work?"

"It'll either make 'em shit their guts or it'll make them so
stunadu, they won't give us any trouble."

"What's *stunadu?*"

"*Stunadu,*" Vernazza said. "It's Italian. For dopey. Stupid."

"*Stunadu,*" Kallstrom said. "Great. Whatever."

In his car down the street from the Maniac Club once again,
Jimmy watched the whole thing unfold just like two nights earlier: Vernazza tiptoeing across the empty street, the dogs going
nuts, Louie lobbing the meatballs one by one over the fence.

He let five minutes go by. "What's going on?"

One of Damon's agents came back on the radio less than a minute later. "The dogs just went inside, boss."

Vernazza came up on the radio next. "All quiet in there. Quiet as a tomb."

Kallstrom waited another five minutes, then gave the order. "Okay, let's move it."

The lock guys hit the front door of the Maniac Club seconds later, and it soon became clear that Donnie Shacks had not invested heavily in top-notch hardware: We were inside in no time.

Next up was Vernazza's tech team, the guys who would string the mikes inside the club. Joe Cantamesa was the team leader.

Kallstrom heard from him just before he went inside.

"I fucking hate dogs, especially big ones."

"Let's *go*, dammit!" Kallstrom hated waiting around.

"Moving, boss. We're moving."

Inside the club, Cantamesa and his team found the two rott-weilers—comatose. Before they had passed out, however, the dogs had relieved themselves with the force of what appeared to be several fire hoses. The club was a mess.

It took Cantamesa an hour to guide his team in and out of the club without disturbing the swamp of fecal material.

The microphones, however, were finally in.

The next day, we picked Donnie Shacks up on the Title III at his house. "The fucking dogs shit all over the place," Donnie told Gerry Lang. "They're fucking outta here."

I don't think Donnie had any idea that we had anything to do with the shitting rottweilers, but he was so spooked by now that he paid an electronics expert that same day to sweep his home and the Maniac Club for bugs. The guy didn't find our micro-phone in the house, but he did get the one in the club.

This was too bad, but when you've got a guy as rattled as Donnie Shacks was, the only thing to do is keep playing with his head. So even though the bug was disabled, it was still our equipment, and the bean counters back at Headquarters would never hear of our leaving it behind. The electronic gear was expensive, and we'd have to retrieve it. Since his guys had to go back in, anyway, Kallstrom figured they ought to make the best of the opportunity. Kallstrom dispatched one of his ballsiest supervisors, a guy named Pat Colgan.

Pat showed up at the Maniac Club a few mornings after the Night of the Shitting Rottweilers. He was with one of his agents, a guy named Tom McShane. The two agents were dressed as workmen and carrying a ladder, and they walked right in the front door of the club. They were there to do some "patchwork," Colgan told the mope behind the bar. Never mind that nobody had ordered any patchwork; the guys in the club knew exactly who Colgan and McShane were. They let them in, though.

None of them was prepared to screw with two FBI agents, at least not in broad daylight.

Five minutes later, Colgan and McShane were on their way out, but not before Pat had a chance to mess with Donnie Shacks's mind. "Well, I'm glad they found this one," Colgan said to McShane in a voice clearly audible to the wise guys at the bar. "I was getting sick of listening to all this shit the last six months." With that, Colgan and McShane made their exit.

Within minutes of their departure, Damon Taylor's surveillance agents watched from outside the Maniac Club as Donnie Shacks's friends proceeeded to rip every phone in the place off the wall. The pay phone wound up in a Dumpster out back, and then a bunch of wise guys came running out the front door. There was a van parked across the street from the Maniac Club, and the wise guys apparently thought it was our guys, only it wasn't. Whoever was in the van, though, got a hell of a rough time. The wise guys started kicking the thing, then rocking it like they were going to turn it over. Finally, one wise guy screamed at the driver, inviting him to "get the fuck out of here."

Some people have no sense of humor.

• • •

What Pat Colgan had done on his way out of the Maniac Club was something we call "tickling the wire." The idea is to rattle a target. Donnie Shacks and his guys knew Colgan and McShane were FBI agents. What they didn't know, though, was that we had more than one Title III listening in on their conversations. So Colgan's smart-ass remark was intended to provoke Donnie and his pals, to get them talking. With any luck, some of the talking would be done either on phones that we had tapped or in places where Kallstrom had his little mikes.

This is exactly what happened.

Indeed, from the talk we picked up in Donnie Shacks's house, we learned that Donnie and Gerry Lang were into some kind of business with Anthony "Fat Tony" Salerno, the boss of the Genovese Cosa Nostra family. After Paul Castellano, Fat Tony was the most powerful mob boss in America.

That Gerry Lang and Donnie Shacks were somehow tied up with Fat Tony was damned interesting, but we didn't know quite what to make of it just yet. What we did pick up, though, was a lead that would elevate our investigation of the Colombos to a whole new level. From the tap on Donnie Shacks's phone, we heard Donnie and Gerry Lang discuss the subject of payoffs that were to be made at a meeting that same day. Damon Taylor's guys were on the case, and they followed Donnie and Gerry Lang out to Brooklyn to a place called the Casa Storta Restaurant, a hole-in-the-wall joint on Twenty-first Avenue.

We knew from nothing about the Casa Storta, but we were about to learn plenty. Since we had no basis to go ask a judge for a Title III on the place, we were stuck with physical surveillance, but since a restaurant by definition is a public place, there was nothing that said we couldn't send our agents in for a few good meals, and what was the harm if they had a look around and eyeballed some of the other diners?

What we did was send couples in, male and female agents posing as starry-eyed lovers out for a romantic Italian dinner. Never mind that the Casa Storta wasn't exactly everyone's idea of a hot date, what was important was the wise guys in the place. Donnie Shacks and Gerry Lang were regulars. So was

"Fat Angelo" Ruggiero, a heavy player in the Gambino family, and Anthony Scarpatti and Ralph Scopo, soldiers in the Colombo family.

Scopo was especially interesting. In addition to being a Colombo family soldier, he was a heavyweight in one of New York's powerful construction-union locals. Our agents in the Casa Storta spotted him spending a lot of time with Gerry Lang, huddled in conversation. How, we wondered, does a mere soldier wind up breaking bread with a Casa Nostra underboss?

Another interesting thing our agents noticed was this: Most of the wise guys tended to show up at the Casa Storta about eight at night, when they would gravitate to a table in the back near the kitchen. This was table 1, of course. By nine o'clock, but certainly no later than nine-thirty, the Casa Storta's owner, a fat guy in a shiny suit, would start clapping his hands, a signal for his patrons to finish up and get the hell out. I'm pretty sure they don't teach this technique at the Culinary Institute of America, or wherever the hell it is they teach restaurant management. But that's what the Casa Storta's owner did, and since our people were curious about the ritual, they began trying to push the envelope, as it were. Some of the agent-couples would wait to order dessert until nine or later. A nervous-looking waiter would then confer with the Casa Storta's *padrone* sitting back there at table 1 with his buddies.

Our couples got the dessert a few times, but when they asked for coffee, they were shot down immediately—the nine-thirty rule was ironclad, it seemed. As they were being hustled from the restaurant at nine-twenty-nine, our agents noticed one more interesting thing: The waiters of the Casa Storta had just begun delivering huge steaming platters of food to the men dining at table 1.

24

ON October 14, 1982, a very peculiar thing happened.

President Ronald Reagan stood up in the Great Hall of the Department of Justice, one of the grandest and most humbling rooms in America, and began to talk about crime.

Specifically, he talked about organized crime.

Say what you want about the Gipper, but the guy could cast a spell. He did that day; I know that.

I had helped develop the plan Reagan was unveiling in the Great Hall, so naturally I watched the speech. The Justice Department was right across Pennylvania Avenue from my office in the J. Edgar Hoover Building. I could see the place from my window on the third floor, but I didn't go. With everything we had going on the Colombo family, I wanted to stay close to the phone. So I watched the president on CNN.

Behind Reagan, Atty. Gen. William French Smith, and the other top officials whose faces would grace the front pages of the newspapers the next day, I spotted Rudy Giuliani. He had risen a hell of a long way since his days as a junior prosecutor trying our crummy FBI gambling cases back in New York. Two years earlier, Rudy had been named associate attorney general, one of the top jobs in the Justice Department. Since we were friends and since our offices were so close, Rudy and I spent a lot of time together in Washington. When I got down to Headquarters, in fact, one of the first things I did was look up Rudy and give him a fill about our strategy for RICO, long-term Title IIIs, and the rest of it. Rudy had been a valued ally, carrying the message to the innermost councils of the Justice Department, and that's why, for both of us, Reagan's speech that day was a watershed event.

"Today," Reagan said, his voice echoing in the Great Hall, "the power of organized crime reaches into every segment of our society. It is estimated that the [organized crime] syndicate has millions of dollars in assets in legitimate businesses; it controls corrupt union locals; it runs burglary rings, fences for stolen goods, holds a virtual monopoly on the heroin trade; it thrives on illegal gambling, pornography, gunrunning, car theft, arson, and a host of other illegal activities."

"Amen," I said to the TV.

The president then ticked off the depressing crime statistics I knew by heart. Between 1977 and 1980, illegal drug sales had jumped roughly 50 percent, to some $79 billion a year; the numbers were climbing still. Sean McWeeney and I had looked at the numbers as we were drafting the president's plan. Drugs were the big thing; Reagan wanted us to focus on them. Ten months earlier, he had ordered the FBI to take a lead role with the U.S. Drug Enforcement Administration (DEA) in the war on drugs, reversing a Bureau policy that had been in effect since the Hoover days; fearing corruption of his agents, Hoover had always resisted pressure to have the FBI work drug cases.

By the early 1980s, however, drugs had become such a pervasive evil in America that there was no way the country's leading law enforcement agency could stay out of the war against the traffickers. Reagan's rationale made sense on that basis alone. But his decision to bring the FBI into the drug war was actually born of a different calculus.

Since its creation in 1973, the DEA had been the lead federal agency working illegal drugs. State and local police worked drug cases, too, obviously, but at the federal level it was mainly a DEA show.

And the DEA had its problems. For one thing, in its early years, it was primarily what we called a "buy-bust" organization. What that means, basically, is that DEA agents would go out on the streets and take some of Uncle Sam's money and try to buy illegal drugs with it. Once they succeeded, the DEA guys would then arrest the sellers and haul them off to jail, where they would soon be released on bond. If this sounds an awful lot like the way the FBI pursued gambling cases, it should.

The irony of the Reagan speech that morning, as I watched it on the little TV in my office, is that someone in the very building where I was sitting, someone very high up indeed, had sold the president and the attorney general a very clever bill of goods. The argument went something like this: Only the FBI could conduct the kind of strategic investigations that would cripple the international criminal organizations behind the drug trade. There was still a role for DEA—out there on the streets, busting the dope sellers. But if the president wanted an agency to go after the big international traffickers, one that would strategically target the organized criminal enterprises engaged in the illegal narcotics trade, there was only one answer, and that was to call in the FBI.

Reagan had agreed, in principle. And with his speech in the Justice Department's Great Hall, the Gipper had put his money where his mouth was. The administration, the president said, would give FBI director William Webster millions of dollars in new funding to hire and train nine hundred new FBI agents. The new agents would be deployed on twelve FBI-DEA task forces around the country to fight the criminal organizations that were poisoning the nation's kids. "The time has come," Reagan concluded, his voice stern, "to cripple the power of the mob in America."

"Amen," I said again, and then laughed out loud.

The only strategic program the FBI had on the criminal side of the house—the spy chasers are another story, and they don't apply here—was in the Organized Crime Section. And the only reason the Bureau had even that infant program was because a few of us, a very few, had taken on the old Hoover bureaucracy a decade earlier and forced it to change. Had it not been for a few visionary people—people like Joe Pistone, Louie Freeh, Tom Emory, Jim Kallstrom, Jim Kossler, Sean McWeeney, and Neil Welch—there would have been no way on God's green earth that Judge Webster could have sold the Bureau as the heavy strategic firepower for Reagan to deploy in the drug war.

Irony is a seductive thing. It would have been easy for all of us to stride the corridors of Headquarters, smirking like heroes. It would have been easier still to bask in the praises that Judge Webster and the brass were suddenly lavishing on the organized-crime program. But the truth of the matter was, there was no time for that. With the conviction of the Bonannos and the long jail sentences we had won against them, the Bureau had finally scored that one big win Kossler and I had been talking about, and the brass had basked in the glowing news-media accounts of the investigation. With the Colombo case, we looked like we were on our way to another big win, and things were shaping up nicely in still another investigation, of the Gambino family's unsavory criminal doings in New York.

"Success breeds success," I had told Sean.

We had had our first big success already with the Bonannos. But with President Reagan's speech in the Great Hall that day, we had scored a success that nobody could take away from us. For a bureaucracy like the FBI, it should come as no surprise, there is no bigger success than when one of its programs wins accolades—and dollars—from the chief executive. With the Reagan announcement that morning, that is just what happened to the FBI. Against its will, the Bureau had developed an effective program for fighting crime strategically.

Now there was no turning back.

Dogs seemed to be becoming a theme for us.

A few weeks before Christmas, in December 1982, Bruce Baird, our attorney on the Colombo investigation, presented an application for an installation of a concealed microphone at the Casa Storta Restaurant in Brooklyn. The judge reviewed the paperwork carefully and signed the order. Jimmy Kallstrom knew right where the mike would go—right over table 1.

If only we could get past Nina.

"We don't know if she's part bear, part werewolf, or what, but she's definitely trouble." Kallstrom had been keeping me abreast of the Nina problem on the phone from New York, and I had the feeling he was getting obsessed by it."

"It's just a fucking dog, Jim."

"Easy for you to say, sitting in Washington."

"So try Vernazza's meatballs. I bet Nina *loves* meatballs."

"No way." Kallstrom laughed. "None of the guys wants to deal with the meatballs and the fucking dog shit again."

"So what're you going to do?"

"I don't know, I don't know. We sent Art Guy up to the Bronx Zoo today."

"What're you, kidding?"

"Listen, we're desperate here. Art's supposed to meet with their top guy on animal anesthesiology."

"I don't fucking believe it."

"I told you, Jules. We're desperate."

"So Art's supposed to knock Nina out with, what, a hypodermic, some headache pills?"

"Something like that. I don't know. When he gets back, he'll let us know. Then we'll see what happens."

"Jesus Christ."

"You got a better idea, you got my number, okay?"

"Yeah, right."

Art Guy took his assignment very seriously. Art went up to the Bronx and came back with a tool kit complete with a blowgun, darts, and something that looked very much like a boat hook with a very big needle on the end—the hypodermic. Art was partial to the blowgun, Kallstrom told me; whether for aesthetic reasons or not, Jimmy didn't know. I was in New York about a week after Art got back from the zoo, and I got a look firsthand. Out in the bullpen area on the twenty-fourth floor of 26 Federal, there was Art, practicing with the darts and the blowgun.

"Just be sure you don't kill anyone out here, huh, Art?"

"Sure, Jim, no problem." Art nodded at Kallstrom and me, then went back to reload.

The night of the installation at the Casa Storta fell just before Christmas and was one of the coldest days of the year. The deal was the same basic setup we had used at the Maniac Club, the three teams of agents: the team for the locks, Kallstrom's Special Ops squad, and the guys from Damon Taylor's squad who would handle the surveillance.

Lou Vernazza had rigged the undercover van for the lock guys with a propane heater so that they could keep warm while they worked the locks. The entry team had to get through a metal roll-up gate that covered the front of the Casa Storta; the gate was secured by two heavy-gauge steel padlocks. Behind the gate was a thick glass door with still more locks.

Behind that, of course, was Nina.

Despite what you may have seen in the movies, cops who engage in these kinds of surreptitious entries don't actually "pick" the locks; honest cops don't, anyway. Our guys actually work on a lock with a blank key, identifying every bump and groove in the lock's chamber until they "create" a key of their own that will turn the lock. This, as you might imagine, is not a quick or easy procedure. And it is complicated by the fact that the guys working the locks always have to make several trips back and forth between the door they're trying to get through and the fancy key-making equipment they keep rigged out in the back of their undercover van. Since security is so important on these kinds of operations, the lock guys have to coordinate with the surveillance teams every time they need to scurry back and forth between the target and the van.

Black-bag jobs, then, are not only not for the faint of heart; they are not for anyone who isn't unusually well endowed in the patience department. I, for instance, would not have made a very good black-bag agent.

On the night we moved on the Casa Storta, the lock guys got started at about two in the morning.

By 3:30 A.M., they were still at it, and the propane tank Lou Vernazza had so thoughtfully installed for them in the van had long since run dry. Since we obviously didn't want to keep the engine running and attract attention to ourselves, the inside of the van soon became about as comfortable as a meat locker. The agents working the metal keys with their ungloved fingers just kept on going, though, blowing on their hands every few seconds and grooving the new keys until they got them right.

Just before four o'clock, they were ready.

"About fucking time," Kallstrom said. As usual, Jimmy had gone along on the installation. He was parked just up the street from the Casa Storta, blowing on his hands behind the wheel of a Bureau-owned Ford Crown Victoria.

From their cars and vans around the Casa Storta, Damon Taylor's agents radioed the all clear: No wise guys in sight.

Kallstrom radioed the entry team next: "Let's go!"

Special Agent Mike Utaro was one of the lead agents on the entry team, and as he moved toward the restaurant, he suddenly fell to the street, writhing.

"Agent down," someone radioed.

Lou Vernazza and another agent ran to Utaro's side.

Utaro was grabbing frantically at his legs.

"What the fuck, Mike? What the fuck . . ."

"My feet, Lou. My feet, goddammit."

Utaro pulled and tugged at his heavy work boots. Vernazza helped him yank them off, and as Louie watched, Mike ripped his socks off, too. Now he was barefoot.

"Excuse me," Lou Vernazza said. "But are you fucking crazy or what, Mike?"

Utaro ignored him. Sitting in the middle of the empty street, Utaro examined his wool socks. The socks had brown burn marks on them, like someone had tossed them on a hot grill. Mike turned the socks upside down, and two batteries fell out. "The fuckers. They must've shorted out."

"Yeah," Lou Vernazza said. "I see."

Kallstrom's voice rattled over the radio. "Gentlemen, can we move it with this fucking three-ring circus, or are we gonna stay out here until we freeze to death?"

"Let's go, Mike." Vernazza gave Utaro a hand up off the asphalt, and somewhere they rustled him up some new socks.

The entry team, meanwhile, was through the two big padlocks

and the metal gate and was starting to work on the double locks on the restaurant's plate-glass door.

On the other side of the door, Nina was going nuts.

"You ready, Art?" Lou Vernazza hadn't been too keen on trying his meatballs again, but he did have some definite doubts about the blowgun and the Bronx Zoo game plan.

"I'm ready, Lou. No problem."

"Yeah, well, good luck."

"Thanks, just give me some room here, okay?"

For all his practice with the blowgun and the darts back at 26 Federal, Art Guy had decided, unbeknownst to any of Vernazza's squad, that he wouldn't tranquilize Nina if he didn't have to. Art was a gentle soul, good with kids and animals, and he figured if he could talk to Nina quietly and settle her down, he could get Mike Utaro and the rest of the installation team past her without too much of a fuss.

With Utaro, Vernazza, and the rest of the squad behind him, Art Guy opened the front door of the Casa Storta a crack.

Nina lunged for him, jaws slashing.

"Good dog. *Gooood* Nina."

"Good dog, my ass."

"Quiet, Lou. Please." Art tried the restaurant door again. "Okay, Nina, *ooookaay*."

Nina lunged again.

This time she got Art by the foot.

"Shit!"

Behind him, Utaro and Vernazza grabbed Art Guy by the shoulders. A second later, he kicked himself free.

Utaro slammed the door to the Casa Storta.

"Goddamned dog!"

"What're you fucking around for, Art?"

"Shit, I was trying to be nice."

"Well, no more nice, okay? We're dying out here, okay?"

"Okay, just give me a minute."

Less than sixty seconds later, Art was back with the boat-hook thing with the big syringe on the end.

"You gonna jab her, then, huh?"

"Fucking-A right."

"Okay, then—go, man."

Utaro held the front door for Art while he jabbed through the opening between the door edge and the jamb.

"Shit, goddammit."

"The dog's no dummy."

Art Guy swore again. Each time he jabbed with the boat-hook thing, Nina jumped backward, just out of range.

"You get her?"

"No, damn it."

"What're you gonna do?" Utaro had shut the restaurant door again, and he was stamping his feet and blowing on his hands.

"Give me a minute. I'll be right back."

This time Art Guy returned with a tire iron.

"What're you gonna do with *that?*"

Art Guy tapped the tire iron against the plate glass of the Casa Storta's front door and nodded toward Nina. "What I'm going to do," Art said, "is kill that fucking dog."

"Oh, *man!*"

"You got a better idea?"

"Wait a minute, wait a minute."

"No, fuck it, let's do it."

"Wait, I said!"

This time, Utaro ran back to the undercover van, and when he came back, he was carrying a small red fire extinguisher.

"What the fuck is *that* for?"

"Watch out, okay?"

Art Guy stepped back alongside Vernazza and the rest of the squad, and Mike Utaro opened the door of the Casa Storta a crack. Nina lunged for him, but Mike's timing was perfect: He caught the beast full in the mouth was a blast of CO_2 foam.

"Bingo!" Vernazza yelled.

"Give it a second, Lou." Utaro gripped the fire extinguisher tighter. Then he opened the glass door wider.

On the other side, Nina growled, but there was a whimper mixed in there with it, too.

Mike stepped halfway inside the door.

Nina took a step closer, and Mike hosed her again with the CO_2 foam. Nina howled as if burned.

"Son of a bitch, you got her!"

Mike looked behind him at Art Guy and Lou Vernazza. Then he kicked the door open, and the squad queued up. "Let's go!"

Nina by now had retreated to the Casa Storta's coatroom, and Mike laid some CO_2 covering fire down into the doorway.

"I'll watch the dog. Stick the fucking mike in there, and let's get this nightmare over with."

Vernazza and his team were in and out of the Casa Storta in under thirty minutes. Finally, we were inside.

PART TWO

PART TWO

25

THE last thing I want to do is leave anyone with the impression that we were working these cases one at a time, family by family; that's the way I have tried to explain them, but the reality is, we were doing everything at once.

Or trying to, anyway.

With the ten organized-crime squads we had in the New York office, we had approximately 270 special agents of the FBI and another 100 New York City police officers and detectives targeting all five of the Italian Mafia families in the city. The FBI-NYPD task force was a model of cooperation, and besides the five families, it worked a bunch of other organized criminal activity related and unrelated to the Italian Mafia. It was a colossal effort, and I tried to remind myself every day what an honor it was to be running such an operation.

Of course, it was also damned complicated and involved juggling a thousand balls at once. We had active investigations open on all of the five Cosa Nostra families in New York, and within families we had multiple investigations going. Sometimes—many times, in fact—leads we developed on one family led to another, but the overrriding strategy remained the same in every case: We were not going to bust wise guys just to bust them; we were going to go after the families strategically and take them out just as if they were a crooked bank or corporation.

The approach required time and patience, but the picture we were developing of the Italian Mafia's stranglehold on New York was more detailed than any that had ever been drawn before. Just as we had shifted gears in the Bonanno case, aiming the Vinnie DePenta undercover operation at the Colombos after the murder of the three Bonanno family capos, we had informant information coming in almost constantly on one family that led us to see ties among the others. The families maintained discrete business operations, and they were plenty conscious of their turf. But there was a lot of spillover, too. We were beginning to see that with the cement business, for example. What we were learning about the commission also indicated that the families had more going on with each other than we knew—a lot more.

The cases we opened in the early 1980s matured at different speeds, and there were reasons for that. In the Bonanno investigation, for instance, the murder of the three capos and the undercover work of Joe Pistone gave us the biggest head start of any case. The other families were tougher to crack.

They took longer.

Everything took long, it seemed. The hangover from the years of mismanaging the organized-crime problem by earlier FBI brass meant that most of our agents working the problem in New York were starting from ground zero. Back in 1979, for example, we had formed an O.C. squad we called BQ-5. The squad's offices were located in the FBI's Brooklyn-Queens office out on Queens Boulevard in Rego Park. Bruce Mouw had been promoted as supervisor of BQ-5, and his job description was as simple as it was daunting: identify, target, and neutralize all of the criminal activity conducted by the Gambino family. The Gambino family was not just the largest Mafia family in New York; it was the largest in the country.

So Bruce didn't exactly have what you would call a nine-to-five job. A 1965 graduate of the U.S. Naval Academy at Annapolis, a decorated submariner who had come a long way from his boyhood home back in landlocked Iowa, Bruce was tall, patient, and soft-spoken. It is a term that has fallen out of fashion, I know, but in Bruce's case it happens to be true: Through and through, the man was a gentleman. No matter what kind of scum he was forced to deal with because of his work on the Gambinos, Bruce was unfailingly polite and solicitous. Guys like myself swore all the time at the office; Bruce never once did. In fact, I don't think I ever even heard him raise his voice. The placid exterior fooled some guys but not me. Behind the shy smile was a cop who was a stickler for detail, a hardball detective who didn't miss a trick. A pipe smoker like Jim Kossler, Bruce was a man constitutionally inclined to the long view of things, an investigator whose fundamental nature gave him an intuitive appreciation of the strategic approach to a case.

One day, I was visiting Bruce out in his cramped corner office on Queens Boulevard, trying to get a better fix on what we had going and how much more we had to do on the Gambinos.

"What've you got, Bruce? Give me a fill."

"Well, Jules." Bruce had a deadpan delivery, and when he wanted to, he could use it very effectively to put me in my place. "We've got Paul Castellano; he's the boss—as you know." Bruce tugged on an ear and looked at me significantly.

I returned the look, saying nothing.

"Then we've got Neil Dellacroce, Jules. He's the underboss."

I smiled then. "That's great, Bruce. What else?"

"Then, Jules, we've got Joe N."

"The *consigliere*," I said helpfully. Joe N. Gallo was one of the Cosa Nostra's true untouchables, though he was no relation to Crazy Joey Gallo, the notorious wise guy who had died many years before, his life bleeding away on the floor of Umberto's Clam House down in Little Italy.

"That's right, Jules. Joe N is the *consigliere*."

"Shit, Bruce." I shook my head. "What else you got?"

Bruce gave me one of his best big Iowa farmboy grins and said, "That's it, chief. That's what we got."

"Listen." I got up and tried to see if there was any air in the little office uncontaminated by Bruce's damned pipe smoke. "If that's all you got, you got a hell of a lot of work to do."

"That's right, Jules." Bruce dispatched a puffy blue smoke ring past me on its way to the ceiling and studied it as if it were a work of art. "We've got an awful lot of work to do."

A lot of the work was records work.

Going back through what the FBI called its "92" Files, investigative case files where agents simply dumped information on criminal suspects and organizations, a lot of what Bruce and his BQ-5 agents turned up was junk. Oh, there was some stuff on who attended which mob wedding or funeral, which wise guy was sleeping with which mob bimbo, that kind of thing. But even that—in fact, most of what was in the FBI's 92 Files—was no more than unconfirmed, arrant gossip. What a waste. Bruce Mouw and his BQ-5 squad would have to start totally from scratch.

It was slow going, but by the time we were beginning to make progress on our case against the Colombo family, Bruce Mouw and his agents were finally getting ready to tee off on the Gambinos. BQ-5 had opened an investigation of the Gambino family crew that operated out of something called the Bergen Fish and Hunt Club, in a Queens neighborhood called Ozone Park. What these Gambino family wise guys knew about fishing and hunting you could put in a tackle box, a small one at that; what they did know was sitting around on their fat asses, drinking and bullshitting—around which activities they fit in an impressive schedule of extortion, loan-sharking, and strong-arm robberies. The Bergen Fish and Hunt crew included John Gotti, Jr., and his brother Gene as well as our John's lifelong buddy, Angelo Ruggiero, the same guy who spent so many evenings commiserating with Gerry Lang Langella at table 1 at the Casa Storta.

Some sportsmen.

At the same time we were working the Gotti brothers—and this is an example of how we really had to keep multiple investigations going not just of different families but of different members of the same family—Bruce Mouw's agents were opening up investigations of a number of Gambino family capos. These were guys like Joe N. Gallo, Jimmy Failla, and Frank D'Appolito. Bruce even assigned one of his agents, Joe O'Brien, to open up a case on the boss of bosses himself, so we had a fat file, too, on

Paul Castellano. They may have been starting from scratch, but our guys weren't afraid to think big.

They inspired the hell out of me.

One of the things we tried to teach agents and supervisors alike was how to pick investigative targets. Under the old Hoover system, this was a simple business: An agent would get wind of someone involved in a criminal activity and then either conduct surveillance or develop evidence from informants or cooperating witnesses and then make the arrest. Easy, right?

Except that strategically this made no sense. By simply making an arrest as soon as he or she had sufficient evidence, the FBI agent had no opportunity to understand how the criminal fit into the larger scheme of things. Who were his colleagues? His bosses? Was the criminal part of a bigger operation?

With all our squads, Jim Kossler and I worked hard trying to develop this kind of thinking. With guys like Bruce Mouw, as I say, it came naturally. But even then the decisions weren't always easy ones. Sometimes we'd get lucky, of course. Vinnie DePenta's coming to us for help—that was luck. But with an organization as big and as complex as the Gambino crime family, luck would carry us only so far. What this meant was that we had to look long and hard at all the players in the family and decide which one was most likely to give us the most complete picture of the family's criminal operations.

There are several factors that go into making an evaluation like this. Obviously, we're talking about installing Title IIIs, so the first thing you look for in a strategic target is a family member who's in a position to know about the full range of criminal activities the Gambinos are into. Guys like Neil Dellacroce and Joe N. Gallo certainly fit the bill, but they were also very careful about who they talked to and what they talked about; they were not easy targets. Go too far down the chain of command in the family, on the other hand, and you run the risk of recording a whole lot of conversations that are based on third-hand gossip and bullshit. That becomes a waste of time and worse, with agents chasing their asses on leads that go nowhere.

Another thing, as I mentioned, is getting a guy who likes to talk. Since we're basically going to be developing evidence by recording conversations, you want a guy, ideally, who likes to flap his gums. You find that guy, then satisfy yourself that he genuinely knows what's going on with the family's business activities, and you've probably got your best target.

Bruce Mouw and his agents reviewed the bidding on all the Gambino family members they had under the microscope. In just a few years, they had come a long way from the dusty 92 Files. Thanks to aggressive physical surveillance, good informant-development work, and the kind of nuts-and-bolts police discipline that doesn't make the network news but does make for solid investigations, Mouw's BQ-5 agents had substantial files now on more than two dozen Gambino family members. They knew who these creeps met with, where they took their meals, and what kinds of businesses they were into. They even had some rudimentary but useful psychological profiles on some of these guys.

Taking all of this together, Mouw and his agents made a few basic decisions. Clearly, the best information we were getting on the Gambino family was on the Bergen Fish and Hunt crew. Unlike the higher-ups, guys like Neil Dellacroce and Joe N. Gallo, the guys in the Bergen Fish and Hunt crew were on the street nearly every day. That meant we could watch them, see where they went, who they met with. We had better informant information on the Bergen Fish and Hunt crew than on any other Gambino family crew.

These guys we had a definite line on.

Gotti himself didn't strike either me, Bruce, or Jimmy Kossler as an ideal target, mainly because of his lifestyle. Even way back then, the man who would eventually become known as the "Teflon Don" was a gambler, a drinker, and a womanizer. These pursuits didn't rule Gotti out on ethical grounds, only practical ones. His busy social life didn't leave the guy a hell of a lot of time to tend to business and talk on the phone.

We needed another member of the crew.

The guy who basically ran the Bergen Fish and Hunt crew for Gotti was Angelo Ruggiero. He and John had been friends since grade school; they had fought alongside each other as members of the same New York street gang, the Fulton-Rockaway Boys.

Unlike a lot of the wise guys with whom he hung around, Angelo Ruggiero was not content with merely scraping out a living. Though he was closer to Gene Gotti, Ruggiero saw in John the potential to become a major player in the Gambino family. The way Ruggiero saw it, one day John might be the boss of the Gambinos; he, the underboss. In John Gotti, Angelo Ruggiero saw someone who would open up new opportunities to make money.

That was the key.

So Ruggiero did for Gotti what Gotti needed doing. It was Angelo who called Gotti at eleven o'clock sharp each morning to rouse him after another boozy night on the town. It was Angelo who made sure that meetings occurred on time, that collections of gambling and loan-shark debts were prompt, that anything Neil Dellacroce wanted he got and got quickly. Like the Gotti brothers, Angelo Ruggiero didn't like Paul Castellano. Like the Gottis, Ruggiero pledged his allegiance to Dellacroce, the Gambino family underboss. Ruggiero, in fact, was Mr. Neil's nephew.

That would explain a lot.

The harder Mouw and his squad looked at Ruggiero, the better he looked as a target. Because of Gotti's extracurricular exertions in the seedier bars and bedrooms of Brooklyn and Queens, more and more of the work of running the Bergen Fish and Hunt crew fell to Ruggiero, to the point where it looked like he was handling virtually all of the crew's business.

Bruce subpoenaed Ruggiero's telephone record and was amazed to find phone calls not just to John Gotti, which he expected, but to Neil Dellacroce, Joe N. Gallo, and other Gambino family capos. Clearly, while Gotti drank and gambled and whored around, Angelo Ruggiero was taking care of business. Amazingly, Bruce found that Ruggiero was also telephoning members of other Cosa Nostra families, acting, as far as we could tell, as the Gambino family's outside liaison to the rest of the mob. Since we already knew how much he liked to talk, these other connections put Angelo Ruggiero over the top once and for all as our strategic target in the Gambinos.

Bruce wasted no time going after him.

We had gotten permission to install our first Title III in Angelo Ruggiero's house back in 1981. Angelo had moved after that, and we put another recording device in the kitchen of his new house out on Long Island, in a town called Cedarhurst.

Monitoring Title IIIs is one of the most tedious and thankless tasks in all of law enforcement, but in Angelo Ruggiero's case, there probably wasn't a day that went by where he didn't surprise or entertain us with something. For starters, we could always count on the 11:00 A.M. wakeup call to Gotti. Lunchtime was approaching for the rest of his neighbors but not for the chief of the Bergen Fish and Hunt crew. Angelo would call, and Gotti would send his alcohol-fogged voice rumbling back down over the phone line to Cedarhurst: "Helloooo!"

"John, how you doin'?"

"Okay, Ange, okay."

"It's eleven, okay, John?"

"Yeah, Ange, okay, okay."

If it had been a particularly rough night, Ruggiero could usually tell, and he would call Gotti back a few minutes later just to make sure the future don was up and stirring and heading in the general direction of a cup of coffee and a brisk shower. Besides Ruggiero's obsessive gossip about who was up and who was down in the family, there were some rare treats. Though he didn't like the boss of bosses, Ruggiero found an excuse just about every other Sunday to trot out to Paul Castellano's mansion in Staten Island. After his visits to the Castellano White House, Angelo would usually drive straight home to Cedarhurst and spend the next few hours on the phone, relating to his wiseguy pals everything Big Paul and he had talked about. For us, this was not just intriguing but important—for reasons I'll explain in just a minute.

In May 1982, Ruggiero was informed that his brother Sal had been killed in an airplane crash. At the Bureau, we knew Sal Ruggiero for exactly what he was—no good. Sal sold heroin, he was a fugitive from justice, and he was a tax cheat; other than that he was a hell of a nice guy.

What we didn't know was that for all the time we had been listening in on Angelo Ruggiero's telephone calls, he had been bankrolling Brother Sal in the heroin business. With Sal gone, Angelo assumed control of the business.

It was big business, too. In the space of just six months, Ruggiero, Gene Gotti, and another member of the Bergen Fish and Hunt crew, a killer named John Carneglia, collected somewhere between $1.4 million and $2.6 million in drug profits.

For wise guys, now, this *was* a lot of money. It made a $50,000 extortion payment look like spit on a sidewalk. It also made a wise guy like Angelo Ruggiero feel like he was superman. "Who's gonna bother me?" Ruggiero crowed to Eddie Lino, another great American from the Bergen Fish and Hunt crew. "If I go on an appointment, I go with four or five guys. They wanna whack [me], they gotta whack four or five of us."

Ruggiero laughed hysterically.

But this was no laughing matter. Paul Castellano had issued an edict against drug trafficking, and violations were punishable by death. "You deal in drugs, you die," the boss of bosses had said. I knew the Castellano edict was a crock of shit, at least as it applied to himself. Remember when Sonny Black Napolitano went out to Castellano's house before the murder of the three Bonanno capos? In exchange for Big Paul supporting him in the Bonanno family feud, Sonny Black had promised the boss of bosses a generous cut of the family's heroin business; Castellano had agreed. That had not stopped Paul, however, from applying the edict to the wise guys who worked for him. This was the sentence that had been imposed, in fact, on a Gambino family associate named Little Pete Tambone.

Little Pete was a good friend of Angelo Ruggiero's. The two had grown up together, and their wives were best friends. When a wise guy named Frankie the Wop told Paul Castellano that Tambone was in the heroin business, Ruggiero was devastated.

Castellano made it clear immediately that Tambone would have to be dealt with, and Ruggiero—who was up to his own eyeballs in heroin with Gene Gotti and some of the other guys from the Bergen Fish and Hunt crew—started working like hell to get the death sentence on Tambone lifted. Ruggiero talked to Neil Dellacroce, the Gambino family underboss. Mr. Neil got the Tambone issue brought before a meeting of the Mafia Commission.

From the tap on the phone in Ruggiero's kitchen, we got a virtual blow-by-blow of the proceedings.

"Hey, shithead." Gene Gotti didn't have what you'd call a gracious telephone manner, though he did spend a lot of time on the phone in Ruggiero's kitchen.

"Hiya, buddy."

"Hey, all this fucking trouble you're putting us through?"

Tambone sighed. "Ah, what could I do?"

Ruggiero interrupted on an extension. "I told Neil how you got fucking trouble."

"Yeah?"

"Paul can say no," Ruggiero said, referring to a cancellation of the murder contract, "and Neil will know."

"You tell John what happened?"

Yeah, Ruggiero says he told the elder Gotti. "Johnny says, 'Are you kidding me or what?' I says, 'I'm telling you the fucking truth.' He says, 'This motherfucker [Frankie the Wop]!' Then he starts screaming. I told Gene, God forbid if something happens over here: We'll *all* be right in the fucking soup. . . . You know what I'm saying, Pete?"

Tambone said he understood.

"If they tell us [there is nothing they can do], I'm telling you, Pete, take off! You know, they're supposed to give us an answer by Wednesday or Thursday. What's going through these people's minds? This is what I'm thinking—that maybe they're thinking that you and me were partners."

"Right."

"But what's happening now, you hit it at the wrong time. Now they're looking to set examples. Ah, *Madonna!* This guy's watching here. This guy's watching there."

Two days later, Ruggiero got word of the commission vote: The families had split two-two. With the Bonannos out of business, thanks to Pistone, Barbara Jones, and Louie Freeh, they didn't have a vote, so Tambone got spared, in effect, by a hung jury.

In addition to the phone tap at Ruggiero's place in Cedarhurst, Kallstrom's Special Ops guys had placed a tiny microphone in his kitchen, and the recorder-transmitter gave us a nice run-down of the Tambone victory celebration.

"Everything is okay; it's over."

"I'm glad, Angelo. Thanks." Ruggiero's daughter offered Tambone a glass of soda, and Little Pete thanked her.

"So that's it. Forget about it. They had a commission meeting this week. Twice already."

"Everybody's in it?"

"Well, there was a vote, two-two."

Tambone took a sip of soda.

"Pete, listen to me, I wanna tell ya. You don't have to watch out no more. You can go out. Nobody's gonna bother ya. The only thing is, Pete . . ."

"I'll go no further."

Ruggiero nodded to his friend and folded his hands in front of him like a judge. "Nothing," he said.

Pete Tambone nodded back.

His days as a heroin dealer were over.

26

"COME on in, guys. Sit down."

Kravec and Cantamesa sat as instructed.

"What do you have, boss?" Cantamesa was more equably disposed toward new challenges than his partner, Kravec, which is to say that Joe didn't look upon every new assignment as a shining opportunity exactly, but he didn't look at it as a high-speed express ride straight to hell, either.

Kallstrom removed his feet from his scarred desktop and leaned toward his two supervisors. "What we got"—he looked from Kravec to Cantamesa and back again—"is the fucking seventh game of the World Series, and you guys are on deck."

"What inning is it?" Kravec shifted uneasily in his seat.

"Not the first. But not the ninth, either."

"Shit." Kravec looked like he was going to be ill.

"Start over, boss, will ya?"

"Sure, Joe." Kallstrom replanted his feet on his desk. "What we got is the opportunity of a lifetime here."

"Ah, Jesus." Kravec knotted his fingers around his belly.

"By which I mean we're just about to get our court approval for a Title III at Paul Castellano's place."

"Shit, that's great, boss," Cantamesa said.

"Yeah, you want us to wire the Vatican first, though?"

"Just wait a minute, okay?"

"No, maybe we'll hit the Kremlin. *Then* the Vatican."

"Will you shut up, Joe?"

"Yeah, after that, we'll knock over Windsor Castle."

"Okay, just listen, all right?"

"Sure, boss, we're listening."

"Yeah, we're all ears."

"Okay." Slowly, Kallstrom explained how Bruce Mouw and Joe O'Brien had reviewed the take from the Title IIIs on Angelo Ruggiero's place. Like me and Kossler, Joe and Bruce were both convinced that the Ruggiero stuff was dynamite, and not just because of all the talk about the drug business and the commission meetings. Nearly every Sunday, by our count, Ruggiero paid a visit to Paul Castellano's mansion on Todt Hill. Ruggiero didn't like Castellano, as I mentioned. But Paulie was the boss of bosses, and Angelo wanted to make sure he stayed in his good graces. After his Sunday visits, anyway, Ruggiero would drive back home to Cedarhurst and phone up his wise-guy pals to tell them what was on Castellano's mind. Angelo was just playing the big shot, Kallstrom explained, but in doing so, he had given us a hell of a lot on Castellano's various illegal businesses.

"So we got the okay on Paulie?"

"We're right on the verge, John."

Kravec shook his head. "How soon do you want it in?"

"I'm not looking for miracles. Let's see what it takes. It doesn't have to be this week."

"That's good, boss." Cantamesa stretched his legs and looked down at the antlike bustle of Lower Broadway twenty-six floors below. "Because I still got Christmas gifts left to buy."

Kossler and I talked that afternoon.

"It was your basic spin-off, Jimmy. No big deal."

"Yeah, right. Except that we're spinning right off into Paulie Castellano's goddamned living room. Or whatever."

"Well, we're not in yet."

"Yeah, well, once we get in, if Paulie is talking the way Angelo says he's talking, this is fucking pay dirt, I tell you."

"We got no reason to doubt Angelo."

"I know. But without the Title III at his place, there's no way we get into Paulie's. I'll tell you that for nothing."

"That's the beauty of it, Jim. The spin-off."

"Yeah, well, now all we have to do is get inside."

"Ah, don't worry about that."

"Yeah, you're right, Jules. That's Kallstrom's problem."

What Kallstrom did was talk to Bruce Mouw, for starters.

More than a year earlier, Bruce had assigned Joe O'Brien to open a case on Castellano. O'Brien was a big Irishman who went about six five, a guy who was not especially inclined to take a lot of bullshit from anyone—especially from any wise guys. Joe had essentially proceeded to conduct an in-your-face investigation of Castellano, watching the gates of his house to see who came and went and generally making a pain in the ass of himself by tailing people and asking obnoxious questions every time he spotted some wise guy coming or going.

Mouw sent copies of O'Brien's surveillance reports on the Castellano White House over to Kallstrom, and Jim studied them at length. Then he ordered his own surveillance on the Castellano White House. Kravec and Cantamesa were right to have their doubts about their chances of getting inside the mansion. Kallstrom wanted to find out just how long the odds were.

As it turned out, they were long as hell.

Just after the New Year, Kallstrom's surveillance teams came in with their reports. They had watched the Castellano mansion every day, twenty-four hours a day, for nearly two weeks, and there wasn't an hour when there wasn't someone inside the mansion. If Paulie went out on a rare piece of business, his little Gloria would be there. And if Gloria and Paulie happened to be out together, Castellano's wife would be on guard.

Kallstrom read the reports, asked his secretary to make copies of all of them for Kravec and Cantamesa, then told her to have both of them in his office first thing the next morning.

"You got everything, I hope." It was only eight-thirty, but already Kallstrom's necktie was askew, hanging a good two inches below and to the left of his unbuttoned collar.

"We got it, boss."

"Thoughts?" Kallstrom turned from Kravec to Cantamesa.

"First off"—Kravec looked at Cantamesa, then at Kallstrom—"Joe's going to be the one going in."

"Okay—Joe?"

"Yeah. That's what we decided."

"So, how do you want to work it?"

Cantamesa took the lead. "The way we figure it, boss, something's got to happen at the house where he's got a problem."

"Yeah. We can't just show up, like, pretending we're a couple of workmen." Kravec shifted his bulk in his chair.

"Okay."

"Only the problem Castellano's gonna have, it's not really a problem, if you know what I mean."

"It comes and goes, sort of." Kallstrom smiled.

"Right, boss."

"But we're the ones that make it come and go." Kravec tried again to make himself comfortable in the narrow chair.

"So maybe he's having a problem with his TV or something?"

"Yeah, something like that. He can't get the fucking Giants on the tube."

"So he calls for a repair guy."

"Right." Cantamesa smiled. "Us."

"I like it." Kallstrom dropped his feet from the desk to the floor and leaned forward again. "Okay, dope out a scenario."

It took another four months, but by the time they hammered it out, Kallstrom, Kravec, and Cantamesa had the script down cold. Because of the way we got the Title III inside Castellano's house and because the FBI continues to use the same tactic to this day, we can't give the details of the installation except to say that Joe Cantamesa and Paul Castellano had a lot of earnest conversations together and that Castellano never had the slightest reason to believe Cantamesa was anything but a well-meaning repairman out to service a customer's complaint.

In fact, Joe played the part so well that he got Castellano's driver and aide-de-camp, Tommy Bilotti, to actually ask him to do the supposed repair work that finally allowed Joe to install the bug. Bilotti was a killer, literally, a big, muscular guy whose one sign of weakness was a ridiculous toupee that could not have possibly cost him more than twenty-nine dollars. Mention the toupee to Bilotti and you were a guaranteed dead man. Castellano, in any case, had ordered Bilotti to follow Cantamesa around the White House as he surveyed the work that needed to be done for the repair job.

"See those cobwebs there, sir?"

Bilotti studied a kitchen baseboard suspiciously. "Yeah?"

"They can screw up an electrical connection like you wouldn't believe—your phone, your TV—just about anything electronic."

"No shit, is that right?"

"Yeah, it's not too well known."

"Whaddya gotta do to fix it?"

"Well, you gotta clean the cobwebs out first."

"Yeah?"

"Then you gotta look at the wiring, check it over, and see if any of it needs to be replaced."

"Yeah, I see, I see."

"So if this is the problem"—Cantamesa pulled some wires with clips on both ends from a pocket—"I can jump over the bad section here like this." Cantamesa snapped his little alligator clips around a suspicious piece of electrical cord that connected to the little television in the kitchen. "Then the problem with your interference and all, it should disappear."

Tommy Bilotti clicked on the TV and swore. "I'll be goddamned," he said. The picture was clear as day.

"See what I mean?"

"Yeah, unbelievable. Fucking cobwebs—who fucking knew?"

"So, you want me to take care of it?"

"Yeah, yeah. Do what you gotta do."

Cantamesa did what he had to do, neglecting to inform Tommy Bilotti that his partner, John Kravec, was on a telephone pole outside the Castellano mansion about a block away, monkeying with the electrical gizmos that created the problems with the television in the Castellano kitchen. Cantamesa and Kravec were hooked up by a little wireless radio set so that John could hear just about every word that passed between Cantamesa and Bilotti. Every time Cantamesa said something like "See this problem here?" or "Any better when I do that?" Kravec would monkey with his wires, and Bilotti would see whatever we wanted him to see.

The charade finally over, Cantamesa completed his work at the Castellano mansion and took his leave of Tommy Bilotti.

"Thanks a lot, guy. You take it easy, okay?"

"Yeah, you bet, mister." Cantamesa thanked Bilotti and turned to leave. "You have any problems, let me know, huh?"

"Okay, guy. Thanks again."

"What did we get, what did we get today, Jimmy?" Once we got the Title III into Castellano's kitchen, I was like a kid on Christmas morning, every day phoning Kallstrom up for the news.

"Shit, nothing, Jules." Sounding like a man who had been working on a speed bag way too long, Kallstrom explained that they had hours and hours of tapes from Castellano's house but all the tapes gave us was the all-news AM radio station.

The boss of bosses had us foxed.

"Come on, Jimmy, you're the Special Ops guy. Isn't there something we can do?"

Kallstrom, as I have explained, had no special training for the high-tech, I-spy job he had been given. A Vietnam-era grunt like myself, Jimmy had done what very few other people could have ever done. Starting from a knowledge base of zero, with no more than an order from Neil Welch to develop a Special Operations Branch, Kallstrom had educated himself in the arcana of electronic eavesdropping to a point where he had become the FBI's guru on matters involving I-spy surveillance. For most people who have absolutely no understanding of the field, this is sort of the equivalent of you or me moving from a level-one high school algebra course to a Ph.D. level in quantum physics—and doing it all on your own, teaching yourself.

I was damned proud of my friend.

Physically, Jim Kallstrom is a bear of a guy, and though he was a hell of a lot more patient than I ever was, when he was stymied or frustrated, he could react exactly like a bear. I had no way of knowing it, but my question about knocking the radio noise out on our Title III at Castellano's place had suddenly brought out the bear in Kallstrom.

"I shouldn't say this, Jules." Kallstrom paused for a second, then plunged straightaway with what it was he shouldn't be saying. "There is something we do have, only it's never been used on the criminal side of the house. It's only for the FCI [Foreign Counter-Intelligence]."

"National security," I said. The foreign counterintelligence side of the Bureau had a lot of fancy electronic gear the criminal side of the house never got to see, the reason being that the stuff was all supersecret.

Kallstrom snorted. "National security, my ass. The fucking Russians'll be coming out of the East River any day now, right?"

I said nothing, smiling.

"I tell you what, Jules. How about national security here in New York City, huh? How about that? That's the problem. We worry too much about things that'll never happen and not enough about the fucking business at hand."

"So get the fucking machine, whatever it is."

"That's just what I'm going to do, Jules. You watch."

"Well, do it, then."

"I will. Screw the Russkie bullshit and screw Headquarters. We got a fucking opportunity here."

"Go for it, pal." I hung up a second later, glad I wasn't on the other end of the line for Kallstrom's next call.

Less than a week after Kallstrom and I talked, Bruce Mouw and one of his BQ-5 agents, Bill Hansen, picked up two strange-looking guys and a couple of odd-shaped suitcases at a hotel in midtown Manhattan and drove them out to Staten Island. The two guys looked like they had spent the better part of their lives peering into microscopes or living under fluorescent lights. They had the plastic pocket protectors in their shirts, the eyeglasses that looked like the bottom of Coke bottles, the whole deal. These were the Bureau's electronic wizards.

They didn't say a word the entire way out to Staten Island.

Posing as a businessman, Bill Hansen had rented a room for us in a warehouse a block or so from Paul Castellano's house. With the two electronics guys still keeping their counsel in the back of the Bureau car, Hansen pulled in behind the warehouse; then he and Bruce helped the other two guys lug the funny-looking suitcases upstairs into the warehouse.

"You guys just tell us what to do, okay?" Polite as ever, Bruce Mouw was just trying to be helpful.

"Don't touch the equipment. Please." The older of the two electronics geeks bore more than a passing resemblance to Harpo Marx, and he turned his back on Hansen and Mouw as he began unlocking the heavy leather suitcases.

Mouw looked at Hansen and shrugged his shoulders.

The younger of the two electronics geeks moved to the window and began fiddling with something there.

For the next half hour, with no one saying a word, Hansen and Mouw watched as Harpo Marx and his partner assembled a bank of what looked like stereo receivers, amplifiers, and loud-speakers—so much equipment, Bruce thought, it looked like they were ready to broadcast a rock concert.

Harpo Marx manipulated a dial and twiddled a lever, then looked at his partner. "Okay."

It was the first word either of them had spoken since they began working.

The man at the window did something with an antenna thing that Bruce and Bill couldn't see because he was holding the antenna between them and the window.

Harpo Marx moved another dial. "Now try."

The man at the window shifted his feet, and Bruce and Bill looked from him back to Harpo Marx.

"Again," Harpo said.

Behind them, one of the loudspeakers crackled, and Bill and Bruce spun around.

"What the heck?"

"Shhh!" Harpo Marx glared at Mouw.

Bruce stared at the loudspeaker, then at Hansen.

Bill turned his palms toward the ceiling, raised his eyebrows, and mouthed the words "Phil Rizzuto."

And damned if it wasn't the Scooter, too, broadcasting the first of a twi-nighter at Yankee Stadium. Bruce listened more closely, and sure enough there was Rizzuto's partner, Frank Messer, and the noise of the crowd he would recognize anywhere.

By now Bruce knew better than to ask questions, so he listened to the game. The Yankees were playing the Indians, and so far there was no score.

Across the room, Harpo Marx was on his knees in front of a black box that might have been an X-ray machine for all Hansen and Mouw knew. Harpo had clamped a set of thick green earphones on his head, and he looked even more otherworldly than ever. As Bruce and Bill watched and the Scooter called balls and strikes from the stadium twenty miles away, Harpo moved a series of tiny levers, one lined up next to the other.

A minute or two later, Rizzuto's voice began to fade out.

The sound of a pot dropping next jolted Mouw and Hansen.

Harpo Marx moved another lever.

"You want coffee?"

Mouw stared at Hansen. He couldn't believe it. The voice belonged to Gloria Olarte, Paul Castellano's live-in maid and full-time girlfriend.

"Nah, maybe later, Gloria. Thanks."

That was Castellano himself, the boss of bosses.

Harpo Marx moved one more lever.

Phil Rizzuto and the crowd noise from the stadium had disappeared entirely.

A second later: "There any more of that pie left, Gloria?"

"Yeah, hang on. I'll get you a slice."

A dish clattered on a table a few seconds after that, and Harpo Marx gestured to his silent partner near the window, then looked at Mouw and Hansen. "Okay," he said. "I think we got it."

27

NEW Yorkers have a thing about restaurants. Discovering the next new place for egg rolls, Mongolian pork chops, or who knows what, carpaccio of sea bass, is like a crazy obsession, and for a lot of people in the city, the stranger and the more out of the way the place, the greater the appeal. Don't ask me why; it's just one of those things about the city.

I mention this because a passerby strolling the grimmer reaches of Twenty-first Avenue out in Brooklyn during the course of the dinner hour back in early 1983 might have easily persuaded himself that the Casa Storta Restaurant was another one of the city's undiscovered culinary gems. The place was certainly crowded. Between the agent-couples we were sending into the place each night, the parade of wise guys who began showing up at around eight o'clock, and the neighborhood people who wandered in merely in search of a nice plate of pasta and clam sauce, the Casa Storta was doing a hell of a trade. Of course, once you got inside, the food wasn't much to talk about. It wouldn't kill you, but it wouldn't send you out the door singing an aria, either.

What was outstanding at the Casa Storta was the quality of the table talk in the place. This was of interest, of course, only to people like FBI agents, but given that caveat, the wise-guy talk at the Casa Storta's table 1 was worth an easy five stars in my book. In fact, if there was such a thing as a Michelin guide to Mafia hangouts, the Casa Storta would have definitely been, as the Michelin people like to say, "worth the detour." In the Bureau, of course, we had another term of appreciation for places like the Casa Storta.

We called it hitting pay dirt.

With the Title III in Paul Castallano's house, we were looking at the potential for pay dirt in our investigation of the Gambino family. With what we were already getting from the Title III in the Casa Storta Restaurant, the pay dirt was confirmed. Our investigation of the Colombo family was rolling.

I'll give you an example. One night back in January 1983, the conversation at table 1 had turned to the subject of extortion. Our agents listening on the muffs were interested, of course, but they weren't really too impressed. By wise-guy standards, the amount of money at issue was pretty modest, just $50,000. What *was* interesting, though, as the agents followed the table talk— trying to distinguish the wise guys' grunted half sentences from the continuous belching and slurping of Chianti—was the fight that was going on over the extortion money. An enforcer from the Colombo family had demanded the $50,000 from a construction company called DeGaetano and Vozzi. Mr. DeGaetano was understandably disturbed at the prospect of seeing $50,000 of his hard-earned cash going out the window like that, and lucky him, he availed himself of an option most ordinary Americans just don't have. DeGaetano had a cousin, a guy named Pete Beck, who was a member of the Lucchese crime family, and DeGaetano asked Cousin Pete if he couldn't do something about the fifty K the Colombos had demanded as a condition for his continued health and well-being. Since it was for a blood relative who was a nice guy and all, Pete Beck went to see the boss of the Luccheses, a hardnose named "Tony Ducks" Corallo. Tony Ducks made a decision: DeGaetano didn't have to pay the $50,000; if he paid half, that would put him square with the Colombos.

This was tricky business. As the boss of the Lucchese family, Tony Ducks couldn't actually "decide" what DeGaetano would or would not pay the Colombos. What he could do was recommend—something that naturally didn't put him in the greatest favor with the Colombos, who were under the day-to-day command now of Gerry Lang Langella. With Carmine "the Snake"

Persico still in prison and an aging Tommy DiBella overcome with his many health problems, Gerry Lang had become the acting boss of the Colombos. Because Tony Ducks was a full-fledged boss, he had more clout than Gerry Lang, who naturally took it as a personal affront that the old bastard would stick his nose into a lousy $50,000 extortion deal, then try to screw him out of half of it.

The five families in New York, together with the rest of the Cosa Nostra families operating across the country, had evolved a mechanism for dealing with these kinds of problems. "The commission"—essentially a Mafia board of directors—adjudicated all interfamily disputes like that involving Mr. DeGaetano and his $50,000 problem. Naturally, there was no provision for appeal. The dons' word was final.

We had long heard rumors about a Mafia Commission, and we had even heard Fat Angelo Ruggiero talking about commission meetings. But just about everything we had was hearsay; to make a case against the commission itself, we would need a hell of a lot more than that.

From the conversations we recorded at table 1 at the Casa Storta, we got our first good glimpse of the commission in action. On January 26, 1983, the commission members reviewed the pleadings in the DeGaetano extortion matter and decided that Tony Ducks was right and that Gerry Lang was not. Mr. DeGaetano would pay the Colombos the $25,000, the commission members said; Gerry Lang could forget about the other twenty-five.

For Gerry Lang this was a big black eye, and he bitched about it to Angelo Ruggiero and Donnie Shacks Montemarano one night over dinner at the Casa Storta. We picked it up on the microphone in the ceiling over table 1.

"Those bosses," Gerry Lang vowed, "I'll make them eat shit, I'll blow their asses off."

There was a pause as Lang caught his breath, and Kallstrom's mike transmitted background noise—the slurping of sauce, the guzzling of wine, the bread being ripped apart as if by rooting hogs. Were it not for the odd clink of tableware, the noise in the

Casa Storta could have passed easily for the soundtrack of a *National Geographic* wildlife documentary.

Ruggiero says he understands, he just talked to Neil Dellacroce, his uncle, about the matter. "I says, 'Neil, what's the matter?' And see, he tells me this story, about, you know, the fifty thousand."

"Yeah?"

"He says, 'I hate this fucking construction.' And he said, 'You believe I asked this guy four times for the fifty thousand?' And he goes, 'Would I say something like that? This guy comes from my friend Tony Ducks [Corallo]. And the guy tells him, 'Forget about the fifty.' "

"Cocksuckers." Gerry Lang took a sip of wine.

Donnie Shacks interrupted, telling Ruggiero how he and Gerry Lang had met with the bosses on the matter. "Now they're talking about the fifty thousand, and Gerry says, 'I want the fifty, you don't think I got it coming? If youse feel that way about it, hey, maybe, I don't want it now.' "

Gerry Lang: " 'Waive it,' I said."

Donnie Shacks: "That's it, that's it."

Ruggiero: "Neil said he didn't know about it."

Donnie Shacks: "Bullshit."

Gerry Lang: "He couldn't back Tony Ducks down."

Ruggiero: "I don't know, I don't know . . . I'm gonna tell Neil you and me talked and say you gave me a message, that you asked us for a little time but that your only alliance is with us. That you ain't got no alliance with any other family."

Gerry Lang: "And tell him Tony Ducks didn't sway me."

"Okay," Ruggiero said.

A minute later, Ruggiero turned the conversation to the bad blood between Neil Dellacroce and Paul Castellano and how Angelo's buddy, John Gotti, was right in the middle of it. "Johnny told [Neil] last night, Paul forbids anyone to go see him. Remember I told you, I said there's gonna be a bid out?"

Gerry Lang: "To get Paul outta here."

Ruggiero: "I think Paul's looking to whack Neil, but Neil told me just yesterday, he says, 'What the fuck is Paulie gonna do?' I said, 'Why don't you just do it and forget about it? Go in and fucking smoke him.' "

"Yeah."

"But Neil says, 'Ah, this guy [Castellano], he don't know his fucking way. This guy's gone crazy; he's a legitimate fucking nut.' "

"Don't I know it?"

"I swear on my mother."

"With the fifty, maybe Paulie's looking for my head, that big fucking dope."

"Nah, I don't think he's doing that. The guy's too fucking old for that."

Gerry Lang drank some more wine, then leaned across the table to Ruggiero. "I don't know, Ange, but I'll tell you, your boss is breaking our balls. This prick is gonna fuck us. And I'm telling you, don't repeat this because I don't want nobody to think I'm a fucking wacko." Lang nodded across the table at Donnie Shacks. "What did I say, Donnie, after the holidays, what would happen?"

"That Neil and Johnny Gotti will die."

"That's it. I made a prediction, and you know what?"

"That's just what you see that's going on."

Ruggiero nodded. "It's getting worse and worse, too."

"They laughed when I said, 'The man comes with his guys with guns, and you know he ain't comin' down easy.' "

"No, I know, Gerry. And Neil knows it, and Johnny knows it. I'll tell you what. If anything happens to Neil and Johnny, I'll come and see you, 'cause I don't trust Paulie and those other fucking assholes."

"I don't blame you."

"I don't trust nobody else."

"I don't blame you. It's not a nice way to live today. And you know what gets me?"

"What's that?"

"Paul."

"Yeah, I know."

"I think I told Neil, 'You know this cocksucker's bad-mouthing you.'"

"To me, he bad-mouths *you*. He bad-mouths everybody. He bad-mouths his own family even."

"He ain't gonna get away with it no more, I tell you, Ange. Somebody's gonna—"

"I know." Ruggiero finished his wine and placed his glass firmly on the table. "Believe me, Gerry, I know."

"Well, fuck him, anyway."

Ruggiero continued: "Where's the honor, Gerry? I mean, where's the fucking honor?"

Gerry Lang pulled a fifty-dollar bill from his wallet. "Here's the honor, Ange. Right here."

"Money?" Ruggiero sounded depressed.

"Yeah, that's it. That's your fucking honor."

Over the next few weeks, the talk at table 1 got more interesting. The conversations involving Ralph Scopo proved especially so. A known Colombo family soldier, Scopo was among the first of the Casa Storta's nightly diners who attracted our attention, and he threw everyone for a loop. The first time we spotted him, Scopo was sitting with Gerry Lang back by the kitchen at table 1, chewing the fat like the two of them were long-lost buddies. What's wrong with this picture, as I mentioned, is that pissant soldiers like Ralphie Scopo don't typically sit down and break bread with generals like Gerry Lang Langella. Just doesn't happen.

So something else is going on, and it takes Damon Taylor's agents several days to figure out that Ralphie Scopo, the Colombo family soldier, is also none other than Mr. Ralph Scopo, president of the New York District Council of Cement and Concrete Workers Union. In a city like New York, where there are several billion dollars in construction projects under way on any given day, this is a very big deal indeed. As president of the District Council, Scopo controlled the laborers who mixed and poured the concrete for every significant building project in the five boroughs of Manhattan. As a loyal soldier of the Colombo crime family, Scopo could use this same influence on the cement and concrete workers to extort millions of dollars from developers, contractors, subcontractors, and even from his own union bosses. Fail to pay Ralphie Scopo on time and suddenly trucks stop trucking, workmen stop working, and your multi-million-dollar construction project is running way over budget and behind schedule. Time is money, and if you ever want proof, just ask a guy who's trying to put up a multimillion-dollar sky-scraper in a major metropolis somewhere when his crews and trucks suddenly fail to show up one morning.

We didn't have a good picture yet on exactly how Scopo was jobbing the cement business, but we knew it had to be an extortion racket. The money involved had to be enormous.

Obviously, what we were looking at here was a huge criminal conspiracy involving, at the very least, tens of millions of dollars. People look at numbers like that and assume the people behind it must be geniuses, but it's just not so. Listen to a slug like Ralphie Scopo describing his day at the office, and no matter how much money he's bringing down, it doesn't take long to see that he's doing it the same way as the cheapest sort of street-corner strong-arm artist.

In his wildest dreams, Bob Blakey had never imagined a criminal corporation with the reach and scope of the one we were hearing about from Ralph Scopo and his friends in the Casa Storta. As the tapes from the Title IIIs continued piling up, Kossler and I began conferring daily.

What we had here went light-years beyond what we had been dealing with in the Bonanno case, and we had to be careful. Here timing could be everything. Attack too soon and we might end up getting just part of the cancerous growth; wait and do the job right, though, and we had a chance to pull the whole damn thing out by the roots.

We decided to watch and wait.

28

AT approximately one o'clock on a breezy Saturday morning in May 1983, Special Agent Denis Maduro was sitting alone in the darkened FBI command center on the twenty-fourth floor of the Jacob K. Javits Federal Building on Lower Broadway when the red light on his secure phone began winking.

The command post was packed with state-of-the-art electronics, and it looked like a fancy operating theater in a big hospital. None of this held any interest for Maduro. The lead agent assigned to the Colombo family investigation, Denis had pulled a rare tour of night supervisory duty, a midnight-to-eight shift that even the most senior people got stuck with every once in a while. Maduro was just thirty years old, but his blue-eyed, blond-haired good looks made him look considerably younger, like a college kid, almost. His assignment to the Colombo squad was a prestigious one for such a young agent, but Denis had earned it through pure hard work. No matter how much he had on his plate, Denis was always volunteering to help other agents with their cases, just because they sounded interesting. It was also not unusual for Denis to work two cases at a time, finishing up with one at the end of what most people considered a normal business day, then starting in on the second case at seven or eight o'clock at night. On the midnight shift in the command post, Denis could have dozed or read the newspapers or whatever, but instead he was using the time to catch up with the mountains of paperwork a case like the Colombo investigation generates. The phone call was a welcome break from the tedium.

"Supervisor Maduro, may I help you?"

The man on the other end of the line spoke fast. He had borrowed a lot of money from some people, he told Maduro, and now he was afraid these people would be coming to visit him shortly and that they would harm his wife and kids.

"Hold on, hold on, sir." Maduro got the man to slow down, and he finally identified himself. His name was Frankie Ancona, the man said. The name meant nothing to Maduro, so he asked the next obvious question. "Who are the people to whom you owe this money, Mr. Ancona? Who's threatening you?"

Ancona sighed deeply and began rattling off names. Maduro copied the names down carefully. When Ancona mentioned Gerry Lang, Denis sat bolt upright in his chair. Shit, he had been working the Colombo case so hard, he had had dreams about Gerry Lang. "Who? Could you repeat that last name, sir?"

Frankie Ancona identified the acting boss of the Colombo family again, and Maduro asked him to hold on a second. This was the kind of luck you think never happens, Maduro thought, at least not to you. Anyone at all could have pulled the overnight shift that evening, an agent from one of the white-collar crime squads, from one of the terrorism squads. Gerry Lang's name would have meant nothing to them, and Frankie Ancona's plea for help would have been routed through the normal Bureau channels for follow-up. Maduro didn't know Frankie Ancona from the man in the moon, but if he was legitimately on the hook to Gerry Lang, this was a lead of solid gold. With Ancona on hold, Maduro called Damon Taylor at home, roused him from a deep sleep, and gave him a quick fill on the call from Ancona.

"No shit," Taylor said. The supervisor of the Colombo family squad ordered Maduro to get out to Ancona's place as soon as possible and find out what the hell was going on.

Maduro got back on the line to Ancona. He would be out there first thing in the morning, he said. He couldn't leave the command post until his relief arrived at 8:00 A.M. "Keep the lights out," Maduro told Frankie Ancona, "and don't answer the door for anyone until I get there."

"Okay." Ancona hung up. The guy sounded like a wreck.

Frankie Ancona's place was in Staten Island, and Maduro got there just before nine in the morning. A padlock tumbled on the other side of the thick door, and as soon as Denis stepped inside, he could see that Ancona was a guy in some very big trouble. First of all, there was not a stick of furniture in the house—nothing. There was a refrigerator, and Denis took a look inside. Total contents: a bag of potato chips and half a bottle of Pepsi. Ancona's three kids—two girls and a boy, ages six through twelve—sat crying on the floor while Ancona's very nervous wife tried to comfort them. Ancona himself was as much of a wreck as he sounded on the phone. He was a fat guy, tremendously overweight, and he had all of four teeth in his mouth, and those didn't look like they had been brushed any too recently. While the kids cried and his wife wrung her hands, Ancona chain-smoked Pall Malls. The phone on the wall in the kitchen rang every few minutes.

"It's them." Ancona gestured at the telephone with his burning cigarette.

Maduro answered the phone several times and used a tape recorder to catch the words of one caller. The man promised to end Ancona's miserable life in a particularly macabre fashion.

Enough of this shit, Maduro thought. He disconnected the phone and sat down on the floor, away from the mewling kids. It was time to take down the story of Frankie Ancona's travails.

Ancona spoke like a man defeated. Things at one time had looked very promising for him and his family, he told Maduro. The woman he had married was the daughter of Joseph "Joe Butch" Corrao, an influential capo in the Gambino crime family. Ancona had used the connection to borrow nearly $250,000, he said, telling Maduro how he had proceeded to put the money out on the street in high-interest loans. In Frankie Ancona's world, being a loan shark was simply a means of making one's way in the world, of providing for one's family; the law wasn't a consideration.

Maduro took careful notes.

The problem with Frankie Ancona's business plan, of course, was that Ancona was not especially bright; he was able to neither read nor write, and he had trouble communicating in simple sentences. More to the point is that, like our old friend Vinnie DePenta, Frankie Ancona simply wasn't enough of a tough guy to go out and collect on the debts he was owed; he came calling for his money, a little fat guy with four teeth in his mouth, and people just laughed.

The wise guys from whom Frankie Ancona had borrowed the quarter of a million dollars didn't suffer from this particular problem; they weren't much inclined to laughter, either. Three days before Ancona's fortuitous phone call to Maduro, one of the wise guys had paid Ancona a visit. Frankie had two days, three at the outside, to come up with the quarter mil, the shylock said. If he failed to come up with the money, the shylock warned, he would burn down the house. Frankie Ancona remembered the second part of the shylock's threat word for word, and he repeated it for Maduro's tape recorder. "Before I burn down the house," the shylock said, "I'm going to tie you up in a chair, and I'm going to rape your wife and daughters in front of you. After that, then I'll burn the fucking place down."

Following the visit from the shylock, an understandably shaken Frankie Ancona had taken himself down to one of the wise guy's social clubs to plead for more time, a flexible payback period, anything. When he walked into the place, however, one of the wise guys broke a bar stool over his back and added the cost of the chair to Ancona's $250,000 bill—just for good measure. Ancona had limped out of the place, his head in his hands, the weight of the world on his chubby shoulders.

Maduro recorded the sad facts of Frankie Ancona's story one by one. Ancona's relationship with Gerry Lang was particularly intriguing. The would-be loan shark was so far into the acting boss of the Colombo family that Gerry Lang had forced Ancona to sign over the deed to a house he owned in Staten Island and then made him and his family move out that very night; the place they were in at the moment was a rental.

The more Ancona talked, the more Denis saw that he had the makings of a genuine grade A witness on his hands. Not only was Ancona related to the Gambino family through his marriage to Joe Butch Corrao's daughter; his own uncle was Anthony LaStorta, the proprietor of the Casa Storta restaurant. As if this weren't enough, Ancona said he was tight with Carmine "the Snake" Persico, the boss of the Colombo family, then in jail. Ancona was also a friend of another major league mob guy, a thief named Anthony Scarpatti, and he knew dozens of other half-assed wise guys—members, made guys, and wannabe wise guys like himself.

Maduro concluded the interview and quickly made arrangements to keep Ancona and his family on ice and out of harm's way for the next few hours. Like a lot of the agents we worked with, Denis had a soft spot for kids. Ancona's two daughters and the six-year-old boy—he kept calling Denis a "BFI man," reversing the letters—really touched Maduro. Before he ran back to the office in Manhattan, Denis raced out to find an automatic teller machine, took $250 of his own money out, then took Ancona and the family to a grocery store so they could get some food in the house and give the kids a decent meal. After that, Denis hotfooted it back to the Javits building at 26 Federal and huddled with Damon Taylor and Jim Kossler. I was on the speakerphone from Washington. Everyone agreed: Ancona was definitely worth the risk. If we put a wire on him and aimed him at Gerry Lang, Donnie Shacks, and that crew, there was no telling what he might bring us back.

The guy was clearly a loser, but he was a desperate loser, and sometimes those guys make the best informants. Of course, we would have to make sure Ancona started making some sizable payoffs on the debts he owed, but I could take care of that at Headquarters. We wouldn't pay back the entire $250,000, of course; despite what the wise guys had told him, if Ancona started making serious payments, he was worth more alive than dead. Even the idiot wise guys could understand that.

So we decided to put Frankie Ancona in play.

• • •

In addition to being a hell of a hardworking agent, Denis Maduro was also something of wise-guy word maven. Denis had
known plenty of wise guys before Frankie Ancona, and more
than most of us, I guess, he had been struck by their peculiar
way of talking. So much so that Denis actually began putting
together what he called a wise-guy *Dictionary of Terms and Mal-
apropisms.*

It exists, to this day, in the FBI's files.

I'm not sure even Denis remembers the exact conversation
that prompted him to begin consigning the wise guys' linguistic
gems to paper. It might have been when Frankie Ancona,
touched by Denis's kindness to his wife and kids, confided that,
should Denis die an untimely death, he would personally be
honored to be a ball bearing at Denis's funeral. What Frankie
meant, of course, was that he would be honored to be a pallbearer, but the way the wise guys talked, pallbearer became ball
bearing, and if anyone was confused, it didn't make a hell of a
lot of difference; at least it didn't to the wise guys.

There was no explaining some wise-guy locutions. "Put the
doorknobs on the paper," for instance, was an expression intended to mean "Let's lay out all the pertinent facts and have a
frank discussion." Go figure.

Similarly with "Let's put the water underneath the barrel and
be friends." This was wise guy–speak, believe it or not, for someone who had perjured himself previously in testimony to the
FBI but who was now prepared to tell the truth.

Some of the stuff Denis recorded can be attributed to wise-guy
stupidity. A "Sony bath" was a sauna, much beloved by older
wise guys after a long day of bullshitting in some dumpy social
club. "College cheese" was cottage cheese, something few wise
guys were known to favor, just as few had ever been identified
anywhere close to America's precincts of higher education.

Some of the stuff in the wise-guy dictionary was peculiar. A
"topaz," for instance, was a male hairpiece, usually of the cheap

variety, like the kind worn by Tommy Bilotti. A "mercy room" was an emergency room, a place with which the wise guys did tend to have some degree of familiarity. A "parakeet" was an attractive woman, but the converse for some reason was a "barracuda." A "deli" was a union delegate, and as Denis recorded it, a "ham-and-cheese samich" was a payoff to said delegate.

There were references to money too numerous to mention. "Make fucking money," Denis noted, was the Cosa Nostra's "short-range strategic goal."

"Fuck everybody" was, as Denis recorded it, the "Cosa Nostra philosophy so long as it results in making money."

It could make you laugh or cry, the stupidity of what the wise guys said. You flip through Denis's dictionary, though, and instead of laughing or crying, I think you just come to a simple conclusion: These were people with few, if any, redeeming social values. These guys were bums.

29

SPRING has always been my favorite time of year, and I couldn't remember a brighter one than 1983. The kids were growing up straight and strong, Linda was happy and settled into the quiet routine of our life in suburban Virginia, and working with Sean McWeeney and the higher-ups I had to deal with at Headquarters was getting easier and easier. The successes, as I expected, had helped a lot in that regard.

But what was even greater to think about as spring blossomed into summer was the future. It looked brighter than ever. With the wire finally up and working in Paul Castellano's place and the lucky break we had had with the phone call from Frankie Ancona, our investigations into the Colombo and Gambino families were now both picking up steam. We had gotten enough of a whiff of the dealings of the Mafia Commission, too, that Kossler and I had begun to dream of an even bigger case. It was a dream so big it scared both of us sometimes, but we also felt that it was nearly within our grasp. Way back at his seminar on the wonders of RICO up in Ithaca, New York, Bob Blakey had planted the seeds of the dream in our heads, and without our ever realizing it, his dream had somehow become ours. "I dream," Blakey had said, "of an indictment of every boss."

Yeah, right, Kossler and I thought at the time. But now we were thinking differently. Why *not* an indictment of every boss?

Why the hell not?

With the Bonanno family on ice and the investigations of the Gambino and Colombo families progressing nicely, we had solid evidence of the criminal activities of three of the five Cosa Nostra families in New York, and we were working hard on the other two, the Lucchese and the Genovese families. With what we knew about the commission's decision on things like the DeGaetano extortion payment, the Pete Tambone narcotics problem, and—most intriguing of all—the mob's control of the construction industry, we were getting the clearest picture ever of the Mafia's operations in New York. We didn't know every-thing, of course; there were nights Kossler and I would go home cursing ourselves for our inability to figure out how things fit together.

Still, it was coming together.

All of us, if we care about what we do and if life means any-thing at all, nourish ourselves with dreams. That's what Kossler and I did, and I know that's what our best agents and prosecu-tors did, too. Joe Pistone, Barbara Jones, Louie Freeh, Denis Maduro, Damon Taylor—there were dozens of them, and they shared the dream. An indictment of every boss? It would take time and a hell of a lot of work. But why not?

Why the hell not, indeed?

I'll tell you one thing that helps you dream the big dreams, and that's a big-play operation like getting the Title III into Castella-no's house. Think of any athlete you want, and the ones who genuinely have a shot to go all the way—not the big mouths who just posture and talk about it—are the ones that pull off the big play in the clutch. That's what we had with the Castellano installation.

It made the dream seem reachable.

Being able to listen in on the boss of bosses, while it was a coup that resulted both from luck and from some phenomenal police work, also made some of us kind of queasy. As I said earlier, I don't share the view of some people in law enforce-ment, those who believe there's a kind of mystical bond between cops and criminals. Crooks were crooks, and wise guys were the worst, at least in my book. I also didn't share the view that some of my colleagues had of Paul Castellano, either, the idea that he was the last of the old gentleman dons, that his "prohibition" against drug trafficking was a ban born of principle. I've already told you that Big Paulie's ban, when it came to himself, was total bullshit. And as to being a gentleman, the only thing I would say to that is: Yeah, compared to a punk like John Gotti, Paul Castellano could be called a gentleman, sure. But then compared to John Gotti, even the inhabitants of the monkey house in the Bronx Zoo could lay a better claim to the title: They were dumb, not evil.

I mentioned earlier that the wise guys were pathetic. Guys like Gerry Lang and Angelo Ruggiero, moping over their Chianti and pasta, bullshitting each other, boasting, stroking each other's stupid egos. That's the way I saw those guys, as total losers, really. In a sad way, though, I think maybe the biggest loser of them all was Paul Castellano. Here's a guy who controls this big business enterprise worth millions and millions of dollars, and over the years he grows more and more reclusive, more remote from his friends, more remote from his wife. Well, that happens, you say: People change.

Maybe. But people I know don't go out and hire a flighty little maid into the house where they're still living with their spouse of several decades and then set up housekeeping with the girl. They also don't spend thousands of dollars on medical specialists so they can restore their virility so as to better disport themselves with the hired girl—while the wife lays dozing upstairs. Some people may say this sounds cruel, but facts are facts, and when I take a look at the public ledger and see all the bullshit that has been written about generous dons and glamorous wise guys, my inclination is to try and set the record straight, and if that means speaking unkindly of the dead, so be it. The wise guys were not nice guys.

They were worthy adversaries, though, I'll say that.

And they did know how to steal. From what we learned from the Title IIIs in the Casa Storta Restaurant and in Paulie Castellano's house, we were getting a better fix on the Mafia's control of the construction industry, and it was clearer than ever that Ralph Scopo was the key to it.

It would take another year to fit all the pieces together, but the general outlines of the scam soon became clear. From what we could tell, it looked like four of the Cosa Nostra families in New York acted as partners in the construction-industry scam; the Bonannos had pretty much been cut out of all the shared wise-guy action in New York.

Basically, the way the construction business works is that a general contractor will supervise all the building work for a project developer. The G.C. will subcontract to a concrete construction outfit for superstructure work on the building, which is all of the structural work above the foundation. For the foundation and the superstructure, the main ingredient is ready-mix cement, and in New York, all ready-mix cement was delivered by members of Teamsters Local 282. On the job site, the guys who got the ready-mix into the right holes in the foundation and then up onto the superstructure were represented by the Laborers International Union (LIU), primarily by Locals 6, 6A, and 18.

As it happened, Ralphie Scopo controlled the LIU locals, while Teamsters Local 282 was run by two other thugs, guys named John Cody and Bobby Sasso. Cody and Sasso had other ties, mainly to the Genovese and Gambino families.

So this was a tidy little arrangement, and it was mostly controlled from the top by none other than Paul Castellano. Going back a few years, to the late 1970s, Castellano had arranged for the consolidation of Manhattan's ready-mix cement business to the point where it was totally dominated by one company, S&A Concrete, which was run by a money-hungry scrounge named Nick Auletta. Working from the other end, on the labor front, Ralph Scopo, John Cody, and Robert Sasso put the squeeze on the construction companies, using the threat of job actions, mob violence, and whatever other options popped into their fertile brains. As a result of these pincerlike pressures, by the early 1980s not only was there just one source for ready-mix cement in New York City; there were only six concrete construction companies that would be allowed to bid on the biggest construction jobs within the five boroughs.

To me, this was unbelievable. I remember how angry I was when I first heard about Frankie "the Beast" Falanga's no-show job at the construction company out in Brooklyn and how the Colombo family there was tacking on $800 to each little middle-class house just to ensure labor peace. How much worse was this stranglehold the mob had on the entire construction industry in New York? Literally, Ralph Scopo, Paul Castellano, and the bosses of the other three Cosa Nostra families were holding up the entire city of New York, adding countless millions of dollars to the cost of living and working in the city. There was not a thing you could think of—from advertising copy to Sabrett's hot dogs to little kids' shoes to Cartier jewels—that didn't cost more because of the hidden costs the mob added to the real estate in which these things were sold or produced.

This was crime so big it nearly defied imagining. It also nearly made me sick. These assholes had to go, I thought.

We couldn't make it happen soon enough.

At Headquarters, Sean McWeeney gave me a free hand to run the show in New York; in fact, however, there were things I got involved in on my own and things that Sean got me involved in to help him kick the FBI's organized-crime program into shape in other parts of the country.

The first was totally on my own initiative. After Joe Pistone helped Barbara Jones and Louie Freeh nail the Bonanno family to the wall, the FBI, in its magnificent wisdom, had assigned Joe to the Bureau's Dallas field division, where he was immediately treated like the greenest, dumbest first-office agent to come down the highway in a hundred years. Dallas then was a typical mixed-bag FBI shop. It was long after the Kennedy assassination and just before the worst of the savings-and-loan (S&L) screwups started bubbling to the surface. Pistone, in any case, wouldn't have been much help on S&Ls or JFK. That wasn't his thing. Joe Pistone was the FBI's most accomplished and heroic undercover agent in history—period. And what the Dallas office of the FBI treated him like was shit. The office has a wiretap set up somewhere outside of Dallas—in a prison, of all places. And who do they want to send in to monitor the damned thing? You got it, Joe Pistone. Who could believe such stupidity? Sending Joe into a federal prison—who knows who might recognize him in there?

What was worse was that Headquarters—my favorite place, right, with all those wonderful, warmhearted bureaucrats—had reaffirmed Dallas in its treatment of Pistone.

I wouldn't stand for it, and neither would Sean, and together we waged a nasty little war on Joe's behalf.

Tom Kelly, the SAC in Dallas, received the brunt of our attack. Tom may have been good enough to be chosen as a SAC by Headquarters, but he had fucked up big-time with Pistone, and I wasn't going to put up with it. His attitude toward Pistone, whom he believed to be a prima donna, was that Joe should be treated like any other FBI special agent—as if any other FBI agent had ever worked six years undercover and infiltrated the hierarchy of the Italian Mafia. As much as Tom Kelly pissed me off, Floyd Clark disappointed me by backing Kelly up. Floyd was then the deputy assistant director of the Criminal Division and had, because of his personal friendship with Kelly, refused to take a stand in the matter at first; eventually, he sided with Kelly against Pistone. Floyd knew damn well and good the sacrifices Joe had made and the phenomenal work he had done. It is not my intention here to beat up on anyone individually, but there is something rotten in any corporate structure—government, the private sector, or whatever—when the powers that be will sanction, or allow by sheer indifference, the unfair treatment of someone like Joe Pistone. To this day, that episode is among the most unhappy remembrances of my time in the FBI.

The episode so enraged Joe and his family that he resigned from the FBI. Years later, he would be rehired and assigned to the FBI Academy in Quantico, Virginia, where he would go on to become the Bureau's intellectual godfather for undercover training, operations, and strategy. With Pistone in Quantico,

FBI undercover operations would make a real quantum leap forward.

As much as I was aching to be back in New York, there were other reasons for staying on at Headquarters. Just as Kallstrom, Kossler, and I had discussed on that beautiful spring afternoon coming back from lunch so many years ago, for us to be able to do what we needed in New York, we had to have someone at Headquarters to watch our back, to be our spy, to get us what we needed with a minimum amount of bullshit.

As fate had it, that role had fallen to me, and I was determined to see it through. For all its success, New York, I knew, still needed a guardian angel at Headquarters. There was still an amazing amount of opposition. Bureaucracies, I often thought, were like weeds. Chop them down or dig them up and the next thing you know they're back again, bigger than ever. The FBI bureaucracy was a hell of a tough weed, and the reason was the goddamned inspection system J. Edgar Hoover had instituted so many years before.

The inspectors would simply not leave us alone. While we were putting the Bonanno family out of business and rolling ahead on the investigations of the Gambino and Colombo families, the New York office had a visit from the geniuses in the Inspection Division. I had tried to prewire this, explaining how the brass on the seventh floor had blessed our new "strategic" approach to organized-crime investigations. It was like talking to a wall.

Shaking their heads like missionaries back from the field after having discovered some new and unfathomable heathen abomination, the inspectors proceeded to claim, in the wonderfully dense and impenetrable prose of the government timeserver, how the New York office had far too many Title IIIs up and running; several must be shut down—immediately.

"What're you going to do now? You're Mr. Fucking Inside." Jim Kallstrom had as much use for the inspectors as I did, but here they were attacking his life's work, the major weapon in our strategic effort. "These assholes, I can't believe it."

"Easy, Jim, easy." I told Kallstrom I would put the inspectors on ice for a while. All they needed to know was what I told them. Besides, the inspectors wouldn't be coming around again for another eighteen months. So screw them.

"Beautiful, Jules. You're a beautiful human being."

"Yeah, right."

What I worried more about—although, I'll tell you, I didn't worry about it too much—was the money we were spending. The way the Bureau was set up, I could authorize only so much money on my own for informant payments, undercover operations, whatever. If we wanted to take some heat off a guy like Frankie Ancona, for instance, I could, on my own signature, get him $1,500 immediately. If he needed more than that, I needed Sean McWeeney's signature on the cash requisition form. But Sean could authorize only up to $5,000. Everything else up to $100,000 had to go through a series of approvals, in ascending order, from the deputy assistant director in charge to the assistant director in charge to the executive assistant director in charge. Anything over $100,000 required a lengthy memorandum that had to be approved by Director Webster himself. With all that bullshit we had to go through, the wise guys would have grown beards.

Getting sign-offs from busy guys like Sean, Floyd, and up took time, and it got in the way of doing business. Besides, they trusted me—a lot further than any of them actually knew at the time. What the FBI had for cash requisitions was your classic government form in triplicate, each copy color-coded, skinny black carbon sheets nested tidily between each one. What I did was simple. When Kossler or Kallstrom or Bruce Mouw or Damon Taylor called me with a problem, I listened, and as was the case with poor Frankie Ancona, I simply made a decision. Shit, why bother the bosses? They were busy.

What can I say; for me the FBI system didn't work.

Say someone in New York legitimately needed $30,000 overnight? No problem. I signed the form, then threw away the two duplicate copies and the carbons. Then I initialed the authorizing memorandum, sent it up to New York, and the money was there for whoever needed it the next day. No red tape.

Speed—it could make or break an investigation.

I would like to say that at some level Headquarters really understood this, but I'm not sure that was the case. I understood it, and that's why I did what I did. But for a place like the FBI, where rules and discipline are enforced with an awesome swiftness and rigidity, I was skating about as close to insurrection as it was possible to get. It wasn't that I deliberately went courting trouble; it was just that I wanted to make things happen, and having a big goddamned sit-down at Headquarters every time an agent in the field needed a few thousand bucks just struck me as a waste of time.

So I short-circuited the process. And I gave my bosses plausible deniability, but I didn't worry about it because I knew we would be successful, and once that happened, there wouldn't be too many people coming around asking questions.

There were other parts of Headquarters life that came with the turf, and I didn't enjoy them as much as I did strategizing with New York. Some were downright silly.

There was the time Nancy Reagan wanted to invite Frank Sinatra to a state dinner at the White House, for example, and one of President Reagan's aides raised the subject of Sinatra's alleged ties to the mob. I don't know what the truth of the matter is with the gossip about Sinatra and Mrs. Reagan, and I don't care. But evidently she was pretty insistent on having Old Blue Eyes at this state dinner, because the next thing I knew, James Baker, who was then President Reagan's chief of staff, was hustling over to FBI Headquarters, and I was summoned up to Judge Webster's office for a sit-down.

At Judge Webster's request, I reviewed the Bureau's entire file on Sinatra, some seventy-five or eighty pages of it. You never saw such junk. The FBI has taken its lumps over the years about the way it collects information on people, and from what I saw in the Sinatra file, the criticism is richly deserved. The mob stuff was what Baker was interested in, but to get to that I had to wade through pages and pages of other bullshit. There were allegations, for example, that Sinatra had ties to the Communist party, of all things. Total bullshit. According to the Bureau's file, the allegations surfaced time and again through the 1940s, starting right after he divorced his first wife, Nancy Barbato, and married Ava Gardner. Sinatra was no more tied up with the Commies than the pope. You want to know the sole basis for the charge? In 1946, Sinatra had registered as a member of a group called the Independent Citizens Committee for the Arts, Sciences and Professions, and the California Committee on Un-American Activities, one of the many McCarthyite nut groups that were springing up back then, called the organization a Communist-front group. It was not.

The mob stuff was more substantive, I saw from the file. Over the years, various informants had linked Sinatra to wise guys like Charlie and Rocco Fischetti, leaders in the Al Capone crime family. Other reports had Sinatra linked to a New Jersey wise guy named Willie Moretti, a guy who was ultimately shot and killed on the personal order of Vito Genovese. Still other reports linked Sinatra to Sam Giancana and Tony Accardo, Chicago mob bosses in the 1960s and 1970s. The most interesting of the alleged ties between Sinatra and the mob, however, had Old Blue Eyes palling around with Frank Costello, one of the most powerful New York mob bosses until his death in 1973.

On a sunny spring afternoon, a secretary ushered me into Judge Webster's big corner office on the seventh floor of the Hoover building, the judge introduced me, and Baker rose from his chair in front of Webster's desk to greet me.

The judge invited us both to sit, and I slowly walked Baker through the reports on Sinatra, starting with his childhood in New Jersey, working forward through the nonsense about his ties to the Communist party, and finally the mob stuff.

President Reagan's chief of staff was a good listener. He took one or two notes but didn't interrupt.

In an effort to compress the briefing, as I had been requested to do, I lumped a lot of the supposed mob incidents involving

Sinatra together. "Mr. Baker, you should know that the file I reviewed has a lot of reports of this type."

"I see."

"But the reports are only that."

"How do you mean?"

"Well, sir, they're not evidence. Sometimes they barely rise to the level of hearsay."

"The Bureau collects them, though."

"Yes, sir." I nodded, but I wasn't going to get into that thicket if I could help it, not in Webster's office, anyway.

Webster interrupted. "Is there anything else, Jules?"

"Yes, sir. There was one incident—but again, it's like the others, not really much more than gossip."

"And what was that?" Baker leaned an inch or two closer.

I checked my notes. "On the fifth of November, 1954, sir, we had a report that Mr. Sinatra, accompanied by the baseball player Joe DiMaggio, was questioned briefly by the authorities after attempting to break into an apartment in Hollywood owned by a girlfriend of Marilyn Monroe."

Baker pondered the information a second. "She was married to DiMaggio at the time?"

"Yes, sir. Only according to the file, Monroe was in the process of trying to obtain a divorce from DiMaggio, and the file says he was apparently looking to obtain some unflattering information on her from the girlfriend."

"I see."

"And that's it—end of story."

"That's it?"

"Yes, sir. It's like I've been trying to say, a lot of what's in these files is just junk." I kept my eyes averted from Judge Webster and continued. "And if you want my opinion, sir, there is nothing unusual about entertainers and Mafia people hanging around together. Why that's so, I don't know, but I can tell you that on surveillance after surveillance our agents working organized-crime cases see it time and again."

"I see."

"The wise guys, I think, like to be around entertainers like Sinatra because it impresses their girlfriends. And the entertainers like to hang around the wise guys because they think maybe it makes them look tough or something."

Baker nodded, paused, then looked at me directly. "What you're saying, then, if I understand it correctly, Agent Bonavolonta, is that there is nothing in the FBI's files indicating that Mr. Sinatra is what you would call 'a made guy'?"

"That's exactly right, Mr. Baker. And if I might add something?" I looked from Webster to Baker.

"Please." Baker still had me fixed with his pale blue eyes.

"I was just going to say that if you look at all these reports the Bureau has collected over the years, there's nothing in any one of them that says Mr. Sinatra ever did anything more than hang around with these wise guys."

"He never did anything with them, you mean."

"Exactly. And my point is, in this great country of ours, it's still not a crime to hang around with or associate with people of questionable character." I paused. "In other words, not only is there no basis, as far as we know, about Sinatra being involved in organized crime; there's no basis for convicting him of anything based just on who he associates with."

Baker nodded. "So there's no problem, you're saying."

"What I'm saying, sir, is that Mr. Sinatra is entitled to the same presumption of innocence as you or me. No, sir, to answer you're question, Mr. Baker, I see no problem at all."

Baker thanked me, then Judge Webster did, and I was escorted to the door. I read later in the papers that Old Blue Eyes had a grand time at the White House dinner.

Other parts of the job at Headquarters were more important, and I took them seriously. After the convictions in the Bonnano trial, Sean had me traveling around the country to talk to agents and supervisors in other offices about the New York strategy and how we were planning to implement it nationwide, not just in organized-crime cases but in narcotics cases as well, since it was precisely for this kind of expertise that Ronald Reagan had ordered the FBI into the drug war.

I wasn't much on traveling or public speaking, but this was important. It is one thing for Ronald Reagan to stand up in a handsome room in the Department of Justice and make a speech about how revolutionary change was afoot in the war on crime and how the FBI would now be leading the way for everyone else. The way the revolution actually worked, however, was by supervisors and agents like Bruce Mouw, Damon Taylor, and Denis Maduro changing the way they went about their jobs. And the way that happened was by spear carriers like me flying around the country to try and instill a vision of the future the way Bob Blakey had instilled his vision in Jimmy Kossler's head and mine.

From the depths of my soul I believed in our strategy.

Now I wanted the rest of the FBI to believe, too.

30

BASED on the conversations we recorded in Angelo Ruggiero's place in Cedarhurst, Long Island, we indicted Ruggiero, Gene Gotti, and eleven other losers from the Bergen Fish and Hunt crew on a sweltering day near the end of August 1983. Instead of the feelings of triumph you might have expected among Kossler and me and the agents working the case, however, there was frustration and anger—the feeling of a job done not nearly as well as it could have or should have been.

I felt sick.

Two months earlier, Jim Kossler, Bruce Mouw, and I had met, and we all agreed that we were ready to go with the Ruggiero indictment. We had enough from the Title III after the death of Sal Ruggiero to bring a massive narcotics-trafficking case against Angelo Ruggiero and his slimy friends. Bruce and his squad put together what we called a pros memo, outlining the reasons the U.S. Department of Justice should proceed with a criminal prosecution. At Headquarters, Sean McWeeney and I reviewed the memo carefully and suggested a few changes. Then we kicked the thing up to the seventh floor and across the street to the blue suits at Main Justice. We got the word back almost immediately: Full speed ahead, go for it.

Maybe it works this way in every line of work, but my guess is that few things are as screwed up and as unnecessarily complicated as they are in Uncle Sam's government. The way things worked in my little end of the government was like this: We jump through all the little hoops they set in front of us, making sure we get the proper sign-offs on the pros memo; but that's not enough. Even after the big brass are signed off on which wise guys we can indict and when, the local federal prosecutor still has to give his blessing before our agents can actually go out and arrest said wise guys.

In the case of the Ruggiero indictment, this last hoop gave us fits. The U.S. Attorney for the Eastern District of New York at the time was a big, handsome Irishman named Ray Dearie, a guy who could be as stubborn as a mule if you were doing something he didn't particularly agree with.

One thing Dearie definitely did not approve of was our preference for bringing our big organized-crime cases to the Southern District of New York, in Manhattan. This preference was based not on personalities or whim or because we happened to like the courtrooms in Manhattan better than those in Brooklyn. It was based on simplicity. Because of a quirk in the way the Justice Department was set up, the Organized Crime Strike Force in Brooklyn didn't report to Dearie; it was answerable directly to Main Justice, in Washington. The practical result of this setup was that the strike-force chief and the U.S. Attorney pretended to cooperate with each other, going through this elaborate Alphonse-and-Gaston routine on nearly every organized-crime case; but even if they did manage not to screw each other up, Main Justice in Washington was not only permitted but required to stick its oar in the water. You want a recipe for trouble and headaches, the Eastern District was a surefire winner. And I didn't want any more trouble and headaches. I had plenty already.

Across the East River in Manhattan, relative sanity prevailed: The strike force there reported to the U.S. Attorney, and all prosecutions, strike force and everything else, came through that office. I liked that. If you're sitting in my chair and you've got to figure out whether you want to deal with one office or maybe two or three on a particular case, my guess is you're going to go with the one office, if only out of deference to the historic KISS principle: Keep it simple, stupid.

That's what I had been doing since I had gone down to Headquarters. That the strike force in Brooklyn was so caught up in the media frenzy over the Abscam case just made my aversion to the Eastern District all the stronger. That made the problems between the U.S. Attorney in Brooklyn and the strike force there even tougher to deal with. And the FBI was caught in the middle, it seemed, almost every time.

With the Ruggiero indictment, we were bound to go with the case in Brooklyn for a lot of reasons, and Ray Dearie was not about to make things easy for us. He knew about the Title III we had up in Paul Castellano's kitchen, and he sure as hell knew what we had gotten from the installation at Angelo Ruggiero's place out in Cedarhurst. Being an astute guy, Dearie also knew about a lot of the other stuff we had working; being an ambitious guy, he naturally wanted a part of it.

What Ray Dearie most certainly did not want, however, was to let our agents make the arrests of Angelo Ruggiero, Gene Gotti, and the other eleven defendants in the drug case until his senior narcotics prosecutor got himself up to speed on the investigation. Jimmy Kossler and Tom Scheer, Kossler's boss, who headed the Criminal Division in the New York office, went around and around with Dearie on this, but the guy wouldn't budge. In Washington, I pushed every button I could, but rules were rules, I was told: When the U.S. Attorney says you can make the arrests, you can do so—not before.

The timing would have been no big deal except for one thing: We wanted to make the busts of Ruggiero and Company while we still had our Title III up and running in Castellano's kitchen, and we were beginning to have technical problems with the thing. If we were up on Paulie when the indictment was returned, there was no telling what kind of leads he might give us. Castellano's ban on drug trafficking may have been bullshit, but once he learned what his guys in the Bergen Fish and Hunt Club were up to, the boss of bosses would be livid.

We knew about the bad blood in the Gambino family from our Title IIIs. What we didn't understand was how bad things had actually gotten in the family. They were ready to go to war.

The Gottis, not the smartest of guys, understood that. Gene

Gotti explained as much in a conversation with Angelo Ruggiero. We got it on tape.

"You're making me ask you, like a fucking hard-on, for a favor. I'm begging you—"

"It's a different story now. Not even Neil, no more. It's Paul."

"Oh, Paul's thinking about doing something."

"Oh, oh, oh, oh, oh . . . [They] made a pact: Any friend of ours that gets pinched for junk, or that they hear of anything about junk, they kill them."

What Paul Castellano had planned, as we would find out, was more strategic than that. The rift between him and Neil Dellacroce was growing deeper, and the Bergen Fish and Hunt crew was clearly aligning itself with Mr. Neil. As the most violent crew in the Gambino family, the Gottis and the other members of the Bergen Fish and Hunt crew would be tough adversaries. Castellano came up with an idea: The crew would be disbanded.

Thanks to the electronics wizards from Headquarters, we had fixed the problem with Castellano's radio, so Phil Rizzuto was no longer interfering with our listening in on the conversations from Paulie's kitchen. The problem we couldn't fix was a technical glitch that made the transmission part of the Title III cut in and out, depriving us of whole chunks of conversation. John Kravec and Joe Cantamesa had gone out to Castellano's mansion two or three times over the past few months to try and fix the thing. Each time, Paulie—or Tommy Bilotti in his crummy toupee—would greet Cantamesa warmly at the door, and Joe would explain how he was just checking up on the repair job, making sure everything was okay. Paulie thanked him and shuffled off to more pressing matters with his little Gloria. Alone, Cantamesa fiddled furiously with the balky transmitter—to no avail.

The law on Title IIIs is very clear. As long as you maintain probable cause, you can keep the bug or microphone up and working; lose the probable cause, though, and you have to pull the Title III out. With the Title III in Paul Castellano's kitchen malfunctioning, we lost our probable cause. It was heartbreaking, especially to Cantamesa and Kravec, who had worked so hard to get the thing inside the Castellano mansion in the first place. But rules were rules, and despite what some of these oddball conspiracy theorists would have you believe, the FBI played by the goddamned rules.

Three weeks before Ray Dearie finally gave us the go-ahead to arrest Angelo Ruggiero, Gene Gotti, and the others, the order was given to pull the Title III out of Castellano's house. There was nothing we could do about it. So we took down more than a dozen high-powered Gambino family members, and that did hurt the family. But a terrific investigative lead had been blown, and for no good reason that I could understand.

The troubles we were having in Brooklyn wouldn't even be worth mentioning except that they were a small part of a bigger problem, and that problem was bad and getting worse.

Several years earlier, New York Police Department detectives from Queens had succeeded in obtaining a court order allowing them to install a secret listening device inside the very same Bergen Fish and Hunt Club that Bruce Mouw and his BQ-5 agents were working on now. Unfortunately, the Title III the cops had installed hadn't yielded enough information to bring an indictment. What it had done was energize a very talented young federal prosecutor in Brooklyn.

Diane Giacalone was born in Ozone Park, not much more than a mile from the Bergen Fish and Hunt Club. The Giacalone family and the Gotti family shared the same neighborhood, but whereas the Gottis turned out to be scum, the Giacalones turned out Diane, a tough and extremely dedicated public servant. Smart and aggressive, a ferociously hard worker, Giacalone was an Italian American who was basically motivated like me and Joe Pistone and others to go after the Cosa Nostra and go after them hard. More than a year earlier, Giacalone had won approval from Ray Dearie to pull together a task force to see if she could bring a case against the Bergen Fish and Hunt crew. On the task force were two FBI agents, several agents from the U.S. Drug Enforcement Administration, and a half-dozen investigators from the Queens district attorney's office and the Queens detective squad.

For all its good intentions, the Giacalone effort was flawed from the start. First of all, here was a classic organized-crime investigation, but it was being worked not by the Brooklyn strike force but by the U.S. Attorney's office. This meant that the wires on the investigation would be crossed right from the very start. Second, with no disrepect to anyone on the task force, only the FBI had any real expertise in making the kind of case Giacalone wanted to make, a RICO case that would take out the entire Gotti crew. Even the two FBI agents on the task force, both of whom were terrific investigators, were not organized-crime specialists. The two agents had come in on the Giacalone task force, in fact, through a back door. They had been investigating an armored-truck hijacking, and the leads had led them to the Bergen Fish and Hunt crew.

Either one of these issues could have been resolved happily, in my opinion, if Diane Giacalone turned up enough evidence in the old Title III files and if her task force could develop enough new evidence to bring an indictment. In that case, I would have supported Giacalone's effort 100 percent. Where our paths were going to part real quickly, though, was if Giacalone's investigation of the Gotti crew began to jeopardize our strategic investigation of the Gambino family. In that case, as I told Bruce Mouw and Jim Kossler, all bets were off.

Bruce Mouw and his agents had developed a handful of grade A informants on the Gambinos, and we had had terrific success with the Title IIIs at Angelo Ruggiero's place and at Paul Castellano's house in Staten Island. We would not, under any circumstance, jeopardize those kinds of assets simply to go after one pissant group of wise guys. Going after a crew went counter to our strategy—which was now the strategy that had been blessed by FBI Headquarters. It also went counter to the core of the Blakey religion to which Kallstrom, Kossler, Mouw, and so many of our other agents and supervisors had converted.

In short, it was just not going to happen. After all we had had to go through to get the strategy in place, we were not going to throw it out for one case no matter who the defendants were or how much we pissed off the higher-ups at Justice. We had come much too far to start screwing around now.

There was a parting of the ways, as it turned out, and it was not a pleasant one. After it became clear how things were shaking out with the Giacalone task force, Jim Kossler and I discussed the situation, and a decision was made to pull our two agents out. There were recriminations then and later that the FBI was sandbagging Giacalone, that we had "double-crossed" her. The theories behind these complaints were nonsense. The FBI wanted John Gotti for ourselves, our critics said, as if John Gotti were worth devoting that kind of time and effort to. For my money, there was no way in the world Gotti was big enough or important enough to make him an investigative target if it would jeopardize a broader investigation that would give us the Gambino family. The way I saw it, guys like Paul Castellano and Ralph Scopo—wise guys who controlled the really big stuff—were worth a dozen miserable mutts like John Gotti.

No matter what you do, there are always going to be critics in life, and my basic rule is to simply pay them no mind. They could bring in the whole damn New York Police Department to investigate a guy like Gotti if they wanted and I would still say the same thing: Sorry, you people are missing the big picture. Besides, without the FBI, there was no way Giacalone and her task force were going to get the goods they needed to bring a case and win a conviction.

That was simply a fact of life.

And that's what I tried to deal in—facts.

The problems with Brooklyn would just not go away. Happily, our investigation of the Colombo family was developing nicely, the heart of our case the racketeering and extortion counts aris-

ing from the Mafia families' manipulation of the cement industry. On top of that, the conversations Frankie Ancona started
pulling in enabled us to build an even broader case.

As an informant, Ancona was a lot of trouble. He was in and
out of the Witness Protection Program, not once but three times.
He drove poor Denis Maduro nuts, showing up outside his Manhattan apartment once in the middle of the night, for example, going up and down the street crooning, "Denis, Denis
Madurooo! Come out, come out, wherever you are." Denis
thought Ancona was in some kind of trouble again, but it turned
out the guy just wanted to talk, so Maduro walked him down
the street and bought him a cup of coffee at an all-night diner.

For all his nuttiness, Ancona did get us some awfully good
conversations. And as sorry a guy as he was, a lot of our guys
genuinely liked him. A bunch of agents took up a collection to
buy clothes for the Ancona kids one Christmas, for instance;
Frankie got all choked up.

As for what Ancona gave us that was indictable, it was good
stuff, not central to the case but helpful. Some of what happened
to Ancona also shows what absolute lowlifes the wise guys were.
Take Gerry Lang, for example. Back in 1978, Ancona had borrowed $3,500 from Lang at an interest rate of 4 percent a week.
Religiously, Ancona had dropped off the weekly vigorish payment at the club where Lang was hanging out at the time; the
bartender would write down a note with Ancona's name on it,
wrap it around the envelope with Frankie's cash in it, then throw
it into a big fishbowl on the bar. Ancona remembered the fishbowl. "There were a lot of envelopes with notes on them in the
bowl," Ancona told Maduro. "It was a goddamned big bowl,
too."

Frankie Ancona had lousy luck. He got sick, went to a hospital, then after the wise guys came calling around to his em-
ployer, a fuel-oil company in Queens, his boss fired him. "By
phone," Ancona remembered. "While I was in the hospital."

A guy like Gerry Lang didn't give a shit. Lang had all these
fancy suits, but he couldn't spare the time of day for a schmuck

like Frankie Ancona. After he found out Ancona had a mortgage on a little house out in Queens, Lang simply ordered Ancona to sign the deed over. Ancona, knowing nothing and scared out of his mind, agrees. But he asks, can he go into the house first, get some clothes for his wife and family, maybe pick up some of the kids' toys.

No way, Gerry Lang says. Leave now.

This is the dead of winter, by the way, February, and Frankie Ancona, his wife, and his three kids have to leave their home that very afternoon. They slept in the family car for the next ten days, and it's a wonder the kids didn't die of exposure or something. Anyway, we planned to put all that in the affidavits and other court documents supporting the indictment. Let the world know what kind of people these wise guys were.

A bunch of assholes.

31

AS much as there were genuinely serious problems with some of the people we worked with, there were pluses too—big pluses —and it's not just the rosy vision of hindsight, but the pluses far outweighed the problems.

Take the New York City Police Department detectives we worked with, for example. The NYPD gets its share of knocks, and God knows it has had its problems. All I'll say is that the one hundred or so police officers and detectives we had working with the nearly three hundred FBI agents we had targeting the mob in New York were the best.

Of course, it's easy to take good things like that for granted and focus on what isn't going right. The problems we were having with the strike force and the U.S. Attorney's office in Brooklyn, for instance, made me crazy because they forced us to waste so much time and energy.

But in the rare instances when I could sit back and take stock, I tried to put those problems into perspective. Sure, there are rough patches in all our lives, but it would be unpardonable to let my problems blind me to all the blessings I had received. My family, first of all—Linda, Maria, and Joe—had given me love and support unstintingly, no matter how hard the going got. There were the friendships I had been blessed with, too—with people like Kallstrom and Kossler, with Joe Pistone, Barbara Jones, and Louie Freeh. And then there were the friends and teammates I worked with every day. Take the dedication of a Bruce Mouw or a Damon Taylor for granted? You do and that's when life really runs off the rails.

For all the frustrations of life at Headquarters, for all the setbacks we had suffered in trying to implement our strategy against the Cosa Nostra and then make big cases, I tried to remind myself how easy it is to lose perspective. Time can drag like a long string, but I'll tell you one way to cut it short: Focus on the pluses, not the problems.

This little motivational tape actually popped out of my head as I thought about Ron Goldstock. Goldstock was in charge of the New York State Organized Crime Task Force, and he was as committed to the war against the Italian Mafia as any one of our agents and supervisors. A product of Harvard Law School, Goldstock had gone on to what we then called the Rackets Bureau in the office of the legendary New York district attorney Frank Hogan. After leaving the D.A.'s office, Ron had gone up to Ithaca, where Bob Blakey was preaching the gospel of RICO in the frozen wastes of northern New York State. Blakey, as I've said, was a gentle man with the soul of a warrior. The same can be said for Ron. He could have coasted on an academic sinecure up in Ithaca for as long as he wanted, but by the time I got to New York in the late 1970s, he was back down in the trenches again, running the New York State Organized Crime Task Force.

By late 1983, while we were moving hard against the Colombo and Gambino families, Goldstock had zeroed in on the Luccheses, and unbeknownst to us, he had hit pay dirt of his own. The boss of the Lucchese family was an old Mustache Pete named Anthony "Tony Ducks" Corallo. There were a couple of explanations for Tony Ducks's nickname. I had always heard that he got it because he had ducked so many grand jury subpoenas over the years.

The important thing, in any case, was that Goldstock and the detectives who worked with him had spotted the old man time and again being driven around the city by a Lucchese family capo named Sal Avellino. Avellino was something of a showboat, and he drove a handsome Jaguar sedan, in a color the manufacturer described as "British Green." Goldstock and his guys had to jump through the same hoops we did on these things, but after a lot of hard work, Ron finally developed the probable cause he needed to install a Title III in Avellino's Jaguar.

That was about midway through 1983, and a few months later, Goldstock and his guys were ready to actually do the installation. Like Jimmy Kallstrom—these Special Ops enthusiasts are a strange fraternity, a combination of cops, spooks, and gadget freaks—Goldstock left nothing to chance. Somewhere he got himself an exact duplicate of the Jaguar XJ-6 Avellino drove. Then he got his team of black-bag guys together and held a stopwatch on them while they disassembled the car, installed the secret listening device, then put the automobile back together again.

Goldstock's tech guys had approached the job like a team of NASA engineers. The Title III would have to rely on power from the Jaguar's battery, so they studied that issue: How to install the bug so as to drain the least amount of energy possible? Then there were the other problems, the usual ones we had with Title IIIs: where to install the thing to get the best reception possible. Goldstock's guys monkeyed around with the demo Jaguar long enough to figure out what they wanted to do—the recording and transmission device would go behind the sedan's inside heating and air-conditioning vents. Goldstock kept the stopwatch on his guys, and by the time they finally got their shot, they had the whole thing down to under five minutes—disassembly, installation of the bug, reassembly of the car, and cleanup.

The Title III went into Avellino's Jaguar on a rainy night out on Long Island, and it started producing almost instantly. Tony Ducks and Sal Avellino sure did like to talk.

Ron Goldstock and I had known each other for years, and I was thrilled when he cut us in on his coup. No thanks to me, we now had the boss of the Lucchese family wired for sound.

That made it four of five families under the gun.

Anthony "Fat Tony" Salerno was the only one of the five New York bosses we didn't have directly in our sights, and that was a source of considerable discussion between me and Jim Kossler. Fat Tony was the boss of the Genovese family, and after the Gambinos, there was none bigger.

From the Title IIIs we had at the Casa Storta, from what Vinnie DePenta had heard over at the D&M warehouse, even from what crazy Frankie Ancona was revealing to Denis Maduro, we had a hell of an intriguing picture of Fat Tony and the influence he wielded. As the boss of the Genovese family, Fat Tony had a seat on the commission, we knew that. But we were also picking up information about the clout he had with the Cosa Nostra in Chicago and Buffalo and about how he was actually running the mob's entire operation out in Cleveland.

The commission stuff alone had goosed us into action. A lot of what we had picked up on the Title IIIs was hard to make sense of, with the way the wise guys talked in shorthand or in grunts and half-swallowed idiocies. Sometimes, even if they were speaking the King's English—a rare thing, believe me— technical problems like the kind we had on the Castellano wire or background noise of the type we had in the Casa Storta made it difficult to figure out what the hell was going on. Even with those problems, though, the sheer volume of the conversations we were picking up at table 1 in the Casa Storta indicated very clearly that Fat Tony was the boss a lot of the wise guys turned to when they had a problem to hash out.

Jim Kossler put one of our best supervisors on the Genovese investigation. Dave Binney was a West Point graduate who had served some very tough duty in Vietnam. He had joined the Bureau not long after that and started working for me almost right away. It didn't take a genius to see that Binney had the tools of an exceptional special agent. As the supervisor of Squad C-22 in the FBI's New Rochelle office, Binney had played a key role in our investigation of the Pizza Connection case. The Pizza case was still going strong, and we had developed some promising spin-offs from it, but Kossler and I both felt we had to stick to the strategy we had outlined on the Cosa Nostra, and that meant going after all five Mafia families hard.

So Binney and his C-22 agents got the Fat Tony case, and it was something of a letdown. It wasn't as sexy as the Pizza Connection case, for one thing. And Binney and his people would be starting just about from scratch.

It seemed we were always doing that.

Like the pros they were, though, Binney and the C-22 agents never complained once. Instead, they started spending some very long days and nights up in East Harlem. It is not generally known, even by a lot of savvy New Yorkers, but there is a part of Harlem that lies hard up against the East River just above 110th Street that is as Italian as the back streets of Naples or Palermo. Mention Italian enclaves and most New Yorkers will think of Little Italy, way downtown, where we had set up Vinnie DePenta at D&M. Italian Harlem, as it is known to those who live there, has pretty much the same feel as Little Italy, except, of course, there were no tourists and not as much general bull-shit. There was one other big difference, too, and that was that in Italian Harlem, there was only one guy who was boss.

That guy was Fat Tony Salerno.

Fat Tony lived in Italian Harlem from Mondays to Thursdays. On Fridays he almost always left for the weekend for his farm in upstate New York, in the town of Rhinebeck. When he was in the city, Fat Tony seldom left the old neighborhood, preferring to spend his days shooting the breeze with his wise-guy buddies in one of two social clubs he basically used as his places of business. The first place was the Palma Boy Social Club. That was on 115th Street between First Avenue and Pleasant Avenue. The other place was just around the corner, on First Avenue, just south of 115th Street.

In September 1983, Binney walked into the federal court-house on St. Andrew's Plaza with a thick sheaf of papers in his briefcase. He walked out a few hours later with the signature of a U.S. District Court judge on every page. The paperwork contained applications for Title IIIs—quite a few of them, in fact. Working with Jim Kallstrom, Binney decided to wire Fat Tony's two social clubs, his house, and a pay phone on the street, to mention just a few locations.

Before he prepared the paperwork for the judge, Binney had assigned one of his C-22 agents, a guy named Pete Kelleher, to find places near the social clubs where we could observe and monitor the Title IIIs. A native New Yorker, a veteran organized-crime investigator (Pete had spent something like ten years working for Neil Welch in Detroit), Kelleher had a hell of a job on his hands. Fat Tony virtually owned the neighborhood, so anybody strolling around looking to rent space for some mysterious purpose was going to have a lot of doors slammed in his face. That, or worse. The other reason Pete's job was so tough was that Kallstrom wanted an airtight surveillance of Fat Tony both visually, through several cameras, and electronically, through the hidden microphones and telephone bugs.

Wait till the inspectors catch wind of this, I thought, after Kallstrom told me his plan. They're going to go nuts.

If Jim Kallstrom had decided to become a criminal, you would have had to call him an evil genius. The plan he came up with for the electronic surveillance of Fat Tony was downright diabolical. Not only did Kallstrom want a Title III in Fat Tony's apartment and in the two social clubs he frequented; he also intended to bug the pizza place next door to the Palma Boy; the wise guys sometimes went in to use the phone there. He also wanted a bug on the pay phone on the corner between the two clubs; Fat Tony's guys made calls from there, too.

That was just the beginning, though.

The Kallstrom game plan called for a total of seven hidden microphones or telephone taps and three video cameras triangulated on the front door of the Palma Boy. If only Fat Tony knew what we had in store for him, I thought, reviewing the plan; the old bastard would lose his lunch.

Pete Kelleher, God bless him, somehow got us into every place Kallstrom needed his guys. It wasn't easy, either. First, Kelleher had tried a hospital for the criminally insane. It was just down the block from the Palma Boy, and Kelleher figured it was a good bet, since it was one of the few places in the neighborhood that Fat Tony didn't have his hooks into. The hospital was a no-go, for technical reasons. Kelleher kept working it, though.

He had an easy way about him, and somehow he finally got it done. He found and rented us space in a warehouse on 110th Street; he got us into the upper floor of a bank—the guy just didn't take no for an answer.

The installations, of course, would be as tricky as ever.

By the time Kelleher had gotten us set up with listening posts and camera emplacements, it had turned cold, but Binney and Kallstrom figured that was good: What better time to go busting into a place than the dead of a bitter winter night?

That's the way Special Ops guys think.

At 3:00 A.M. on a frigid December morning, the usual FBI procession rolled out. There was Binney's C-22 squad, Kallstrom's Special-Operations team, and the lock guys to help us get inside. Italian Harlem had never seen such an invasion.

The Palma Boy was tricky. The way Kallstrom's guys had it figured, they would have to disable the alarm that had been installed on the outside wall of the place, then do some drilling so they could get the transmitter seated into the bricks. Positioning the thing like that would allow us to pick up the signal from the transmitter at our listening post down the block in Kelleher's warehouse.

Drilling into bricks in the middle of the night is obviously not a real good way of making a covert entry, but Kallstrom had a solution to that problem. Somehow he had persuaded someone to loan a few of his agents a bunch of New York City Sanitation Department trucks, and just before his entry team broke out their equipment for the assault on the Palma Boy, a half-dozen garbage trucks started rolling up and down 115th Street and First Avenue, FBI agents in grungy coveralls swinging off the back, throwing trash cans into the trucks' giant maws, and generally trying to make as much noise as possible.

As soon as the trucks started rolling, two of Kallstrom's guys, Mike Utaro and Mike McDeavitt, began their assault on the Palma Boy. Slouched in his government car in an alley just off 115th Street, Kallstrom had the heater going full blast, and a fiendish grin played across his face as one garbage truck and then another rumbled past him.

The alarm on the Palma Boy was high up on the outside wall of the club, so Mike Utaro had to climb up on McDeavitt's shoulders; it was faster and less conspicuous than lugging a ladder around. Utaro, you may recall, was the agent who had had his electric socks short out on him when we were going in on the installation at Donnie Shacks's Maniac Club over in Brooklyn. Small but tough, Mike had a black belt in karate, and if the occasion arose, he could take out several guys much bigger than himself. Utaro had started out literally as a kid in the Bureau, working as a clerk to help pay his way through school. Now here he was a special agent working for Jim Kallstrom on what would come to be regarded as one of the most outstanding Special Operations jobs in the history of the FBI.

Except it very nearly wasn't.

As Utaro wobbled on Mike McDeavitt's shoulders, fiddling with the alarm on the Palma Boy, a half-dozen squad cars filled with New York City's finest came roaring down First Avenue the wrong way, sirens off but lights blazing. The marked units were driving up on sidewalks, bouncing over curbs, and before anyone could do a thing, Utaro and McDeavitt were surrounded by a dozen cops, little Mike still balancing up on McDeavitt's shoulders.

Jim Kallstrom, needless to say, was no longer grinning at the garbage trucks. What he was doing was striding briskly from his car across 115th Street and doing a very creditable imitation of the last guy on earth you'd ever want to fuck with.

Against the brick wall of the Palma Boy, Mike Utaro struggled to maintain his perch on McDeavitt's shoulders, wobbling ever so slightly but saying nothing.

The cops and their sergeant eyeballed the two agents wordlessly, their revolvers drawn.

Kallstrom approached the cops rapidly, his breath condensing like steam from a runaway locomotive. "It was weird," he recalled afterward. "It was like back in Vietnam when you're waiting for the mortars to come in and everything's quiet. No one moved. No one said a word."

With the cops and our two agents frozen in place as if on a

Kabuki stage set, Kallstrom grabbed the NYPD sergeant rudely by the elbow and stuck his unshaven chin in the poor man's face. "We're on the job," he said. "Now get the fuck out of here."

The sergeant looked at Jim. Then he looked at poor Utaro balancing up in McDeavitt's shoulders in the bitter wind. "Okay, guys," he said. "Let's get the fuck out of here."

Within minutes, the blue-and-whites had vanished.

Minutes after that, Mike Utaro bypassed the alarm. "Done," he said, blowing on his hands. "Let's get the show on the road."

Kallstrom led the entry team through the grimy bowels of the basement beneath the Palma Boy. Once again, he had chosen John Kravec as his point man.

"Ready, John?"

"Ready as ever, boss."

"Problems?"

"Problems, boss? Nah—only that this'll never work. We're gonna get our asses in a sling, that's all."

"Other than that, no problems, though?"

"Right, boss. Other than that, no problems."

In the basement of the Palma Boy there were big problems, and they came in the form of rats. These were not your everyday, garden-variety city rat, either, the furtive little things that look like a mouse, maybe, but three or four times larger. You've heard the expression "rats as big as cats"; these things in the Palma Boy were bigger than that—and they were mean. Clenching a flashlight between his teeth, Kravec fiddled with the wire he had to run up through the floor of the Palma Boy. "Stop kicking me, boss, will ya?"

Kallstrom had a high-intensity flashlight, and he played on the ceiling above them so that Kravec could see. "I'm not fucking kicking you, John. What're you crazy?"

"What the fuck, then?"

Kallstrom looked down, and a rat the size of a cocker spaniel was chewing on Kravec's calf. Jimmy kicked at it, and the rat lunged for him.

"Fuck it, boss. Let's just get the thing in here, okay?"

THE GOOD GUYS

FBI agent Sean McWeeney (left) with the author at the author's induction into the Italian Historical Society of America.

Bruce Mouw overcame an incredible number of bureaucratic obstacles to finally bring John Gotti and the Gambino family hierarchy to its knees.

G. Robert Blakey, father of the RICO statute and catalyst for our many successes.

Jules Bonavolonta, standing, with tough prosecutor Barbara Jones and undercover FBI Agent Joe Pistone.

Jim Kallstrom built New York's Special Operations Group into the best around and is today the agent in charge of the FBI's entire New York Field Division—the Bureau's largest.

Special Agent Lou Vernazza.

At his judicial appointment celebration: FBI Director Louis Freeh with wife, Marilyn, mother, Bernice, and father, William.

The Colombo family prosecution team: (from left) Aaron Marcu, Bruce Baird, then United States Attorney Rudy Giuliani, and Frank Sherman.

Michael Chertoff successfully prosecuted the Mafia Commission and went on to become a highly successful U.S. Attorney for the State of New Jersey.

Pat Marshall ran the case that would ultimately fulfill Bob Blakey's dream—"to indict every boss."

Special Agent Brian Taylor led the FBI's civil RICO charge against mobsters running New York's Fulton Fish Market.

THE BAD GUYS

Paul Castellano, who was the boss of the Gambino family from 1976 until his murder on a New York street on December 16, 1985.

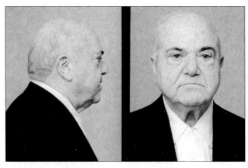

Anthony "Fat Tony" Salerno, Genovese family boss, exerted tremendous influence over the Teamsters Union. He died in prison in 1994.

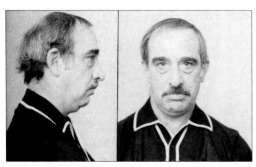

Carmine Persico, also known as "Snake," boss of the Colombo family, is currently incarcerated.

Dominick "Donnie Shacks" Montemarano, Colombo family capo, is currently incarcerated.

Frank "the Beast" Falanga, Colombo soldier and ruthless enforcer, died just prior to standing trial.

Ralph Scopo, Colombo soldier and union business agent, was responsible for controlling construction contracts. He died in prison.

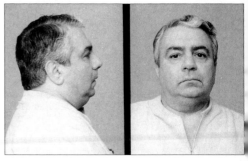

Anthony "Tony Ducks" Corallo, Lucchese family boss, is currently incarcerated.

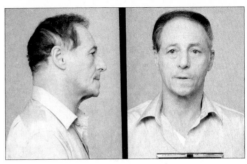

Christopher "Christy Tick" Furnari, Lucchese family *consigliere*, is currently incarcerated.

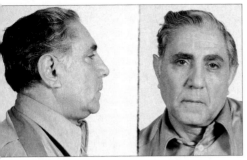

Philip "Rusty" Rastelli, Bonanno family boss who ran the family from prison for several years.

Frank "Frankie Loc" Locascio, Gambino family *consigliere*, is currently incarcerated.

John Gotti, Gambino family boss, currently serving a life sentence.

Aniello "Neil" Dellacroce, Gambino family underboss and John Gotti mentor, died of natural causes in 1985.

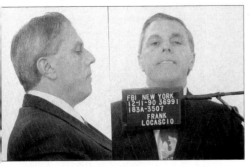

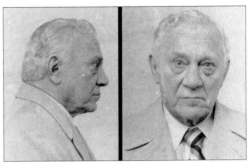

Angelo Ruggiero, Gambino family capo and one of John Gotti's closest friends and supporters, died of natural causes in 1989.

Benjamin "Lefty Guns" Ruggiero (right) with Mike Sabella, Bonanno family capo.

FBI agent Joe Pistone (left), undercover as Donnie Brasco, with Bonanno family acting boss Dominick "Sonny Black" Napolitano in Florida.

From left, Nicky Auletta, Louis De Napoli, Anthony "Fat Tony" Salerno (Genovese family boss) with cigar, and Vincent "Fish" Cafaro, in front of the Palma Boys Social Club in East Harlem.

Sonny Black emerges from a motel coffee shop with Florida boss Santo Trafficante. The two forged a new alliance between the Bonanno and Trafficante families to share gambling and other illegal activities. From *Donnie Brasco: My Undercover Life in the Mafia*, by Joseph D. Pistone with Richard Woodley (New York: NAL Books, 1988).

Sonny Black summoned the top members of his crew to plan emergency strategy regarding the stunning news about "Donnie Brasco." From left: Boobie Cerasani, Nicky Santora, Lefty Ruggiero, Sonny Black. From *Donnie Brasco: My Undercover Life in the Mafia*, by Joseph D. Pistone with Richard Woodley (New York: NAL Books, 1988).

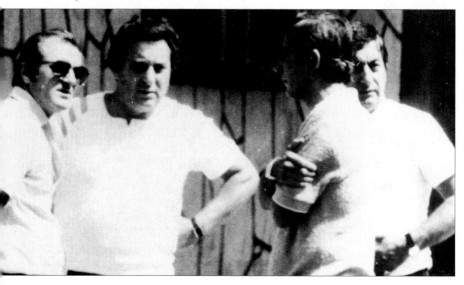

Lefty Ruggiero, Agent Pistone's Mafia "partner" for five years, stands in the doorway of the Motion Lounge as the "Donnie Brasco" revelation sinks in. From *Donnie Brasco: My Undercover Life in the Mafia*, by Joseph D. Pistone with Richard Woodley (New York: NAL Books, 1988).

FBI agent installing a bug inside the Ravenite Social Club, during the Gotti investigation.

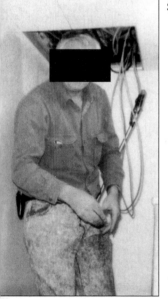

FBI agents during the installation of microphones in the Ravenite Social Club (photos are of John Gotti and Neil Dellacroce).

Kallstrom took a few more swipes at the rat, but he couldn't keep it away from poor Kravec's leg. Kravec kept right on working, ramming the wire through the floorboard above him. It took another ten minutes or so to complete the job.

"Okay, boss, we're in."

"Shit, John, you okay?" Kallstrom took a vicious kick at the rat and sent the son of a bitch flying.

"Yeah, yeah. Let's get the fuck out of here, huh?"

Except for the rats—Kravec emerged from the basement of the Palma Boy with shredded pants and a bloody leg—the installation at the Palma Boy went fine.

On arising the following morning, several residents of Italian Harlem commented favorably and with evident surprise on the sudden tidiness of their streets. It had been years, they said, since the place had been quite so clean.

32

LIKE every other spawn of the Cosa Nostra, the Mafia Commission was the product of greed and violence.

In 1930, the Castellammarese War—it was named for the primary participants in the battle, who hailed from the mob-dominated Sicilian village of Castellammare del Golfo—had left the streets of New York littered with corpses. America's newly transplanted Italian crime bosses had met a couple of years earlier, in Cleveland in 1928, but the war among the Castellammarese prompted the first true meeting of the Mafia Commission. That was on a spring day in 1931, and it was convened by that brilliant misanthrope Charles "Lucky" Luciano. More than three hundred Mafia dons, soldiers, and capos showed up, and the agenda was simple: a discussion of business interests, where they overlapped, and how to avoid future wars.

As Paul Castellano would remind his fellow bosses many years later, wars were bad for business: Families had to learn to get along. It was hard to get along, though, when there were so many greedy and dysfunctional family members. Take Albert Anastasia, for instance. An exceedingly fat man who amused himself by sticking the hands of his loan-shark debtors into a tank filled with hungry piranhas, Anastasia was a psychopath, and he wasn't the worst of the commission members, not by a long shot.

The personalities were not what interested me and Jim Kossler; what had us hooked was what the commission did. Blakey had talked of indictments of every boss. Nail the commission, Kossler and I thought, and we would have all the biggest bosses; more important, we would have the board of directors of the entire Cosa Nostra. That was the goal.

This will give you an idea of how far we had come, not with all the Special Operations stuff, as important as that was. But in the way we were planning to attack the mob now, in the way Kossler and I began diagramming the play we intended to run against the commission, it was almost like the kind of corporate warfare the big investment banks and law firms were playing just a few blocks from our office at 26 Federal. When I talked to Kossler from Washington or when the two of us sat down together in New York, we didn't talk about putting up more Title IIIs or assigning more agents to cases. What we talked about was building a legal architecture that would imprison the members of the Mafia Commission in the facts of their own existence.

Like the loveliest architecture, I like to think ours had the virtue of simplicity. With the investigations we had up and running on the Cosa Nostra families in New York, our squads— Bruce Mouw's, Damon Taylor's, and Dave Binney's—were overwhelmed with the volume of evidence the Title IIIs, the informants, and the agents were pulling in. To make the commission case, we didn't need new evidence—at least not much of it. What we needed was to think like Bob Blakey had taught us. Or, to be more precise, what we needed was to take Blakey's thinking about evidence and strategy and push it to the absolute limit.

With the New York investigations driving ahead under full power, the time to do that was now. The Italian Mafia Commission had been in business for more than half a century.

I figured that was just about long enough.

On a bright winter day near the end of January, I got an early shuttle from Washington's National Airport, grabbed a yellow cab at La Guardia, and was at 26 Federal before ten.

Kossler was waiting for me.

Jim had a small office on the top floor, the twenty-eighth, and we spent countless hours there talking, Kossler behind his desk blowing smoke rings toward the ceiling, me leaning back in a comfortable armchair against the wall to the left of the window.

"So what do we know?"

"The Palma Boy wires are unbelievable, Jules." Kossler fell into his chair and fumbled for matches.

"What do we have, three teams on the muffs now?"

"Round the clock. Binney's got 'em on eight-hour shifts at the warehouse, yeah. It's a killer, but what're you gonna do?"

"Yeah, I know." I didn't mention it, but the inspectors from Headquarters were already making noises about the number of wires we had up on the Fat Tony case.

"We had a little trouble with the wire in the Palma Boy, but Kallstrom's guys got that fixed, so we're in business there again." Kossler got the pipe fired and leaned back.

"Yeah, they're moving, it sounds like."

"Yeah, but what we've got to do next, that's what worries me."

"We've just got to make it happen, though, Jim."

"Yeah, but think of it." Kossler contemplated a perfect smoke ring as it wafted heavenward. "In all the years there's been a Bureau, there's never been a case like this. Never."

"I know, I know. And I know we got about a ton or more of Title III transcripts."

"Literally."

"And no one—not you or me or Mouw or Binney or Damon or anyone—has ever looked through all that shit."

"Well, someone's gonna have to do it now."

"Damn right. If we're ever going to make a case against the commission itself, that's the only way."

"Look, I know. We agree, okay?"

"Okay—but the question is who? Look, we've got guys who can work undercover, string wires, kick down doors, and shoot people if they have to."

Kossler laughed.

"But what we really need here is someone like you, Jimmy."

"Bullshit."

"Bullshit, my ass. What we need here is an intellectual. Someone who can take his time, go through all this stuff, make the historical connections, and make sense of all the different ties among the families and how the fucking commission plays into all of that."

"Look, Jules, I've been thinking about this, too, okay? The first thing we've got to do is settle on the squad, and I think you and I see eye to eye on that."

"C-10, right?"

"Yeah, DeVecchio'll be perfect for the job, I think."

"Shit, Lynn was in New York even before I got here. He knows all the families, all the players."

"Yeah, and he's got the flexibility to take it on where the other guys just don't."

"Well, Binney's clearly got his hands full, like you say."

"And Bruce is up to his eyeballs on the Gambinos."

"The same for Damon on the Colombos."

"Right. Now with the Bonannos, Lynn has no responsibility for the murder of the three capos."

"They're working that in Brooklyn-Queens."

"Right. And after the trial the fucking Bonannos are still trying to catch their breath."

"They're barely in business, the way Lynn tells it."

"Which is why C-10 is perfect for the commission case."

"Okay, but who's the agent? Who's the fucking *case* agent?"

"That's what I've been leading up to." Kossler blew a dough-nut-size smoke ring, then blew a quarter-size ring through it.

"That's sort of what I figured." I pushed the sole of one shoe against the edge of Kossler's desk and rocked back in my chair.

"I've got just the guy, Jules. He's perfect."

I racked my brain, trying to thing of the agents on Lynn De-Vecchio's squad, but came up empty. "Okay, who?"

Kossler leaned forward suddenly and put both elbows on his desk. "Pat Marshall, that's who."

I sat forward in my own chair. "Pat Marshall! That's fucking brilliant, Jimmy. Bingo!"

I knew Pat as one of the most even-tempered agents in the entire FBI. Marshall goes maybe 145 pounds soaking wet, but he's a tough guy and an absolute genius at cultivating, recruit-ing, and developing informants, then pumping them for the very last piece of information he needs to make a case. Pat and Kos-sler were close, I knew, and I should have guessed that was who

Kossler had in mind, especially once he laid out his rationale for assigning the commission case to DeVecchio's C-10 squad.

"You agree, then?"

"Shit, yes, Jimmy, let's do it."

"Okay." Kossler's pipe had gone dead, and he spent a minute relighting it. "I'll tell Lynn this afternoon."

On the shuttle back to Washington later that day, I thought about my conversation with Kossler. What the FBI had never done historically—Hoover's own personality, indeed, had militated against this—was to foster a culture of intellectuality. In the old days we had a hell of a lot of agents—white males almost exclusively—who were content to make their numbers, take their promotions, and go through the motions.

This had changed, oddly enough, with Hoover's decision to accept former military officers into the FBI. That was really where I saw the changes in FBI thinking coming from—from the agents who had served in Vietnam. Guys like Jim Kallstrom and Dave Binney. They had seen the worst of the shit in Vietnam; they had seen firsthand the shameful and outrageous performance of the Pentagon bureaucracy. They wouldn't put up with it again.

Life was too short.

One consequence of this change was that the rigidity and narrow-mindedness that had been stamped on the FBI by Hoover was eroding. There was a time when a Pat Marshall and perhaps even a Jim Kossler might not have been able to make their way in the Bureau. Not because they weren't exceptional investigators with incredible dedication to the job but just because they didn't fit Hoover's narrow conception of a G-man.

The good news here is that the FBI had to change, too. As America transited the two decades from JFK in Dallas to the 1980s and AIDS, crack cocaine, and homelessness, all of life seemed to require more thought and reflection. That was as true for the FBI as it was for any other group of people. Sure, we had problems with discrimination within the ranks, and that had to go; there was no place for it. But the point is, to run the kind of strategic investigative program Kossler and I wanted, we could not have done it without a whole new class of agents—thinkers, innovators, and self-starters.

Lynn DeVecchio's office was two floors below Kossler's, and he called Marshall in the day after I returned to Washington.

Pat took a seat without being asked. "What's up, boss?"

DeVecchio took a deep breath, then launched into a description of the new assignment. Marshall was to review every Title III transcript we had generated on the Gambino and Colombo family investigations. That meant Vinnie DePenta's conversations with Frankie "the Beast" Falanga at D&M, DeVecchio said. It meant the tapes we had pulled from Angelo Ruggiero and Tommy DiBella's residences. It meant the Casa Storta tapes, the Ralphie Scopo tapes, and the tapes from Donnie Shacks's Maniac Club.

"It's a hell of a big job, Pat."

"That's okay, boss. We'll get it done."

"That's not all of it, though."

"That's okay. What else?"

DeVecchio told Marshall he would have to talk to Ron Goldstock about getting ahold of the transcripts from the conversations Tony Ducks Corallo was having with Sal Avellino in Avellino's green Jaguar.

Marshall nodded. "Okay, boss."

"Then I want you to go see Binney and get him to give you everything he's pulling down from the wires on Fat Tony."

Marshall nodded again, this time saying nothing.

"And then I want you to get with Joe Pistone—but check with Jules first—and get him to give you a full dump on everything he knows about how the bosses work together."

"Right." Mentally, Pat totted up the workload that had just been dumped on his back. "Is that it, boss?"

"Yeah, I think so, Pat. That's it."

Marshall paused half a beat, then looked DeVecchio in the eye. "Boss, I don't mean this disrespectfully, but are you fucking nuts or what? These cases—every one of them—they're still ongoing. No one's going to give me shit. What am I, a magician?"

DeVecchio smiled. "This is big, pal, but don't worry. Jules and Kossler want it, and they want you specifically. Anyone gets in your way, you tell me, and they'll fucking roll him, all right? They'll do the downfield blocking."

Marshall shook his head. "Holy shit," he said. "Holy shit."

I had briefed Rudy Giuliani on our scheme for the commission case before almost everyone else. The first time was more than a year earlier, when Rudy was still in Washington and the idea of indicting the Mafia's board of directors really was no more than a dream. Giuliani loved it.

He was going to depose Joe Bonanno, he said. The eponymous chief of the now-discredited Bonanno family, Joe Bonanno had gone to prison, then written a book—called, for some idiotic reason, *A Man of Honor*. As a former member of the Mafia Commission, Bonanno would be a natural witness, Rudy enthused. I don't actually remember him rubbing his hands together, but that's the way I like to remember it. Rudy had other plans, too. He would put Jimmy Frattiano on the witness stand, he said. Jimmy the Weasel was aptly named. He had turned on his wiseguy brethren and testified against them in court. Why not get him to tell us what he knew about the commission?

Sure, Rudy, I said. Anything you say.

Now that we were ready to actually begin building the case, I took it up with Giuliani again. The enthusiasm had not dissipated; if anything, it had fermented like fine spirits, and it was more powerful than ever. After Rudy and I were done scheming like a couple of schoolkids, Giuliani passed the word on to his bosses at Main Justice in Washington, and they were so enthused they phoned across the street to Judge Webster to congratulate him on the plan. The next thing I know, Kossler is on a plane to Washington, and Sean McWeeney and I are hustling up to the seventh floor for a meeting in the judge's big corner office.

"Brilliant" and "inspired" were some of the words I recall being used. I looked at my shoes and smiled. If Headquarters was on board, shit, all we had to do now was make the case.

33

RALPH Scopo was the wise guy who was right in the middle in the cement-industry scam, and I wanted chapter and verse on that operation. For what he would give us on the case against the Colombos and tell us about the operations of the commission, Scopo was critical.

He obliged us nicely.

Scopo, like most wise guys, had no sense of proportion. He liked cars, for example, but I know a lot of guys who like cars, and they don't go out and buy seven of them; that's what Scopo did. He also did a hell of a lot of business in the cars. Kallstrom's surveillance agents and Damon Taylor's Colombo squad had tailed Scopo all over the city as he made his rounds, putting the arm on contractors, threatening job actions and worse if the guys he was talking to were uncooperative.

Seven cars? Wise guys, what are you going do with them?

So Scopo liked his cars. But what he didn't like was our agents tailing him all over the city. Just before noon on March 7, 1984, we picked up Scopo in a Lincoln out in Queens. Ralphie was riding with a mope named Dave Assalti.

"What's that car?"

"Thunderbird, Ralphie."

"Oh, but the fucking agents got a Firebird." Scopo switched lanes. "What's that, a Pontiac?"

"A Firebird—Pontiac, yeah."

"Shit, same color as the fucking agents'."

"It's like a steel blue, they call that. But that car's all right—it's a little too light."

"Well, okay. But these guys, these fucking agents. They pick me up by my house. They follow me all fucking week. That's why I'm using this car, ya know?"

"I figured that."

"Yeah, I got three cars like this."

"Is that right?"

"Yeah, but the Caddy they know so good. Now this one I think they know, too."

"So you got to get rid of this?"

"So I got to get rid of it. What're you gonna do?"

What we did was attack.

Ralph Scopo's approach to his job was numbingly repetitive. One after the next, he would tell a nervous cement contractor how he had just put the screws to one of his competitors and how, if the guy didn't play ball and pay off his friends, all kinds of unpleasant things would ensue.

"Pay them, pay them," Scopo told one harassed construction-company executive. "It's only fucking money. . . . Besides, look, you got a home and a family. I mean, you don't know what these people are gonna do."

The poor guy in Ralphie Scopo's car, of course, knew exactly what the wise guys would do. And he paid up, like the rest of Scopo's pigeons, promptly.

Rules were rules in this game, and Scopo's pigeons were smart enough to know that the price for breaking them would be high.

What *we* didn't know was how the rules worked.

On a freezing day in March 1984, Scopo filled us in. A guy named Salvatore D'Ambrosia, an employee of a company called All-Boro Paving, came hat in hand to see Scopo, and Ralphie took him for a ride in his Lincoln Continental, driving around out in Queens. D'Ambrosia wanted to know if there was any way he could get a piece of a new construction job out at Kennedy Airport. The job was worth about $200 million.

"Kennedy?"

"Yeah, Ralphie. Could I bid it? As a G.C.?"

"Two hundred million?"

"As a general contractor. Sure, why not?"

"Listen, you ain't doin' the concrete."

"Sure I'm doin' the concrete. Why not?"

"How much is the concrete?" Scopo knew his business. On a $200 million construction job, the concrete work would amount to just a fraction of the total; the big money was in steel, framing, and the rest of it.

"Concrete's gotta be nothing, Ralph."

"Yeah, but how *much?*"

"What could concrete be, seven, eight, nine million?"

"The job's two hundred million!" Scopo snorted in disgust. "The concrete's gotta be twelve million."

"Yeah, okay, twelve. So why can't I do the concrete?"

"You can't do it. Over two million, you can't do it." Scopo sighed, regret barely detectable beneath his glib banter. "Under two million, me, hey, I'll tell you go ahead and do it."

"Who do I gotta see? Tell me who do I gotta see?"

"You gotta see every family!" Scopo was not a patient man, and that fact was betrayed in his changed tone of voice. "The families, they're gonna tell you no. So don't even bother."

"What if Tommy goes and talks to them?"

"They'll tell you no—no matter who talks. I know they'll tell you no. I went through this not once but a hundred times. I can't get it for myself, how could I get it for somebody else?"

"What happens if they give me the job a million at a time?"

Not possible, Scopo said. And besides, there was something else to be considered. "Something important, Sal."

"What's that, Ralph?"

"First of all, the job, it costs you two points."

"Two points?" On this kind of job, that was a lot of money.

"That's what they pay." Scopo made no apologies. "On anything over two million dollars. All the guys in the club pay two points."

The club.

For a wise guy, Ralph Scopo had actually laid out the cement

scam with unusual precision. The way that it worked was like
this: On any cement work in New York over $2 million, only six
firms, all of them previously selected by the Cosa Nostra, would
be allowed to bid. In exchange for that privilege of bidding on
the jobs, the six firms had to pay the Colombo, Gambino, Lucchese, and Genovese families two points on every contract they
got. The families would then divvy the money up equally.

The money was big. On a $2 million contract, for example,
the four families collected a cool $200,000. That was $50,000
apiece—for doing exactly nothing. On contract work under $2
million, Ralph Scopo could give the business to anybody he
wanted, and the Colombo family would pocket the payoff from
the "winning bidder." The rationale for this was also simple:
Scopo was the Colombos' guy, and, hey, the cement thing was
his gig.

For the wise guys, this was their sweetest deal.

It was also the one that would send them down the tubes.

Somehow Mike Chertoff had survived growing up in Elizabeth,
New Jersey, where the contaminants in the air were only slightly
less lethal than those at Chernobyl after the disaster there. That
was the good news.

The bad news was that after surviving the rigors of life at
Harvard Law School, Chertoff had turned up in the offices of
the U.S. Attorney for the Southern District of New York, and his
boss, Rudy Giuliani, had chosen him as the workhorse attorney
on the commission case. Rudy would try the thing once we were
in court; Chertoff would do the grunt work needed to get it
there.

That's just how it is between bosses and subordinates.

If Pat Marshall had a killer job assembling the evidence
against the Mafia's board of directors, Chertoff had one just
as tough: He would have to make the evidence stick. That's a
prosecutor's job, of course; the only difference here was that
Chertoff would be in totally uncharted waters, and for lawyers

that's the same thing as taking off in a boat without a depth chart or map. Which is to say, it makes them very, very nervous.

On the face of it Chertoff was not exactly the most logical choice for Rudy to hand the commission case to. Mike had gotten out of Harvard only six years earlier, had gone into private practice after that, got bored with the pay-for-hire business, then joined the Southern District a little over a year before, in the summer of 1983. Rudy had assigned Mike to work with Barbara Jones, and for anyone interested in learning how to convict wise guys and send them away to some chilly upstate prison for a good long time, there was no finer mentor.

So while Mike had been in the office just a short time, he had also learned a hell of lot working with Barbara. He was also a tough son of a bitch by nature, a tremendously hard worker, and a very quick study. So we were in good hands with our prosecuting attorney, no problem there. Still, Rudy had dumped a monster of a case on poor Chertoff.

Because we had given him the case early on, Pat Marshall had a head start on Chertoff. He also had some good help. Lynn DeVecchio saw right away that the commission case would need more than one agent working it, so he had assigned Special Agent Charlotte Lang to work with Marshall. For twelve years after she had graduated from college, Charlotte had been a grade-school teacher, and then she had worked for IBM; what she really wanted, it turned out, was to be a special agent of the FBI. She made her dream come true in October 1981, and exactly twenty-three months after that she was transferred to New York and assigned to the Organized Crime Section.

The commission case was her first assignment there.

By now we had more than 350 FBI agents and more than 100 New York Police Department officers and detectives working organized crime investigations according to the strategic plan Jimmy Kossler and I had developed. It was a small army, but unlike the army I had fought with back in Vietnam, in New York we didn't have a lot of shifters and bullshit artists and people who would find a way to do just about anything but their jobs.

Sure, we still had interference from Headquarters in Washington, but by now I was actually having a pretty good time keeping those assholes at bay.

What we had on the front lines in New York—and the memories will never fade because I have never experienced anything like it before or since—was a team of agents, police officers, supervisors, and prosecutors who were possessed of a sense of mission like nothing you have ever seen. What we were about was doing good work—and doing good: We thought of ourselves, corny as it may seem now, as the good guys.

For most of us, I don't think we have ever felt, before or since, as energized, as bulletproof, as destined, as we did when we were turning the corner in our war against the Cosa Nostra. Kallstrom, Kossler, and I had all come to the job in different ways. For me and Kossler, it was the inspiration Blakey had provided. We had known what we wanted before that; Blakey had shown us how to achieve it. For people like Kallstrom, a guy who wouldn't agree to fight the war if it was going to be a repeat of the farce he had seen in Vietnam, it was a commitment to better equipment and smarter tactics and strategy. For so many of us—Barbara Jones, Dave Binney, Mike Chertoff, Pat Marshall, Charlotte Lang, Louie Freeh, Bruce Mouw, Denis Maduro—it was a sense that the impossible was now just a matter of time. It was going to happen. The whole thing, as I look back on it, was a strange process. It meant learning as we went along, improvising. Sometimes it simply meant putting your head down and just plowing ahead. However we did it, the days flew by, and although there were the frustrations and bullshit you have with every job, every once in a while one of us would stick our head up and take a look around and recognize it: Goddammit, what we had was a team that could not lose.

I could see it everywhere. Take Charlotte Lang and Pat Marshall. The size of the job they had been handed was incredible, a crushing burden, yet they tackled it immediately and without complaint, wading into the mountain of transcripts, meeting with the supervisors of the ongoing cases—Taylor, Binney, and

Mouw—and talking to Ron Goldstock about the conversations he was picking up from Sal Avellino's Jaguar. A lot of people, good people, might have tried, thrown up their hands, and walked away; Charlotte Lang and Pat Marshall just made it happen.

And that's how we built our cases, with agents like that.

By the time they sat down with Chertoff at 1 St. Andrew's Plaza, Lang and Marshall were convinced that an indictment of the Mafia Commission was achievable.

They had their doubts, of course, for they were plowing brand-new legal ground here. On a breezy afternoon in early April, after meeting with Chertoff, Charlotte was walking back across St. Andrew's Plaza to 26 Federal with Marshall. "This is some hell of a case, Pat. What are we going to do for witnesses?"

Marshall shook his head and laughed. "Never mind witnesses, Charlotte. We need a fucking crime."

Everyone working the commission case knew the problem with it. We could and would allege the outlines of the broad criminal conspiracy. The mountain of transcripts we were pulling in from our investigations of the individual families would ensure that.

But to make the case really unassailable, we needed to allege what the lawyers called "overt acts." This is what Pat Marshall meant when he said we "needed" a crime. In the Bonanno case we had had the overt act involving the murder of the three capos. In the Colombo case it was extortion of the cement companies. In the commission case we had no good overt acts, and we had to be careful of two things. First, we had to make sure we didn't charge anyone with crimes for which they had already been indicted in other cases; that was double jeopardy, a no-no. More important, we needed overt acts that we could allege against the Mafia bosses and then describe before a jury. Getting that evidence was what Lang and Marshall had to do, and the first place to start was with the Title III transcripts.

The stuff was there; I knew it.

One of the first claims the two agents staked was a conversation between Sal Avellino and Salvatore "Tom Mix" Santoro, the underboss of the Lucchese family.

Joe Bonanno, after publishing his book *A Man of Honor*, had become a wise-guy celebrity, making the rounds of the talk shows. Rudy Giuliani had read Bonanno's book several times; all of us had pored over the damn thing, amazed at the things Bonanno had committed to print. In black and white, on page after page, Bonanno described how the Mafia Commission issued policy directives, settled disputes among the families, decided on applications for membership in the Cosa Nostra, and occasionally assigned a contract to murder someone who had screwed up or sold them out; it was the commission, indeed, that had issued the contract on Joe Pistone after we took down the Bonanno case.

In any event, the wise guys were not big book readers, so many of them had no clue about the stuff Bonanno had included in *A Man of Honor*. Sal Avellino and Tom Mix Santoro sure didn't have an idea, because in the transcript of the conversation Charlotte Lang and Pat Marshall rooted out and then red-flagged, the two Lucchese family members couldn't stop talking about an appearance Joe Bonanno had just made on CBS's *60 Minutes*.

"I was shocked," Avellino said. "What's he trying to prove? . . . He actually admitted that he was a boss of a family, he was even saying about a commission. He says you gotta see the commission that was first started by Charlie Lucky [Luciano]."

"Yeah, the five bosses from New York," Santoro replied. "That was the original commission. Then they took in Chicago. Then they took in, you know—they were making them all."

Chertoff hooted when he read the transcript. When Giuliani assigned him to the commission case, in Rudy's big office high above St. Andrew's Plaza, Mike had been dubious; not now. Now it was not just a case of relying on the word of a lying sleazeball like Bonanno and what he had written in his book; here we had two wise guys on a Title III confirming it.

But there was more to come—much more.

• • •

From the little microphone John Kravec had braved New York's killer rats to install at the Palma Boy Social Club, Dave Binney's agents in the warehouse down the street picked up a conversation among Fat Tony Salerno, the boss of the Genovese family; Tom Mix Santoro, the underboss of the Luccheses; and Chris Furnari, the Lucchese family *consigliere.*

Binney reviewed the conversation and saw it was of little value to his investigation of the Genovese family, but it was pure gold for Pat Marshall, Charlotte Lang, and Mike Chertoff.

Fat Tony, Funari (who went by the name Christie Tick), and Tom Mix Santoro were talking about the sorry state of the Bonanno family and their attempt to regain a seat on the commission. Phil Rastelli was about to become the boss of the Bonanno family, but thanks to Joe Pistone, Barbara Jones, and Louie Freeh, the Bonannos were still *personae non gratae* when it came to the other Mafia families in New York. They were the only New York family that didn't get a cut from the cement-industry scam and the only family denied a seat at commission meetings.

Rusty Rastelli wanted to change that.

Fat Tony was dead set against Rastelli.

"Look, Tony, did Paul speak to you about it?"

"I haven't seen Paul for five or six months, Chris."

"And Gerry Lang?"

With Carmine Persico in prison, Gerry Lang Langella was the acting boss of the Colombo family and so had one of the four votes on the commission.

"I don't know how they feel about it, the Colombos." Fat Tony pounded the table in front of him. "But I told them up there eighty times or more, he cannot sit on the commission. I don't want to see him on the commission."

"Yeah, they took too many junkies in there, the Bonannos."

"I know all these guys from Canada. They're all in the junk business." Fat Tony pounded the table again. "Now, if Rastelli's allowed on the commission, they'll be coming down here to meet with us. Then we'll all be getting into this fucking shit."

"Wait a second. I seen Gerry Lang yesterday, Tony, and he said he saw Paul, and Paul told him to say that you okayed it."

Tom Mix interrupted: "Did he mention the word 'commission,' Chris? Or was he saying he just okayed him to be a boss?"

"Yeah, did Gerry Lang want him on the commission?"

"No, Tony. He only okayed Rusty to be a boss."

Tom Mix: "But not the commission! Who fucking threw the word 'commission' in?"

Christie Tick: "No, Gerry said he *would* be on the commission, too."

Tom Mix: "No, no. Pay attention to what I'm saying, Chris. He's only going to be the boss. Gerry Lang says it's okay for Rusty to be a boss."

"Wait a minute, wait a minute." Fat Tony pounded the table a third time. "Do youse guys want him on the commission? Does Gerry want him on the commission?"

Christie Tick: "I don't know, but Gerry says it's okay with him [if the other bosses okay it]."

Tom Mix: "He's known as a boss now, Chris—a boss! It's okay for him to be a boss, no problem."

Christie Tick: "Right."

Tom Mix: "Okay . . . but he can't sit on the commission."

Christie Tick: "But Paul said he *could* sit on the commission."

Fat Tony: "*Paul* wants him to sit on the commission?"

Christie Tick: "Yeah, and he's the one that said *you* okayed it."

Fat Tony: "No, he can't say that. I got two witnesses. . . . I'll make them tell what the fuck I really said."

Christie Tick: "Okay, okay. I'm glad we got this squared away."

Fat Tony: "What I don't understand is Paul. Why is he so insistent? Why does he want them on the commission. Why? What does he want to do with these guys? There's nothing but trouble in it for us."

"I don't know." Christie Tick sighed audibly.

"Rusty would like to meet and straighten it out with the other families?" Fat Tony snorted. "He wants to be boss? Let him get fucking balls, then! As far as the commission goes, they don't fucking want him there."

On May 9, at 11:12 A.M. on a very slow Wednesday morning, Fat Tony Salerno was sitting at his favorite table in the Palma Boy Social Club with a wise guy named Giuseppe Sabato, and they were joined almost immediately by a gentleman named John Tronolone. Everyone called Tronolone "Peanuts," but he bore no resemblance at all to the little round-headed kid in the comic strip. Peanuts Tronolone was a crook. He was also something of a showboat. On the cameras and the microphones we had up on Fat Tony, we picked up Peanuts coming through the front door of the club on 115th Street, and he paused to announce his entry.

"The Palma Boy Social Club, hey!"

"Look who's here." Fat Tony's voice boomed over the microphone. "Hey, how you doing, pal?"

"Good, good. Pepe, how you doin'?"

"Look at this guy. He comes in like a fucking undertaker, all the goddamned weight he lost."

"How you feeling, pal?"

"All right, Anthony. How's things?"

"Okay. The last time I wanted you, you was in China."

"Yeah, the fucking China trip; you fucking starve to death. That's how I lost all the weight."

"Is that right?"

"Yeah." Tronolone took a seat across from Fat Tony and got right down to business. "You know Jackie lost all his appeals, Anthony. Now he's going to the Supreme Court."

"Yeah, I know, I know."

"Now this is very, very important. Did anyone come to you and approach you about a guy by the name of Bill Brown?"

"Bill Brown?"

"Yeah. With the Teamsters. There's this guy Schloessinger, and he's stepping down. And this guy Bill Brown, he went to Jackie Presser, and he wants to get Schloessinger's job."

"You sure you got the right name?"

"Yeah, yeah. Now listen to this. So Jackie Presser, he tells Brown, 'You go and see who you wanna, and if they contact me,

then I'll give you a second look or something.' This Schloessinger, he's got the big job under Jackie. Now, this is the guy,
Bill McCarthy [who's going to replace Jackie]."

"Oh, McCarthy, he's from Connecticut."

"Yeah, you've heard of him?"

"He's the head boss of the East Coast, this guy."

"Yeah, now listen to this. This is the message for you, Tony.
You're going to name whoever you want to for Schloessinger's
job. Who do you want to name?"

"I don't know this Schloessinger."

"He's the guy under Jack. And he's a vice president. And
they're waiting for me to come back with any message you give
me."

"Yeah, well, I've gotta leave. There's a commission meeting
this afternoon."

"Well, you go ahead, then. I'm going back to Cleveland tonight. And then we'll see. I'll take care of whatever you want me
to take care of."

"Yeah, okay, thanks. We'll see, okay?"

Down the street in our little room in the warehouse Pete Kelleher had arranged for us, the agents listening in on the conversation looked at each other, dumbfounded. Kate Ball, Artie
Grubert, Bob Tolan, and Pete Kelleher had spent so much time
listening to Fat Tony, it sometimes felt like he was kin. But this
talk about the Teamsters, what the hell was that all about?

Kate Ball talked to Kelleher and the other agents; then they
got the squad supervisor, Dave Binney, on the phone, and by
midafternoon he was listening to the tape himself.

"Goddamn!" Binney said. "Unbelievable."

Like clockwork, Jim Kossler convened a daily 9:00 A.M. meeting
of all his supervisors. There was a small conference room across
from Kossler's office on the twenty-eighth floor, and with the

overlap we were getting from the investigations of one family to the next, and now with the commission investigation moving forward, the morning meetings were invaluable both for avoiding a lot of duplicate work and to develop whatever synergy we could among the squads, feeding leads and evidence from one to another.

At 9:00 A.M. on Thursday, May 10, Binney sat down at Kossler's conference table with a copy of the transcript generated from the previous day's conversation between Peanuts Tronolone and Fat Tony Salerno. Binney started to explain, but Kossler had scanned the transcript, and he was out of his chair already.

"Holy shit, Dave! You see what these guys are doing? These assholes are sitting up there on 115th Street, and they're picking the next fucking Teamsters president!"

The Title IIIs on the Fat Tony case would yield more conversations about Teamsters business in the months to come, and Binney made sure the transcripts were forwarded promptly to Charlotte Lang and Pat Marshall.

The commission case was starting to take shape.

On May 15, 1984, two of Bruce Mouw's agents, Joe O'Brien and Andy Kurins, were down in the South Beach area of Staten Island conducting a stakeout as part of their investigation of Paul Castellano and the Gambino family. The place they were watching was a modest home located at 34 Cameron Avenue. There was nothing particularly sinister about the place; a spindly spruce tree shaded the postage-stamp front yard. The house was owned by a longshoreman named Dewey Gheraldi and his wife, Angelina. She worked for the Board of Education.

The house was interesting for the following reason: Joe O'Brien had an informant, a guy who has only been identified —before or since—as "G." What G told O'Brien was that the commission would be meeting that afternoon at the Gheraldi residence and that the purpose of said meeting was to discuss "construction." O'Brien pressed, but G would say no more.

"You giving me garbage," O'Brien swore, "it's your ass."

"I'm giving you diamonds and rubies."

An hour and a half after the conversation with G, O'Brien was sitting in a dented Dodge van one hundred yards down the block from 34 Cameron with Andy Kurins, and the two agents saw no signs of diamonds and no rubies. O'Brien was the agent who had doorstepped Paul Castellano after he learned of the contract on Joe Pistone, and he could usually be found making his rounds in a starched shirt, quiet tie, and pressed suit. The Cameron Avenue stakeout found O'Brien sporting a paisley bandanna wrapped Gypsy style around his head, a ripped work shirt popping across his broad back, and a single gold hoop dangling from one ear. He could have passed easily for a derelict or a madman.

Kurins looked somewhat better, but no one would have noticed, since both men were crouched in the back of the filthy undercover van, concealed by a cracked sheet of black vinyl and a broken box that had once contained an Amana refrigerator.

So much for high-tech.

On their stakeouts, Kurins was the designated lensman, and he had brought along the 300-mm telephoto for this job. From his perch in the back of the van, the long lens made the front door of 34 Cameron look like you could reach out and ring the goddamned buzzer. The only problem was, no one was coming or going from the front door.

Sometime around four in the afternoon—after Kurins and O'Brien had been crouched in the van for more than two hours —a maroon Chrysler piloted by a man named Frank DeCicco turned into Cameron Avenue, slowed briefly in front of number 34, then drove on. DeCicco was a Gambino family capo well known to Kurins and O'Brien.

"They're in there," O'Brien said.

Kurins cradled the lens and checked his light meter.

Cars started coming and going shortly after that, and suddenly the little house on Cameron Avenue began disgorging a virtual who's who of the Cosa Nostra. At four-fourteen, a gentleman named Alphonse "Funzi" Mosca stepped out the Gheraldis' front door. He was the first to go. Funzi Mosca was a liverish-looking little man who was basically a harmless individual, and he scuttled away down a side street like an overweight beetle. Kurins captured him with the long lens.

The bigger fish were next.

At 4:40, Fat Tony Salerno appeared in the Gheraldis' doorway, stubby cigar shoved in his mouth, a Genovese soldier named Carmine Delacava a deferential half step behind. Like clockwork, Funzi Mosca wheeled a red Oldsmobile to the curb in front of the Gheraldis' place, and Fat Tony and Carmine Delacava quickly stepped inside—but not before Andy Kurins captured the three of them for posterity on Kodachrome with the long lens.

At 4:41, Gerry Lang Langella made his appearance on the Gheraldis' front porch, the acting Colombo family boss dapper in a crisp gray blazer.

Next came Ralphie Scopo, the Colombos' star cement fixer.

Kurins shot both of them, several frames each. "It's amazing, Joe. They're coming out family by family."

Next came Tom Bilotti, Paul Castellano's driver and alter ego, but he was just going for the boss of bosses' baby-blue Cadillac. Kurins snapped him, anyway.

Seconds later, the Lucchese team was on the porch, underboss Tom Mix Santoro followed right behind by a Lucchese family capo named Aniello Migliore.

Kurins snapped them both.

Last was Paul Castellano, the boss of bosses, and he stepped onto the Gheraldis' humble front porch with something like the air of majesty. Castellano was not a good man, but he did have presence. As I look at it today, in the image frozen by Andy Kurins's long lens, the boss of bosses appears to be savoring the fresh spring air, blue smoke from a long Churchill-size cigar curling around his handsome head.

Castellano was no Funzi Mosca, a small man with bad teeth and flickering eyes. The boss of bosses was a crook, and he was an enemy, but he also stood head and shoulders above the other wise guys. It would be easy to dwell on that last fact and make of Castellano more than what he was.

I preferred to dwell on another fact, however: For the first time ever, we had a meeting of the Mafia Commission on film. It would be evidence we could ultimately present to a judge and jury. For the wise guys, time was running out.

34

BRUCE Baird began putting the finishing touches on our indictment of the Colombo family in September 1984, and the grand jury voted to approve a month later. By then, Carmine "the Snake" Persico, Gerry Lang Langella, and Donnie Shacks Montemarano had scattered like sparrows in winter.

Carmine the Snake had been released from prison just a few months earlier, so the Colombo family had its old boss back in place. But Carmine's timing was lousy. Sure, it's nice to be in the driver's seat again, but who the hell wants that when the car you're riding in is about to go off a cliff?

Couldn't happen to a nicer guy, I thought.

Clearly, someone had tipped the Colombos to the indictment, and that was a problem. While we worked that, however, we put out lines everywhere to see if we could locate Carmine the Snake. Him we wanted most of all—so much so that we stuck his ugly mug on the FBI's ten most wanted list.

For weeks, we got nothing.

Then we got a break.

On February 7, 1985, Special Agent Jim Nelson answered his phone in the FBI's sprawling Los Angeles field office on Wilshire Boulevard. "Hello, Nelson."

"Special Agent Jim Nelson?"

"Yeah, this is Jim Nelson. Who's this?"

A long pause. "It's Fred DeChristopher, Agent Nelson, remember me?"

"Yeah, Mr. DeChristopher, sure. How you doing?"

Another pause, longer. "Not too good, sir. But I think I might be able to help you out on something."

"Is that right?" Nelson grabbed a legal pad and a pen.

Nelson and DeChristopher had a history going back a few years, but Jim had no idea what DeChristopher had been up to recently. Twelve years earlier, DeChristopher had married the sister of a wise guy named Andrew Russo. Not long after that, Fred had come to see Nelson to talk to him about his new brother-in-law. DeChristopher told Nelson about a night he and Russo had met a third man in a restaurant out on Long Island. The third guy had pissed off Russo somehow, and as the three of them were sitting in the restaurant sipping their highballs and studying the menu, Andy Russo calmly picked up his salad fork, pressed the tines of the thing against the white part of the third guy's right eye, and made a little speech. "Look, when I tell you to do something, you do it, okay, asshole?"

The third guy, petrified, made an okay like a semaphore.

Andy Russo wasn't finished, though. "The next time you fuck up, I'll push this fork right into your fucking eye."

The third man stammered an apology, and Russo turned to DeChristopher, the little salad fork still in the third guy's eye. "If they fear you, Freddie," Russo said, nodding to the unfortunate man with the fork pressing against his eyeball, "they'll lick your hand or kiss your feet. They'll respect you."

DeChristopher nodded, his own eyes bulging.

"I'm a gangster, see, Freddie? I can lie, and I can cheat, and I can kill," Russo concluded.

DeChristopher nodded again.

Andy Russo finally removed his fork from the third guy's eye, and the three men proceeded to order dinner.

DeChristopher told Nelson he was so nervous he ordered several stiff drinks during the meal, draining them one right after the other.

Pressing the telephone receiver to his ear in his little cubicle in Los Angeles, Nelson tried to remember as much as he could about DeChristopher. Notwithstanding the problems he had with his brother-in-law, Fred DeChristopher was a good guy. He had a good job selling insurance for the Equitable Life Insurance Company. He paid his taxes and his bills on time, had never been in trouble. After approaching Nelson to seek advice about his brother-in-law, however, DeChristopher had gotten cold feet. He was afraid of Andy Russo and definitely afraid of what would happen if it was found out that he was talking to the FBI. So DeChristopher had broken off the relationship.

Nelson hadn't talked to him in five or six years. "Please, Mr. DeChristopher, take your time."

"Okay." Fred DeChristopher coughed. "This is what I got."

"Go ahead, sir."

"Okay. I understand you guys—the FBI, that is—that you're interested in a guy named Carmine Persico."

"Yes, sir, that's right." Nelson sat bolt upright in his chair, then struggled to keep the excitement out of his voice. We had just put Carmine the Snake on the Bureau's ten most wanted list. His police mug shot was hanging in post offices all across the country.

"Well, Carmine—I can tell you where he is."

"Okay, that's great, Mr. DeChristopher."

"See, he was living here until a few days ago."

Nelson was scribbling frantically. "At your place."

"Yeah, he was here maybe two months—no, a little more."

"And when did he leave, Mr. DeChristopher?"

"Ah, two, three days ago. Two days ago."

Nelson checked the calendar on his watch. The date was February 6. "And you know where he went after he left your place, sir? Where Mr. Persico is now?"

"Yeah, that's what I'm saying."

"Okay, go ahead."

"This son of a bitch." DeChristopher coughed again, then went into a long story about how Andy Russo's nephew Jo-Jo had come to his house and told him—told him!—how he was going to be getting a houseguest. Carmine Persico showed up on November 1, DeChristopher explained, and he had not left until February 4. During the entire time, DeChristopher told Nelson, he had been confined to the house—not even allowed out in the yard. And the whole time that was going on, Carmine Persico was sitting around his living room with his feet on the furniture, eating up his food, smoking his smelly cigars.

"That's terrible, it must have been awful for you, sir."

"Yeah, well, anyway. I been thinking about it, and they told me that if for any reason I need to get ahold of Carmine, this is where he'd be staying—like I'd wanna get ahold of the guy after living with him three goddamned months straight."

"So where is it he went, Mr. DeChristopher?"

"Goshen."

"I'm sorry."

"It's a little town upstate in New York."

"Goshen?"

"Yeah." DeChristopher spelled it for Nelson. "They didn't give me a phone number or nothing, but I got the street address and directions how to find the place."

"Great."

DeChristopher rattled off the address and the directions, and Nelson made him repeat them twice, checking his notes.

"This is very helpful, Mr. DeChristopher. Very helpful."

"Yeah, well, good. You gonna go after the guy now?"

"Yes, sir." Nelson was already looking up my direct line at FBI Headquarters. "That's exactly what we're going to do."

I got on the phone to Kossler immediately. He got his secretary to find Damon Taylor, our Colombo squad supervisor, and Damon walked in during the middle of the conversation.

"I got calls going out right now, Jules. We're putting a team together even as we speak."

"Good, good. What do we know about this place?"

"It's a little town, kind of a farming community, maybe ninety minutes from the city."

"Nelson says his guy says Carmine's on a horse farm."

"Yeah, I know. Should be pretty easy to take down, anyway."

"Yeah, okay. Well, let us know as soon as it happens, huh?"

"You bet, Jules, thanks, we will."

• • • •

By the time Damon Taylor's arrest team knocked on the front door of the little farmhouse in Goshen, Carmine the Snake had disappeared. Two days later, Fred DeChristopher called. Jim Nelson had told DeChristopher that if he needed any help at all, if he found out anything else on Carmine Persico, he should call Damon Taylor at 26 Federal. Nelson gave DeChristopher Damon's direct-dial line and his twenty-four-hour beeper number.

DeChristopher got Damon on the beeper. "He's back!"

"Hello, who's this?"

"I'm calling from a pay phone, dammit. It's DeChristopher, and I just got a minute. This is Agent, uh, Taylor, right?"

"Yes, sir—this is about Persico?"

"Yeah, he's at my place. Came back two nights ago."

"Shit." Damon had his arrest team wandering around the woods of this to-hell-and-gone town called Goshen, and Carmine the Snake is sitting back in DeChristopher's living room with his feet up on the furniture—a hundred miles away. "Has he harmed you in any way, sir? You all right?"

"Yeah, yeah. But I don't want him here no more, okay?"

"Yes, sir. Give me your address, please, okay?"

DeChristopher spat out his address. "Look, I gotta go."

"Okay, just sit tight, Mr. DeChristopher. And when you go home, don't do anything unusual. Just make like everything's normal and we'll be there as soon as we can, okay?"

"Yeah, okay, okay. I gotta go now."

"Okay. Just be cool and we'll be right there, okay?" Damon listened for a reply, but there was none.

The line had gone dead.

Damon called Kossler immediately, then started phoning his Colombo squad agents one by one. Two hours after the call from Fred DeChristopher, Damon had a discreet little surveillance team surrounding the goddamned place.

Four days after that, we picked up a phone call from Carmine the Snake to Donnie Shacks Montemarano. The Colombo family boss was inviting Donnie Shacks to dinner.

Kossler and I talked, then Jim gave the order to Damon: No more waiting on these guys. Let's arrest the bastards.

Some of the guys on Damon's squad wanted to kick poor Fred DeChristopher's front door in. They had spent nights and weekends for the past few months looking for Donnie Shacks and Carmine the Snake. After we put Carmine on the most wanted list, that put even more pressure on the squad. Now that it was payback time, some of the guys wanted to see just what tough guys these two Colombo family assholes were.

Damon Taylor would have none of it.

The takedown occurred on a chilly Saturday afternoon, the sun slanting behind pewter clouds, the shadows long on the grass. DeChristopher lived out on Long Island in a pretty little town, and there were kids riding their bikes in the streets, bundled in bright parkas against the chill air.

From a booth a couple of blocks from DeChristopher's place, Damon made a phone call. DeChristopher answered.

"Mr. Persico, please."

Long pause. "Who should I say is calling?"

"It's the FBI, sir. Please call Mr. Persico to the phone."

From his end of the line, Damon could hear a brief silence, then: "Fucking motherfuckers, I don't believe it!"

Then: "Listen, shut up, will ya, Donnie!"

"Those cocksuckers—let's fucking deal with them. Let's just fucking do it."

By now, Damon recognized the voice: There was no mistaking the dulcet tones of Donnie Shacks Montemarano. The stupid son of a bitch wanted to shoot it out with the FBI. What an idiot.

"Wait, Donnie. I said wait!"

A second later, Carmine Persico came to the phone. "Who is this, and what the fuck is this about, please?"

Damon liked that; the "please" was a nice touch. "This is Special Agent Damon Taylor of the FBI, Mr. Persico."

"The FBI."

"That's right, sir. And I am instructed to inform you that I have a warrant for your arrest and for the arrest of Mr. Montemarano as well. We know he is there in the house with you, Mr. Persico, and we would like to make this happen without anyone getting hurt today, okay?"

"Yeah." Persico paused maybe half a minute. "You gonna come to the front door, then, or what?"

"The front door, yes, sir. We'll be right there."

It was a long drive back to 26 Federal, and Donnie Shacks rode in the back of the government car with Denis Maduro; they put Carmine Persico in another vehicle.

After we got the wise guys all squared away—booked, fingerprinted, and the rest—Persico somehow got word downstairs to Denis, who was about to head home after a hell of a long day. Denis checked his weapon with the guards and took the elevator back upstairs to the booking area. Carmine Persico and Donnie Shacks were waiting for him; ominously, there wasn't a single guard around anywhere.

"Excuse me, someone was asking for Denis Maduro?" Even with wise guys in jail, Denis was unfailingly courteous.

Maduro had personally made it his business to make life a living hell for these two guys, and it was clear that they didn't appreciate it a whole lot. Persico stepped forward and stuck his lumpy chin out at Maduro. "Who the fuck do you think you are, anyway, fucking Eliot Ness?"

Denis held his ground—and his silence. There was nothing to be gained by bantering with these two clowns.

A second later, it was Donnie Shacks's turn to play the hard guy. "Just remember something, my friend." He stabbed his fat forefinger at Maduro's chest. "Someday you're going to have to walk the fucking streets by yourself."

Denis nodded but didn't break his silence.

A minute or so later, a guard finally showed up, and Denis summoned him. "I think you want to take care of these two guys," he said. "They weren't looking for me, after all."

• • •

At just after 5:00 P.M. on the twenty-fifth of February, I was on the speakerphone from Washington. Kossler and Kallstrom were on the other end in New York. Tensions were at a pretty good boil.

"Listen, Jules, this is all wrong. All wrong."

"How do you think I feel about it, Jimmy?"

"I know, I know."

"But what the fuck are we going to do? I just talked with the producers at NBC again, and they say they're going with the piece tonight. They don't give a shit, okay?"

"So we bring the whole thing down?"

"You see any other options? Because I sure don't."

Kallstrom chimed in. "What a fucking mess."

"Listen, guys, this stinks, okay, we all agree. But if the bosses get word of the commission indictment before we arrest them, then they're fucking history, and you guys know it."

"Yeah, but there's gotta be some other way. On Fat Tony alone —you, me, and Binney agreed—we want to keep those wires up at least a few more months with all the leads he's giving us."

"Yeah, but what's the other way? NBC says it's going with the piece, and you know as well as I do, we got Fat Tony himself on the wire saying something like 'Hey, the fucking FBI comes after me, I'm going to make myself disappear.' "

"Yeah, I know, I know."

"So we've got to do it, Jim. We don't have to like it, but from where I sit, we've got to do it, and that's that."

Kossler sighed deeply. "You're right, Jules. It's just that this is a tough one. After all the work we put in here."

"I hear you, pal."

"But I got all the squads standing by. We do it, we can bring everyone in in a couple of hours, max."

"Let's do it, then. You on board, Jimmy?"

As I hunched over my desk in Washington, Kallstrom's growl filled my ear. "Yeah, shit. Let's do it."

"Give the order, then," I told Kossler. "And Jim?"

"Yeah, Jules?"

"Just tell everyone not to do anything dumb."

With Carmine the Snake and Gerry Lang, of course, we didn't have to make any arrests. We already had them in custody, so all we did was have Denis Maduro run over to the federal lockup and ruin their evening by serving them with the new arrest papers.

Denis was as polite as ever, calmly informing Donnie Shacks and Carmine the Snake that they had now been named by the FBI as defendants in a second racketeering conspiracy case.

"Shit," Donnie Shacks said.

"Fucking Eliot Ness again," Persico snorted.

Denis Maduro wished the two wise guys a pleasant good evening on his way out the jailhouse door.

Special Agent John Joyce picked up Ralph Scopo out on Long Island as he was about to get into one of his cars.

The little extortionist went quietly.

Joyce read Scopo his rights and hustled him into a Bureau car. The car turned onto the Long Island Expressway, cleared the toll booth for the Midtown Tunnel, and plunged into blackness. Halfway through the tunnel, Scopo turned to Joyce.

"I've always had a thing about confined spaces, you know?"

"You mean like being afraid."

"Yeah, like that."

Joyce nodded but said nothing. Scopo must have had some idea how confined the spaces were we had in mind for him.

Special Agents John Kapp and Tom Sweeney arrested Tom Mix Santoro, the underboss of the Lucchese family with no trouble.

"A real gentleman," Kapp called Tom Mix.

In the booking area at 26 Federal, there was a bit of a backup with all the other wise guys, so Kapp, who was a nut about crossword puzzles, fished one out to pass the time. Over the course of the day Kapp had completed the entire puzzle except for two words. He was stumped on them. Having nothing better to do, Tom Mix Santoro took a peek over Kapp's shoulder, studied the clues, and then gave Kapp the answers, one right after the other. John looked up like he couldn't believe it, but he rechecked the clues, then tried Santoro's answers. They fit.

"Not bad for a ninth-grade education, huh?"

"Not bad at all, sir." Kapp thanked Santoro, entered the last two words with his pencil, and stowed the crossword away.

Just after seven o'clock, Dave Binney, with agents Kate Ball, Bob Tolan, and Pete Kelleher, was standing outside the front door of Fat Tony's apartment building on 115th Street.

Binney pushed the buzzer.

"Yeah, who is it?" Binney recognized the voice immediately. It belonged to Vincent "Fish" Cafaro, Fat Tony's main factotum.

"FBI, Fish. We're coming up."

"Ah, shit." Fish pressed the buzzer. At the top of the stairs he was waiting. "What do you fucking guys want coming around here?"

"Easy, Fish, easy." Across a narrow hallway, Binney could see Fat Tony sitting at the head of the table in a bathrobe; six other wise guys were seated at both sides of the table, waiting to chow down. A delivery man had just arrived, but no food had been placed on the table yet.

"What's the problem?"

"The problem"—Binney placed his nose approximately three inches away from Fish Cafaro's nose—"is that we've got a warrant for Mr. Salerno, and he's got to come with us."

"Son of a bitch! You're gonna arrest him?"

"One way or the other, Fish, that's right."

"Hold on, hold on. Gimme a minute."

"One minute, Fish, that's it."

Fish Cafaro disappeared, and Binney and the other agents studied the old men around the table. Here were the cream of the Italian Mafia, Binney thought. Fat Tony and his boys had cowed the fearsome Teamsters Union as well as several platoons of wise guys from half a dozen states or more. Fat Tony had major crooks like Peanuts Tronolone flying in from all over the country paying court to him like he was royalty. And yet to look at Tony and his guys, they were a bunch of sad-looking old men.

"Tough guys, fucking FBI." Pepe Sabato was a little eighty-year-old crook who passed most of his days sitting with Fat Tony at his table in the Palma Boy.

"Put a cork in it, okay, Pepe?"

Sabato sat down, muttering imprecations.

Fish Cafaro came back a few seconds later with a phone. "Here, it's Roy Cohn for you. Mr. Salerno's lawyer."

"Thanks, Fish." Binney grabbed the phone and started to talk, but Cohn was already going a mile a minute.

"I thought we had a deal. I talked to Giuliani's office, and they said no arrest; Mr. Salerno would present himself for arraignment and booking in the event of an indictment."

"Mr. Cohn."

"Goddammit, I'm gonna call Giuliani."

"Call Mr. Giuliani, Mr. Cohn."

"I'm gonna, dammit. Gimme twenty minutes."

"I can't do that, Mr. Cohn. You call back before we're done here and I'll listen to anything Mr. Giuliani's office has to say. But I have my orders, and my orders say to bring Mr. Salerno in for booking tonight. Now."

"Goddammit, gimmee a few minutes!" Cohn slammed the phone down.

Binney shook his head, handed the phone to Fish Cafaro and walked into the dining room. "Mr. Salerno?"

"Yes?" Fat Tony contemplated Binney from his seat at the head of the table.

"I have to inform you you are under arrest, sir."

Fat Tony nodded but said nothing.

Less than ten minutes later, he was seated next to Binney in the back of an FBI car heading south in light traffic down the Franklin D. Roosevelt Drive. From across the East River, the yellow phosphor-gas lights from the borough of Queens reflected up at the two men from the river's blackness. Fat Tony seemed to find the view engrossing. He kept his face pressed to the car window during the entire trip downtown.

It was dark when Andy Kurins and Joe O'Brien wound their way up the long driveway to Paul Castellano's mansion in Staten Island. The agents walked up the front steps and rang the bell. Big Paul's voice crackled through the intercom.

"Who is it?"

"Joe O'Brien, Mr. Castellano. FBI. I have a warrant for your arrest, sir."

"*Ach.*"

A few seconds later, Castellano appeared at the door, casual in gray slacks, silk shirt, and slippers. "May I ask what this is about?"

"RICO conspiracy." O'Brien produced a copy of the commission indictment. "A dozen or so of your colleagues are being arrested right now, sir."

"Really—right now?"

"Yes, sir."

"Well, come on in."

O'Brien and Kurins trooped into the vast entry hall of the Castellano White House. The godfather led the way into the kitchen. Kurins and O'Brien followed silently.

Inside, the two agents took in the scene: The table was set with Lenox china, a delicate pattern. A rare roast beef, already carved, sat on a platter in the center of the table. There were two other people in the room.

"Dr. Richard Hoffman," Castellano said, indicating the older man in a dress shirt. "He's a friend."

Kurins and O'Brien nodded.

"And Gloria Olarte."

"Hello, Gloria," O'Brien said.

Gloria's eyeballs bulged.

"Be civil," Castellano said. "The man is only doing his job."

"Hees yob! Hees yob! Hees yob is only to make trouble for other people who don't do nothing. I no like thees Meester O'Brien."

Castellano smiled, shook his head, then turned to the two agents. "I'd like to change into a suit."

"That isn't necessary," O'Brien said.

"I know it isn't, but I'd feel more comfortable. I'm asking as a favor."

Kurins and O'Brien looked at each other.

"Sure, why not," O'Brien said.

The ride downtown was quiet—until the all-news AM radio station O'Brien had on in the car interrupted with a bulletin:

This just in: At this moment, agents of the Federal Bureau of Investigation and the New York State Organized Crime Task Force are arresting the reputed leaders of all of New York's five Mafia families. According to U.S. Attorney Rudolph Giuliani, the arrests are part of the most far-reaching mob investigation ever, an investigation aimed at convicting the entire Mafia leadership —the so-called commission—under federal racketeering statutes. Tonight's arrests cap a four-year law enforcement effort, which, according to one highly placed source, included the 1983 bugging of the Staten Island home of Paul Castellano, alleged boss of the Gambino family and the de facto boss of the commission.

Behind the wheel, Andy Kurins watched the road.

Next to him, Joe O'Brien stared straight ahead.

From the backseat, the two agents heard a barely audible groan. Then Castellano leaned forward, staring at the dashboard radio. "Is that true? Did you guys bug my house?"

"Yes, sir." O'Brien kept looking ahead. "I'm afraid it is."

"*Gesù Cristo!* When? How'd ya do it?"

"I'm sorry, we can't tell you that."

"No." The boss of bosses slumped his bulk back into the rear seat of the Bureau car. "I suppose you can't."

Headquarters was virtually deserted by the time Kossler called me back with a fill on the night's events. On the third floor of the Hoover Building, my light was the only one still burning. It was nearly midnight.

"No problem, Jules, we got them all. Every one."

"Tell the guys, great work. Great work all around, Jimmy."

"I will, I will. It turned out okay, after all."

"We'll make it turn out okay; that's the main thing, pal."

"Goddamned right. Good night, Jules."

I thanked Kossler again for all his great work with the squads and the program in New York, then wished him good night.

Driving across Washington's Memorial Bridge ten minutes later, I thought about the day's events and about how far we had come. Ahead of me, the white headstones of Arlington National Cemetery glowed like ghosts in the moonlight, the black Potomac heaving sluggishly on its way to Chesapeake Bay and then to the ocean beyond.

For me, the facts, for once, were less interesting than the theory of the case and even the details of the arrests. With Giuliani's blessing, Mike Chertoff had impaneled a grand jury several months earlier, and he had begun meeting with the members every week to educate them about the Mafia's board of directors and how deep they were into the slime. Chertoff had started with what we knew, things like the dispute over the $50,000 extortion demand from DeGaetano and Vozzi. Then he had moved on to the cement-industry scam and the conversations we were pulling from Ralph Scopo's cars. As Charlotte Lang and Pat Marshall mined new nuggets from the transcript mountain, Chertoff brought them before the grand jurors, too. The photographs taken on May 15 by Andy Kurins from the back of our undercover van were an especially big hit.

The theory behind the indictment was what was so thrilling, though. Go back to what we knew about the Italian Mafia and the commission meeting that had been convened by Lucky Luciano back in 1931 to settle affairs after the Castellammarese War. Then fast-forward from there to what Bob Blakey had pounded into our heads just five years earlier at the seminar on RICO up in Ithaca, New York. Take those two things and use them as bookends. Then place between the bookends everything Pat Marshall and Charlotte Lang had mined from the transcripts —things like Fat Tony Salerno sitting up at the Palma Boy Social Club deciding who the next Teamsters president was going to be. Add to that list what Joe Bonanno had said and written in *A Man of Honor.* Then take everything Joe Pistone had seen firsthand working undercover for more than six years.

Take all that now and what you have is the definition of a monstrous criminal enterprise—my friend Blakey, again—that had maintained a virtual chokehold on much of American life for more than five decades. Take all of that, finally, add it up, and turn it around against the Mafia's board of directors. What you have, the way I see it—the way I see it now, the way I saw it then, the way I had dreamed about it—was something close to revolutionary: a sweeping indictment of the largest criminal enterprise in the history of the United States.

For too long, the wise guys had beaten guys like me at the strategy game; now, finally, we were beating them. Turnabout, as someone once said, really is fair play. When it finally happens to you, it's also a hell of a beautiful thing.

35

THIS is the way the world works, at least the world of the FBI as I knew it. For more than a year Headquarters had been promising me a shot to go back to New York, but the brass had never delivered. There had been plenty of talk and good intentions, but that was it.

The time passed achingly slowly, not just because I wanted to be back in New York running the show but because by now I no longer had to run interference every day at Headquarters for our investigations in New York. Sure, we still had problems with the Inspection Division and with a few hardcase holdovers who would never get used to doing things the new way. But they were nothing I couldn't deal with by phone.

The Bureau owed me New York, I felt. I had set the strategic program in place. Now I wanted to see it through.

Only Headquarters wasn't cooperating.

At home, Linda had some pretty ambitious redecorating ideas, but I had persuaded her to put them on hold. "Any day now," I told her, "I know we'll be getting the word."

That was midway through 1984.

A year later, we were still waiting, and Linda decided the hell with it, she was calling the painters, the handymen, and the electricians. She had waited long enough. A few weeks and a few thousand dollars later, Linda's redecorating ideas were a reality, the house looked beautiful, and Headquarters finally came through with the transfer to New York.

Go figure.

As it happened, both Sean McWeeney and I got our transfer orders at the same time: The FBI's Organized Crime Section would be passing on to new hands. Sean and I had been friends in New York, had gone in separate directions afterward, and through the grace of good fortune, we had been reunited at Headquarters. In different ways and for different reasons we had both come to a kind of vision of a new FBI. We weren't visionaries, either of us. But as young agents we did know what was wrong with the way the FBI worked organized-crime cases, and we had definite ideas about how to fix things.

At Headquarters, despite opposition that was sometimes bitter and never less than stiff, we had made our vision a reality. There had been hard words among close friends and colleagues. The fight over whether and when to pull Joe Pistone out from his undercover role was just one of the many battles we had fought. As we prepared to leave—me for New York and the final push against the Cosa Nostra, Sean to a high-level liaison job in the State Department—the two of us laughed as only veterans of a shared battle can laugh.

It is impossible to place precisely the value of trust in a relationship like Sean's and mine. With Sean's blessing, I had run the New York program as if it were my own, and there was never a step along the way, not a one, where Sean had second-guessed or even questioned something I had done. The vision we shared of a new FBI was based on our own experiences in New York; at Headquarters, we had used New York as a model of things to come. The pariah status that New York had traditionally been accorded in the old FBI had made this a particularly hard sell, but as we prepared to move on to our new responsibilities, neither of us had any doubt that the sale had been made. This was due to Sean's genius, I think, but both of us agreed that we could never have accomplished what we had alone: In unity, there is strength.

In any case, it was clear that the changes we had made in the Bureau's organized-crime program were already changing the way investigations were being run elsewhere in the FBI's Criminal Investigative Division. Against white-collar criminals, terrorists, and narcotics traffickers, the FBI had begun to evolve from a by-the-numbers, reactive cop-shop agency to a much smarter and tougher adversary.

Call the change evolutionary, but for an institution as hidebound and resistant to change as J. Edgar Hoover's FBI, I'd call it revolutionary. It was an amazing thing.

For me it was another one of those August transfers. I showed up at 26 Federal early on a blistering hot day in the middle of the month. The air on Lower Broadway was stale and overheated, the city somehow dirtier than I remembered.

I felt great.

Finally, I was home.

And there was plenty of work to be done. With the indictments in the Colombo and commission investigations, some people might have thought we were in the final rounds of our fight against the mob, but indictments are just that: If you don't make the charges in an indictment stand up in court, the damned things aren't worth the paper they're written on. The commission case was going to be especially tricky.

Still, there was no doubt we had the wise guys on the run.

From a Title III one of Kallstrom's Special Operations teams had installed in Neil Dellacroce's home, we had firsthand evidence that the boss of bosses was more than a little worried about the charges that had been filed against him. Like a lot of the wise guys of his generation, Aniello Dellacroce, the underboss of the Gambino family, did not enjoy anything like good health. Still, we had picked him up on enough surveillances that we knew he continued to be highly active in the criminal affairs of the Gambino family. With the problems we had had with the Title III at Paul Castellano's home, we figured our best shot after Castellano was Dellacroce. Kallstrom's agents slipped the Title III in his house in January 1985.

A few weeks before I got back to New York, in the middle of June, Paul Castellano and his driver, Tom Bilotti, had turned up at Dellacroce's house, and Big Paul, having posted bail after his indictment in the commission case, told the Gambino family underboss that he wanted copies of the tapes we had pulled off the Title III at Angelo Ruggiero's home.

This was interesting, I thought. The way the rules of evidence work is simple. In charging Castellano in the commission case, we were duty-bound to inform the boss of bosses that much of the evidence alleged against him in the indictment had come from tape recordings we had made of the loquacious Ruggiero and his drug-dealing friends, especially Gene Gotti and some of the other wise guys from the Bergen Fish and Hunt crew.

Castellano never let it show among the wise guys, but the way he handled the Ruggiero business told me a lot about the depth of his troubles; this was certainly not the boss of bosses of old. Big Paul knew that Angelo Ruggiero despised him. He also knew that Ruggiero and Dellacroce were tight. Obviously, Castellano could have simply ordered Ruggiero to deliver the tapes to his mansion on Todt Hill. But he didn't play it that way. Instead, he ordered Dellacroce to talk to Ruggiero directly. It was yet another measure of Castellano's troubles that Dellacroce did not rush to carry out the order.

The sources of Paul Castellano's troubles were several. There was the embarrassing relationship with his little Gloria, the obliging live-in maid. That was one. There was the fact that we had installed a Title III in Castellano's home and recorded some rather compromising conversations there. That was two, and it was a big embarrassment. Finally, there was the fact of Castellano's indictment in the commission case. All had served to erode the authority of the boss of bosses.

Wise guys have only two things in common with sharks: One is that, on average, they are every bit as dumb as the beasts from the deep. The other is that they have an uncanny knack of smelling blood in the water. In Castellano's case there was no doubt that he had been grievously wounded by the commission indictment. The only question was whether he could survive.

The sharks had already begun to circle around Castellano. For the boss of bosses, it wasn't sink-or-swim time; it was swim-like-mad-or-be-eaten time.

Neil Dellacroce circled with the other sharks. He had lost out narrowly to Castellano nine years earlier when the old man, Carlo Gambino, had selected his unassuming brother-in-law Paul—over his son Tommy—as the new head of the Gambino family. The loyal and astute Dellacroce had placed a close second to Castellano. Should Big Paul be convicted and sent to jail now, Dellacroce might have been thinking that he would be named acting boss of the Gambino family, and who knows, if his health improved, one day he might even become the boss of bosses. So Dellacroce bided his time, and he didn't press Ruggiero on the tapes Castellano was so eager to lay his hands on.

The tapes, Dellacroce figured, could wait a while.

Not that Dellacroce didn't talk about the tapes a lot.

"I've been trying to make you get away with these tapes," Dellacroce told Ruggiero one evening. "But Jesus Christ Almighty, I can't stop the guy [Castellano] from always bringing it up. Unless I tell the guy, 'Hey, why don't you go fuck yourself and stop bringing these tapes up?' Then we know what we gotta do then. We gotta roll it up and go to war. I don't know if that's what you want."

"I don't want that, no. I don't want that."

All stupid Angelo Ruggiero did want was to avoid giving copies of the tapes to Paul Castellano, because the tapes showed beyond any doubt that he was up to his shaggy eyebrows in his dead brother's heroin business, and bullshit or no, Paul Castellano's edict against drug dealing by wise guys still carried an automatic sentence of death.

"There's things, there's things that were said on those tapes—things which shoulda never been said."

"Like what, Neil?"

"Like about the junk."

"The what?"

"The junk. And that shoulda never been discussed."

In addition to that problem, big-mouth Ruggiero had talked about a lot of other things wise guys shouldn't talk about publicly—things like commission meetings. We listened to John Gotti in Dellacroce's kitchen delivering that lesson to Ruggiero.

"Angelo, you're not supposed to speak to every fuckin' guy about a commission meeting. All right, you ain't the only guy that done it, but you ain't supposed to do it. You could sit here all night and try to justify it, but you ain't supposed to [talk] about the commission."

Ruggiero agreed glumly, but what could he do? He had talked his stupid head off, and now the damage was done.

A few weeks later, Ruggiero took the matter of the tapes up with Castellano directly, and believe it or not, the little weasel tried to strike a moral tone. It might have been funny if it wasn't so offensive, but here is this slimeball heroin dealer explaining to the boss of bosses that he cannot turn over the FBI's wiretap transcripts because doing so would mean selling out his friends and buddies.

"You gotta understand my position as a man," Ruggiero told the boss of bosses. "I was only brought up one way in this life: I'm not a fucking rat. . . . I'm not a fucking rat to cops, and I'm not gonna rat no wise guys. I ain't gonna rat no fucking friends of mine; that's the way I feel."

Castellano shook his head in disagreement.

Ruggiero pressed on. "You got your opinion, and Neil's got his; this is my opinion. . . . I got a moral obligation to myself."

Aside from the rotten taste they left in your mouth, the conversations highlight two things worth noting. The first is that from Paul Castellano to Neil Dellacroce to Angelo Ruggiero, the wise guys were genuinely rattled by our ability to listen to their conversations in homes, bars, just about anywhere; we had them playing defense now. The second is that the order that had traditionally existed within most Mafia families had clearly broken down within the Gambinos. When you have an underboss like Dellacroce referring to a boss like Castellano as an asshole and worse, you know something is seriously amiss. For Paul Castellano this was an ominous development indeed.

Dellacroce wasn't the biggest worry for Castellano, however; his health was lousy. John Gotti, Dellacroce's main ally in the Gambino family and the head of the Bergen Fish and Hunt crew, was the guy we knew Castellano had to watch out for.

Gotti said as much in a conversation with a wise guy named Sammy "the Bull" Gravano. "Sam, if he hits me first, he blows the guy who really led the [Bergen Fish and Hunt Club] ring. . . . That's the guys on the tapes."

"I think he would've hit Angelo and not you."

"Nah, he knew we weren't lay-down Sallies."

In Gotti's view, however, Paul Castellano was a lay-down Sally, or as he put it on another occasion, "a fuckin' faggot."

On a crisp fall morning in late October, Lynn DeVecchio, the squad supervisor on the commission case, walked into my office on the twenty-sixth floor of 26 Federal.

"You got a minute, boss?"

"Yeah, Lynn, what's up?"

"Well, we're still looking for those overt acts Marshall is always bitching about."

"Yeah, I know. How's it going?"

"Too soon to say, but I wanted to give you a fill on what they're working on."

"Sure, go ahead. As far as I was concerned, the theory of the RICO indictment against the Mafia Commission was airtight, the evidence against them was compelling. Still, an overt act—a murder, extortion, or other crime—would certainly help grab the attention of a bored jury.

DeVecchio coughed. "What we're looking at is the hit on Galante.

"Jeez, Lynn, that's going back, isn't it?"

"Yeah, but listen to what we got."

DeVecchio laid it out for me. About forty-five minutes after Carmine Galante was murdered in 1979 by three guys in ski masks, New York Police Department detectives conducting a surveillance outside a mob social club on Mulberry Street in Little Italy spotted two Bonanno family members, Bruno Indelicato and his uncle, J. B. Indelicato, hugging, backslapping, and generally carrying on with Neil Dellacroce and a guy named Steve Cannone, the Bonanno family *consigliere*.

"That was six fucking years ago, Lynn."

"I know, I know, but we've gotten new information since then."

"I'm all ears."

"What we got is informant information saying the commission authorized the hit on Galante."

"No shit."

"Yeah. Now what we're thinking is, if we can link one or both of the Indelicatos to the Galante hit and show that the commission had ordered the hit, suddenly we've got the overt act Marshall has been tearing his hair out about."

"That's great, Lynn. But what kind of odds are we talking here?"

"Who the hell knows? We're just working it. We'll see what we come up with, that's all."

"It's worth a shot, Lynn. Tell Pat to go for it."

"Okay, boss. We'll keep you posted."

"Thanks, good luck."

No one had ever been arrested for the Galante murder, but the NYPD had lifted fingerprints from the getaway car the hit men had used, a beat-up Mercury Montego. The fingerprints had been checked against NYPD files, but for some reason no one had ever lifted what we call "major case prints" from the car. With major case prints, crime-scene technicians record not just prints from the fingertips but from the palms and the sides of the hands. As DeVecchio explained it, Marshall was busy trying to match the prints from the Mercury Montego to a set of major case prints he was having taken on Bruno Indelicato.

A week after my conversation with DeVecchio, Pat Marshall strolled through my office door. Pat was one of the most serious, hardworking agents we had in the Organized Crime Section; he went about his job with the quiet intensity of a monk. Which is why I was so startled by the big grin that split his face as I looked up from my desk.

"What do you want? You look like the fucking cat that ate the canary."

"Never mind, Jules." Marshall made as if to walk out. "You can wait, and I'll let Kossler or DeVecchio tell you. Whenever the hell they get around to it."

"Don't fuck around, Pat. What have you got?"

"Bingo—that's what I got!" Marshall looked like he was ready to dance a little jig, he was so wound up. "The fucking prints matched, Jules! Bruno's our guy!"

"Holy shit, you guys did it. I don't believe it!"

"I don't believe it, either, to tell you the truth." Marshall explained that they had hauled Bruno's sorry ass over from a lockup in New Jersey, where he was awaiting trial on a weapons charge. Prints of the heel of his right hand matched those taken from the right rear door handle of the Mercury Montego. Eyewitnesses at the time had identified a man with a shotgun as having emerged from the right rear door of the car; the man had entered the Italian restaurant where Galante was dining and emerged less than a minute later, Galante no longer among the living. Bruno Indelicato had been the shooter.

"Great work, Pat. Great job!"

"Ah, it doesn't hurt to be lucky sometimes, either."

"Luck my ass, pal." I climbed out of the chair behind my desk and engulfed Marshall in a big bear hug. "Great fucking job, Pat. Just great work."

The commission case was gathering steam now, and our date in court was looming in front of us.

Tragically, Paul Castellano would never make it.

On December 16, with exactly nine shopping days to go before Christmas, three men in trench coats murdered Castellano and his trusted driver, Tom Bilotti, as they stepped out of the boss of bosses' shiny black Lincoln on Forty-sixth Street, between Second and Third avenues in Manhattan. The story of the Castellano hit has been told and retold, and I am given to understand that the precise location where the boss of bosses fell, just outside Sparks Steak House, where Castellano would have dined that evening had the men in the trench coats not made other plans for him, is now among the midtown landmarks pointed out by the tour guides on their bus trips around New York.

Much has been made of the highly public nature of the Castellano murder—appropriately so, I think. This was no run-of-the mill Bonanno family capo, buried in the weeds in a crummy garbage-strewn lot out in Queens. The boss of bosses went out at approximately fifteen minutes before six, at the height of the Manhattan rush hour, in midtown, on a busy street and in plain view of dozens of harried Christmas shoppers, home-rushing office workers, and hungry pretheater diners. That was part of the message—one Paul Castellano had somehow failed to receive when he was alive.

The message, as befits a culture governed by such crude norms as those of the Italian Mafia, was a simple one. Castellano may have embarrassed himself by the unseemly affair with his flighty Gloria, but in allowing the FBI to gain access to his home and then to record the most sensitive and damaging conversations that had taken place there, the boss of bosses had left himself dangerously exposed. The commission indictment had increased that exposure, as had a second investigation of Castellano involving a charge of conspiracy to commit murder.

Exposure to the rigors of the criminal justice system is nothing new to wise guys; it comes with the turf. But Paul Castellano's personal life and his seeming inattention to the repercussions that his own legal troubles were having on others among the wise guys had rendered what might have been a tolerable level of exposure for another Mafia boss to one that ultimately proved fatal for the boss of bosses.

Others, including some of my former colleagues, have speculated that Castellano was murdered because of fear among the wise guys that he was preparing to cooperate with the FBI. Anything is possible, I suppose, but we had no indication that Castellano was about to turn on the wise guys, and I doubt the man was capable of it. I don't say this because I consider Paul Castellano a stand-up guy; he was anything but—a crook, a double-dealer, a man not above ordering the murder of a long-time associate or of throwing several decades of spousal devotion out the window of his million-dollar mansion in exchange for the cheap attentions of his maid.

No, Paul Castellano was not a stand-up guy. What he was, in a very real way, I think, was a sadly delusional man. From Castellano's White House up on Todt Hill, the view of New York is leafy green and clean. The air is fresh, and the panorama conveniently admits of no crack dens, no homeless people, no wretched shopkeepers lying awake nights wondering how they'll make next week's payment to the bull-necked Gambino family enforcer who would be at their door as sure as sunrise. This was the view that comforted Paul Castellano, the one he cherished.

But it also reinforced his delusions. Paul Castellano wasn't a criminal, he told himself; a legitimate businessman was what he was. He had taken drug money from Sonny Black Napolitano, but in his own mind Paul Castellano had shunned the evils of narcotics trafficking and even imposed draconian penalties on any of his confederates who engaged in it. Conveniently ignored in the Castellano rationale was not just the fact that he had taken drug money from Sonny Black but that capos in his very family, the slimeballs from the Bergen Fish and Hunt Club crew, were pumping millions of dollars of heroin into New York every year.

In the end, the way Paul Castellano saw it, it was his far-seeing stewardship that would guide the Italian Mafia out of the bad old days of the Mustache Petes and into the bright new world of legitimate business. It was a fine and inspired vision. The only trouble was, it had almost nothing to do with the reality of the way the Cosa Nostra operated or even the way Castellano attempted to influence its operation.

That, in any case, was the Paul Castellano I saw. And if all that doesn't add up to the definition of a seriously delusional human being, I don't know what does.

On a bitterly cold December morning, Paul Castellano was buried with the pomp and ceremony befitting a man of his station. I had no doubt that the very commission Castellano had once ruled with the stern hand of a paterfamilias had approved his murder. It was, in that sense, a patricide.

But there are casualties of all sorts in war. Patricide or no, I counted Paul Castellano no different from the rest.

36

THE same day Castellano's cooling corpse was drawing a crowd of gawkers on East Forty-sixth Street, we were laying out the picture of mob infiltration of New York's vast business community for twelve citizens honest and true. The place was a hushed courtroom a few miles downtown from where Castellano had breathed his last, and the ladies and gentlemen of the jury were getting an earful about how Ralph Scopo and his fellow wise guys had hijacked New York City's cement and construction industries. The government's case, which would take seven months to present, would introduce the jurors to many of the people you have already met—people like Vinnie DePenta, Frankie Ancona, and Fred DeChristopher. All would testify at length as witnesses for the prosecution. Bruce Baird was the ringleader of this particular circus, and with his fellow prosecutors, Aaron Marcu and Frank Sherman, he would treat the jurors to an unprecedented firsthand look at Mafia control not just of the cement and construction trades but of much of New York's multibillion-dollar restaurant and hotel business as well.

From my office across St. Andrew's Plaza at 26 Federal, I monitored the trial proceedings closely, but not because I was worried about how things were going. We had great agents on the case in Denis Maduro, John Joyce, and the rest of the crew from Damon Taylor's squad. The prosecution team of Baird, Marcu, and Sherman was also top-flight. As to the evidence, it literally spoke for itself. The Title IIIs from Ralph Scopo's cars were devastating. So were the conversations from Vinnie DePenta's conference room at D&M. Ditto the Title IIIs from the Casa Storta and from Donnie Shacks Montemarano's home and club.

Even poor Frankie Ancona's story about losing his house to that slimeball Gerry Lang Langella and having to sleep in his car with his three little kids in the middle of winter—what jury could fail to be moved by that or fail to make the person responsible pay?

A few weeks after the murder of Castellano, Jim Kossler walked into my office at 26 Federal, pipe in hand, chuckling.

"What's so funny?"

Kossler fell into an armchair. "Nothing, just Brian."

"Now what? Someone hit him in the face with a fish?"

"Nah, he's just frustrated, that's all. The case is going nowhere."

"Yeah, I know."

A few months before I got back to New York, Kossler had assigned a supervisor of one of our labor-racketeering squads, a guy named Brian Taylor, to an investigation of the Fulton Fish Market. Brian went five eleven, two hundred pounds, and a tougher guy you are not likely to meet. As an army officer in Vietnam, Brian had won a Silver Star for courage and a Purple Heart for stupidity. But Brian was not stupid; he was fearless.

For years, the Fulton Fish Market was a place where wise guys had operated as if laws and law enforcement did not exist. More than 100 million pounds of fish moved through the market every year, and its wholesalers provided seafood of one type or another to nearly every part of the country. The stuff was not just seafood caught by commercial fishermen along America's East Coast, either; South African lobster tails, Norwegian salmon, and exotic catches from as far away as Alaska and Chile were flown in nightly by jumbo jet to Kennedy Airport and whisked away by truck directly to the Fulton market.

The market's influence extended across the United States. If you have ever eaten a deep-fried shrimp at a fast-food restaurant or a blackened platter-sized swordfish steak at one of America's most elite eateries, the chances are better than even that your meal came through one of the nearly one hundred wholesalers who operated out of the Fulton Fish Market. The chances are also good—because the market was controlled lock, stock, and barrel by the Mafia—that you paid a lot more than you should have for your nice fish dinner.

Mob control of the Fulton Fish Market dated to the late 1920s. A Genovese family capo named Joe Lanza controlled the Fulton market as if it were his personal fiefdom, and not a scallop moved through the place that "Socks" Lanza didn't make a profit on. No pun intended, the guy ran a tight ship.

Lanza's operation was straight out of the Cosa Nostra playbook. Local 359 of the United Seafood Workers Union handled all of the loading and unloading at the Fulton Fish Market; Socks Lanza controlled the local. But that wasn't all he controlled. Lanza's influence extended to the East Coast fishing fleets that supplied the Fulton market. If he had reason to believe that an oversupply of seafood on any given day would drive his wholesalers' prices through the floor, Lanza simply put out the word to the fleets: Dump your catch. Anyone who didn't do as Lanza said could basically forget about getting his fish unloaded at the Fulton market the next day.

More than any other commodity, seafood relies on speed of delivery. You want to see a man about to lose his mind because of circumstances beyond his control, turn up at a place like the Fulton market about midnight and look for the guy with a thousand pounds of fish on his truck when no one will unload it. Socks Lanza knew this, of course, and it was precisely why his extortion racket at the Fulton Fish Market was so successful. All Lanza had to do was look cross-eyed at some poor wholesaler and the guy would pay up, whatever the price. If he didn't pay, the wholesaler knew for a matter of fact that the six unloading crews from Local 359 who worked the Fulton market would simply look at his truck the next time he drove up, then walk right by. By dawn, the guy's fish would be beginning to stink pretty good, the price of his catch plummeting with each passing minute. Which meant basically that not paying was not an option.

Extortion wasn't the only scam Socks Lanza ran on the people who did business at the Fulton Fish Market. When it came to screwing people, Mr. Lanza had a very fertile mind indeed. Lanza's beefy unloaders from Local 359 would frequently steal sizable quantities of fish—and we're talking multihundred-pound loads here, too, not a bushel of scallops. Lanza would then arrange to sell the stolen fish and pocket the profit himself. Then he or one of his emissaries would approach the wholesaler whose fish had mysteriously disappeared, and Lanza would offer to protect the fellow from future thefts of seafood. The guy, needless to say, paid up.

Over the years, after Socks Lanza faded from the scene, the Genovese family kept right on operating the Fulton Fish Market precisely as Lanza had. Socks had set up a crude but highly efficient system whereby just about everyone at the market was getting screwed to the max; the system worked, and the wise guys weren't terribly interested in tinkering with it. As for the people who had to do business at the market—and if you were in the seafood game, the Fulton Fish Market was the only game in town—they had gotten used to wise-guy rules over the years, and they had long since learned that there was no point in going to the cops to complain; historically, law enforcement in New York had given the hoods at the Fulton market pretty wide berth.

Kossler and I intended to change that.

"So"—I blew some of Kossler's pipe smoke away from me—"what'd you tell our friend Brian?"

Kossler chuckled again and drew on his pipe.

"What'd you tell him, Jimmy?"

I look back on it now, and it still amazes me, so many different personalities and how they complemented each other so well—Pistone and Kallstrom and Sean McWeeney, then Kossler and I back together for the final push in New York. Ever since the Blakey seminar up in Ithaca, Jim Kossler had been plumbing the depths of the RICO statute, talking endlessly to Blakey about the ramifications of this or that clause, reading everything he could get his hands on. Whereas I tended to think of RICO as a weighted club, at the ready, Kossler studied the law with the intensity of a reader of ancient texts, eager to unlock the statute's very last secrets. Which is why his answer to my question surprised me, but only for a moment.

"I asked Bri to think about a civil RICO approach."

"Oh, Jesus."

"No, really." Leaning back in his chair, Kossler explained how he had sat Brian down in his office and told him about the civil penalties Blakey had written into the racketeering law and how they might be applied to the wise guys running the Fulton Fish Market and Local 359 of the United Seafood Workers Union.

I shook my head in admiration. Leave it to Kossler, I thought. I understood the noncriminal portions of Blakey's racketeering law, though not nearly as well as Kossler. I could only imagine what Brian must have been thinking as Jimmy walked him through the thicket of legal arcana. Like me, Brian was impatient, action oriented. He was also a younger guy, and he had not been exposed to the Blakey brilliance firsthand, as Kossler and I had. "Shit, Jimmy, what did Brian say?"

Kossler laughed, then snorted through his pipe smoke. "He asked me what the hell a civil RICO was."

"Oh, shit."

"I just told him. I laid it out as simply as I could." Kossler gave me the short version.

While he talked, I considered the merits of the civil RICO approach myself. There would be no busting wise guys at the fish market if we went the civil route; that was a given. We would not be running a criminal case. But the way the Operation Seaprobe investigation had been going, I thought, there would probably be no busting of wise guys at the fish market, anyway. What there would be, if we got lucky on a civil RICO approach, was a petition to the court that would cite the evidence Brian and his squad had already gathered as well as the historical record going back to Socks Lanza, including the 1979 case against Carmine and Peter Romano and the five other Genovese family thugs.

For us, the biggest appeal of going the civil RICO route was the evidentiary standard we would have to meet. Unlike a criminal trial, where we were required to prove "beyond a reasonable doubt" that a defendant had committed the crimes alleged in an indictment, the civil portions of the RICO statute required only that a "preponderance of the evidence" show that our allegations were true. The difference, if you think about it, is sort of the same thing as a vote in your state legislature that requires a two-thirds majority to win and a straight up-or-down vote where you can prevail with a simple majority. The standard, in other words, was an easier one to meet.

The RICO law had been on the books a long time, and we had begun making aggressive use of the criminal portions of the statute; the civil portions had been employed sparingly, however. There would be abuses of the civil and criminal portions of the RICO statute in years to come. But given the facts of the Fulton Fish Market situation, civil RICO was a perfect solution for us back then. If we prevailed, I knew, a U.S. District Court judge would issue a permanent injunction forcing all Genovese family members and associates to divest themselves of all business interests having any relationship with the Fulton Fish Market and Local 359. If we could persuade the judge with a preponderance of the evidence, hizzoner could also remove every last Local 359 official who had ties to the Genovese family and replace them with court-appointed trustees. As to the fish market itself, if the judge bought our case, he could appoint an independent administrator to run the entire show.

As Brian told me afterward, he had sat there slack-jawed as Kossler explained the mechanics of civil RICO to him.

"Any questions?" Kossler asked when he was done.

"Yeah, one, Jim. Can we really do all that shit?"

It was exactly the right response.

Tough guys are a dime a dozen, I've always thought, but tough guys with smarts don't come along too often. A lot of cops get their satisfaction from the job simply by busting wrongdoers. There's nothing wrong with that, of course. But agents like Brian Taylor saw clearly how meaningless that could be. It was exactly the same thing I had felt years before, making all those crummy gambling cases. What did it prove? What I mean to say here is that if we didn't have a few smart, tough guys like Brian —if, in fact, all we had was a bunch of agents whose eyes would glaze over when they heard some mumbo jumbo about something called civil RICO—then a visionary like Jimmy Kossler would have been like a prophet in the wilderness.

But that wasn't what happened.

What happened was that Brian Taylor went after the civil RICO case on the Fulton Fish Market like a man unchained.

And Brian's guys followed. The labor-racketeering squad Brian had working on the Seaprobe case included some of the toughest guys within the FBI and the NYPD, door kickers and guys who didn't take any shit from anyone. They would not be an easy sale on civil RICO, but so possessed was Brian by the possibilities of the approach outlined by Kossler that he spent hours talking with the guys on the squad one-on-one, explaining why this was the way to go. It took some doing, but before too long, the whole squad was chattering away like a bunch of law clerks about the nuances of civil RICO. Within weeks, I became so convinced of the genius of the approach Kossler had suggested that I converted Brian's entire squad—ten FBI special agents and ten top-notch NYPD investigators—into a civil RICO squad. It was the first such squad in the entire FBI.

Putting the theory into practice was interesting.

With ten FBI agents and ten NYPD officers, Brian Taylor descended on the Fulton Fish Market with the zeal of an avenging angel. He was not, as you might expect, received with much cordiality.

The Fulton market was an almost exclusively male domain, and the men who worked loading and unloading the wholesalers' trucks were large, well-muscled individuals. As a rule, these individuals were not especially inclined to put up with bullshit, interference, questions, and the like. These same men were also given to expressions of annoyance, unhappiness, or even just plain boredom with fists, clubs, and occasionally those very large fishhooks the wholesalers used to display their trophy catches.

The fishhooks, indeed, were used on Brian and his squad not long after Kossler talked to Brian about going the civil RICO route. Somehow some of the gentlemen from Local 359 who worked at the Fulton market identified the squad's undercover cars, and they used the big hooks to shred and flatten their tires, break into the car trunks, and generally beat the shit out of the vehicles. There were verbal threats to go along with the abuse, but Brian and his guys gave as good as they got.

The place was a tough one for Brian and the squad to operate in. The way the Fulton market worked, things didn't really get going there until around ten o'clock in the evening, when the trucks from JFK started rolling in, followed close behind by seafood trucks from as far away as the Carolinas and Maine. Buyers would show up at around three in the morning, and before that, the loaders would be in high gear moving seafood from the trucks to the retail stalls.

There was a lot of chaos and bullshit, with everyone running around like mad, and ordinarily that would have been a perfect environment for an FBI agent to work undercover. The Fulton market was such a closed society, however, that everyone pretty much knew everyone else, and Brian and his guys had a hard time conducting surveillances and interviewing potential witnesses. Finding anyone who would even consider talking with us about the wise guys who exploited them was a nightmare.

When Brian took a rare night off from hanging around the fish market, to give you just one example, he was spelled by his primary relief supervisor, a no-nonsense former marine named George Walker. One night, George was hanging around trying to make conversation with a retail fish buyer who did a lot of business at the Fulton market. The man was Oriental, very fit, and George had heard that he had a black belt in karate. George had also heard that the man had put his martial arts training to work not too long before when a Genovese family hood had come around demanding his protection money. The Oriental man basically wiped the floor with the Italian hoodlum, but that was not the end of it, as Walker found out.

The Genovese family member returned to the Oriental man's stall sometime after he had recovered from his kung-fu injuries, and he and a bunch of his wise guy buddies had used the blunt ends of those large fish hooks to beat the Oriental man until he was nearly unconscious. The man had then paid his protection money. As the man's friends told George later, there was no way in hell he would be a witness for us.

Brian and his squad did score a few successes, enough to win court approval of several Title IIIs.

Headquarters, of course, went nuts. Ten agents, ten cops, no indictments, no arrests: In Washington, even after all this time, the arithmetic still did not compute, and as luck would have it, an inspection team from Headquarters was already heading our way when they got the news about the new squad and their Title IIIs on the Fulton market.

Good, I thought. Let 'em come.

Brian Taylor was in my office a few days after the inspectors arrived. "Boss, we're screwed." Red-faced and filling my doorway like an angry bear, Brian was visibly upset.

"What's up?" For a second I wondered if he had decked an inspector.

"We're screwed, boss. They're definitely going to fry our asses this time."

Before I could ask about this latest cause of calamity, Brian was telling me how an aide to the head inspector had been grilling him for the better part of the past hour. " 'What are we doing, exactly?' the guy asks. 'How many arrests we got? Convictions?' We're down there playing twenty questions, and I got no fucking answers. I mean, Jeez!"

I laughed. "Hey, Bri, do me a favor, okay?"

"Yeah, what?"

"Just keep pushing, all right? I'll handle these assholes."

"Sure, boss, whatever you say." Brian flashed me his world-beater grin. "That's why you get the big bucks, I guess."

"Get out of here, will you?"

Brian left, and I had my secretary find the chief inspector's aide. Five minutes later, this kid who was maybe three years out of college was standing in my office, and I confess I read him the riot act. It was a shame to take it out on the poor kid, but I had more than had it with the FBI's Inspection Division, and this young guy, who was really only just doing his job the way he had been taught, caught the full brunt of all that pent-up anger. I still feel bad about it, but who knows, maybe the kid learned a little something in the process. In any case, about twenty minutes later, Brian Taylor was back in my office, cackling like a man sorely in need of a straitjacket and a couple of beefy attendants. "Boss?"

"Yeah, Bri?"

"What the hell did you say to that kid with the inspector?"

"I just talked to him, that's all. Why?"

"I got on the elevator just now, and the kid was with his boss, and he was shaking. I mean literally."

"No kidding."

"Yeah, and the kid was telling the inspector how you were crazy. Fucking crazy, he said."

I laughed. "Oh, yeah?"

"Yeah, but the best thing, the inspector, he looks at the poor kid, and he agrees. 'That fucking Bonavolonta,' he says, 'the guy *is* crazy.'"

Crazy or no, that was my job, the way I saw it, keeping my people happy and productive and not hung up with the bureaucratic bullshit from Headquarters. After that morning, Brian and his squad had no more questions from the chief inspector and his little aide. The squad went back to work coming up with a preponderance of evidence that would put the goddamned Genovese family so far away from the Fulton Fish Market that they might as well be on the moon.

I'm not very superstitious, but the patriarchs of the Colombo organized-crime family might have been as they contemplated their navels in the bowels of various federal penitentiaries around the country.

On Friday the thirteenth in June 1986, U.S. District Court

Judge John F. Keenan ordered federal marshals to usher the twelve men and women who had sat so patiently for the past seven months listening to the evidence in his courtroom back into the jury box. Jim Kossler got the call five minutes before noon and rushed into my office.

"Jules, the jury's back."

Nervous Nellies, the two of us raced across St. Andrew's Plaza and took the elevator up to Keenan's courtroom. Bruce Baird, Aaron Marcu, and Frank Sherman were already there. So were Denis Maduro and John Joyce. The agents and prosecutors had invested the last few years of their lives on the Colombo case, and now it had all come down to this, the judgment of twelve honest Americans on whether or not we had done our jobs properly and well. I leaned forward in my seat to listen.

"Madame Forelady, has the jury reached a verdict?" For his solicitousness toward all parties over the course of the seven-month trial, Judge John Keenan should have been canonized.

"Yes, Your Honor, we have." The jury foreperson rose from her chair to answer Keenan. She was seventy-two, a kindly grandmother who had spent more than thirty years as a teacher and guidance counselor in New York City's tumultuous public schools.

"You may be seated if you wish, Madame Forelady. It's been a long trial, and there are a lot of counts."

"Thank you, Your Honor, but I prefer to stand." With that, the kindly grandmother looked directly into the eyes of Carmine "the Snake" Persico and the other defendants and spoke in a clear, unmodulated voice. "On count one as to Mr. Persico"—a slight pause; count one was the RICO charge—"guilty."

I breathed a sigh of relief and saw Bruce Baird, Denis Maduro, and the others sit a little straighter in their chairs.

Across the aisle at the defense table, Carmine Persico looked rumpled and confused, but it was impossible to feel sympathy for the man. Next to him, Gerry Lang Langella found something interesting to study on the tips of his gleaming shoes. The six other defendants, all members and associates of the Colombo crime family, found other things to stare at in the courtroom

—everything but at the kindly grandmother standing ramrod straight in the front left seat of the paneled jury box declaiming the day's news. "As to Mr. Scarpatti . . . as to Mr. DeRoss . . . as to Mr. Langella, to Mr. Russo, Mr. Cataldo, Mr. McIntosh . . . guilty, guilty, guilty, guilty, guilty, guilty."

There was something about the forelady's unembellished voice as it echoed in the otherwise silent courtroom that thrilled me. Here was an ordinary American, a public servant in the best and purest sense of the term, a woman who had devoted her life to working with kids. For most of that life, though she could not have known it, the wise guys, like those seated before her, had made her city and her country unhappier places to live. For the seven months she and her fellow jurors had listened to Bruce, Aaron, and Frank lay out the FBI's case against the Colombo family, it was impossible for us to know how she or the other jurors felt. Were they bored, confused, tired?

Here, now, was the answer: The jurors were angry.

The wise guys, with their ready-mix cement "club" that had boosted the cost of virtually everything made and sold in New York City, were certainly worthy targets of anger. With their ties to the narcotics traffickers who poisoned the kids on the city's streets, they were worthy objects of rage, too.

In courtrooms, unless I was a witness, I was a silent watcher. I watched then and cheered silently for the ladies and gentlemen of the Colombo family jury. I cheered especially for that ordinary but magnificent jury forelady.

Perhaps her family had faulted the kindly grandmother at one time or another for a voice that was too high or too low, too fast or too slow. For me it was magisterial. It told us not that we had won—the government and the FBI over the wise guys. No, what it said was that the system had won, and if that sounds trite or corny, too bad, because in the end that was what this was all about. Sure, at some important level, the war against the wise guys for me was personal, and there was no way I was going to come in anywhere but first place. But this wasn't about ego or winning and all that crap. What it was about was upholding a system and a society founded on law.

That's corny? Sorry, not in my book.

In his closing statement to the jury before the jurors began deliberating, Aaron Marcu spent some time talking about law and lawlessness, right and wrong. But Aaron had sharpened the barb in his summation, asking the jurors to consider not just the philosophical differences between the polarities but the penalties that ought to be paid by those who chose the latter over the former. "You, ladies and gentlemen, learned an enormous amount in the past seven months about a small but dark segment of our society that, unfortunately, is with us." Marcu spoke in a quiet voice, not lecturing. "It is a shadowy world filled with selfish men, men who have chosen as a way of living, as a profession, crime. You have learned about the criminal careers of a group of men who picked the Colombo family and membership in it over a decent way of life. The years of crime that you have learned about during the course of this case do not come without any responsibility, and the time finally has come to place responsibility for those crimes, for those lives dedicated to crimes, exactly where it belongs."

No, the majesty I heard in the kindly grandmother's voice was not the chrome-plated kind that you find inscribed to the victor on his trophy cup. The majesty I heard grew straight out of a system of justice that can place responsibility, as Aaron Marcu phrased it, "exactly where it belongs." In the end, it was a system that could triumph even over such soulless, vicious criminals as Carmine Persico and Gerry Lang Langella.

After standing for forty-five minutes and reading the verdicts on all counts for all eight of the defendants, the jury forelady sat down, and Judge Keenan thanked her and the other jurors for their service. The jurors were excused, and Judge Keenan then ordered Carmine the Snake, Gerry Lang, and the six other defendants remanded to the custody of federal marshals. The eight Colombo family defendants would eventually be sentenced to more than two centuries in the custody of the U.S. Bureau of Prisons. For the record, the exact number of years to be served was 202.

37

IT seemed like almost no time after the convictions of the Colombo family hierarchy before we were back in court for trial on the commission case. The players who had to make both trial dates were definitely not growing any fonder of our faces.

There was Carmine Persico again, for instance. The Colombo family boss was looking at a total of thirty-nine years in Uncle Sam's prisons on account of the jury's verdict back in June. By the time he showed up for jury selection in the commission case, either Carmine the Snake was broke, tired of talking with lawyers all the time, or just didn't give a shit. Whatever it was, Persico had decided to act as his own attorney at trial. Gerry Lang Langella was another guy doing a twofer on the Colombo and commission cases, and he had even bigger problems than Carmine the Snake. Gerry Lang was looking at a total of sixty-nine years behind bars as a result of his convictions in the Colombo case, so even if he managed to walk on the charges here, there was no way he would be breathing the clean air of freedom again in his lifetime.

The rest of the commission-case defendants were no strangers to a courtroom. There was Fat Tony Salerno, the Genovese family boss, Fulton Fish Market godfather, and patron saint of crooked would-be Teamsters Union higher-ups. The Lucchese family had thoughtfully contributed a trio of defendants to the case. There was Tony "Ducks" Corallo, the Lucchese family boss, lately recovered from his mysterious case of indictment flu. Behind him was Salvatore "Tom Mix" Santoro, a man who we had on more than a few compromising Title III conversations that he would have cause to regret. Behind Tom Mix was Christopher "Christy Tick" Furnari, the Lucchese family *consigliere*.

Of course, no trial of the commission case would be complete without the presence of fat Ralphie Scopo, the can-do wise guy behind the ready-mix cement scam. This crew of heroes was rounded out finally by none other than Bruno Indelicato, the Bonanno family capo and all-around loser whom we had charged in the superseding indictment for the murder of Carmine Galante.

Almost right up until the trial began, Rudy Giuliani had been telling me and just about anyone else who would listen that he was going to try the case himself. Rudy had assigned Mike Chertoff to prepare the case for trial, but Giuliani would put the case to the jury, he said. Barbara Jones's political antennae are second to nobody's, and she knew that in the end Giuliani would not try the commission case. Giuliani kept insisting he would, but Barbara pulled Chertoff aside one day and told it to him straight: "Get ready, Mike, it's going to be your baby." Chertoff was relatively new to the U.S. Attorney's office, but he knew a good tip when he heard one, and he started working nights and weekends to get the case ready.

Rudy Giuliani and I had been friends for a long time, and I knew why he had finally taken a pass on the commission case; I wasn't thrilled by it, but I understood. The big Wall Street insider-trading cases of the 1980s were beginning to come down the pike, and there were a couple of promising political-corruption cases Rudy's people were working. Giuliani was drawn to them, his politician's eye already starting to focus on the kinds of events that would maximize public exposure.

That was fine with me, because in Mike Chertoff, Rudy had given us a first-class prosecutor. The commission case would be Mike's first big prosecution, but just talking with him, you knew Mike had the tools. No question about it.

The commission case, indeed, would set the standard for a stellar career for Chertoff. "Tenacious" and "brilliant" were adjectives that even adversaries used in describing Mike's courtroom skills. Mike would go on to become the U.S. Attorney for New Jersey, a position in which he would handle dozens of high-profile prosecutions with a surefootedness other lawyers could only envy. Handed the commission case by Giuliani, Chertoff would demonstrate every one of those qualities at trial.

Young Mike, indeed, had come loaded for bear, I saw on the opening day of the trial. With Assistant U.S. Attorneys John Savarese and Gil Childers, Chertoff launched a withering attack on the Cosa Nostra's board of directors.

The date was September 8, 1986. I was sitting in the back row, my usual spectator's chair. Damn, I thought, the guy's sure as hell not wasting any time.

In his opening statement, Chertoff spent a few minutes speaking quietly to the twelve jurors and the two alternates who had been selected for the trial. He introduced himself, Savarese, and Childers. Then he introduced Pat Marshall and Charlotte Lang. Then he began outlining the case.

I listened, and as Mike talked about what the FBI's evidence would show, I felt a surge of pride.

What a team we had put together!

Chertoff's words soon brought me back to the reality of the courtroom. The commission, Chertoff told the jurors, was "the ruling council of the Cosa Nostra." The Cosa Nostra was not a charitable organization, Mike explained. It was not a social club like the Elks or the Moose, nor was it an association of businessmen like the Rotarians. Members of the Rotary Club, Chertoff explained, were interested in legitimate business; not so the Mafia Commission. No, Chertoff said, almost in sadness, I thought. "Mafia families have a single overriding purpose, and that purpose is to make money—to make money illegally, to make money criminally, to make money using corruption, fear, and violence."

Chertoff paused and gazed steadily at the most powerful men of the Italian Mafia, then continued: "Corruption of labor unions, extortion, loan-sharking, murder—that is why these men have been brought here before you, ladies and gentlemen."

Chertoff dwelled for several moments on the wise guys and their peculiar affinity for violence, but my thoughts wandered elsewhere. Just months ago, most of the wise guys we were after had no real understanding of the power of the RICO statute. One day, Aaron Marcu, the Assistant U.S. Attorney who helped prosecute the Colombo case, had brought Frankie "the Beast" Falanga into his office at 1 St. Andrew's Plaza to explain the charges on which he had just been indicted. Now, granted, Frankie the Beast was not exactly your brightest wise guy, but he serves as a general barometer of wise-guy intelligence. Anyway, Aaron sat Frankie the Beast down in a chair in front of his desk and started to explain the indictment.

"Mr. Falanga, the grand jury, in its first count against you, has charged you with RICO."

Frankie the Beast flew out of his chair. "RICO? I don't even know any fucking RICO!"

By the time the commission case came to trial, all the wise guys knew RICO very well. As Chertoff concluded his brief opening statement, I thought the Mafia's board of directors could not have been too cheerful about their chances. Overweight, pathetic old men, they still amazed me, however, by their capacity for violence and ruthlessness. Silently, from my usual perch in the courtroom's back row, I cheered the team on. "Get 'em, Mike. Let's put them away, every one."

The trial lasted nine weeks. And with each passing day, the furrows in the wise guys' brows appeared to grow deeper, the frowns as pronounced and tragic as Greek masks.

Fat Tony Salerno in particular seemed prepared for the worst. Fat Tony, you should not be surprised to learn, was a rather indelicate eater, and as the trial progressed and the stack of evidence against him grew higher and higher, he began consoling himself with chocolate bars. Sitting at the defense table alongside Tony Ducks Corallo, Carmine the Snake Persico, and the other defendants, Fat Tony produced a seemingly inexhaustible supply of Mars bars and Baby Ruths from the capacious pockets of his rumpled suitcoat. It was a sight to see but to hear as well. At quiet moments in the courtroom, when there was a break in the action, you could hear Fat Tony sinking his carious teeth into another nutty candy bar. *Ka-runch.*

One of the people who provided invaluable help to us in organizing and cataloging the Title III information in the Colombo and the commission trials was a great guy named Gene McDonald. Chertoff or one of the other prosecutors would promise the jury they would hear this or that defendant incriminate himself in his own words, and presto, Gene McDonald was there with exactly the right tape snippet at exactly the right spot, and Tony Ducks's rattly voice or Carmine the Snake's sinister rumble would fill the quiet courtroom. One day we were waiting for the jury to come in after lunch, and Gene McDonald, purely out of the goodness of his heart, walked up to Fat Tony at the defense table and offered him a granola bar.

"They're really much better for you, Mr. Salerno. Better than all that chocolate."

Fat Tony waved the granola bar away and dipped into his pocket. "Who the fuck cares," he said, producing an Almond Joy and pawing at the wrapper, not even meeting Gene McDonald's eyes. "I'm gonna die in the fucking can, anyway."

So the wise guys had few illusions about how things would turn out, and it was a good thing. In his summation of the case against the wise guys, Mike Chertoff harkened back to one of the few moments of comic relief the commission trial had afforded. Carmine Persico had served throughout the trial as his own attorney, and it was clear that he had not spent a lot of time perusing the thick procedure manuals published by the American Trial Lawyers Association. As a rule, Carmine the Snake's questions to witnesses tended to be rambling and unfocused— and those were the good ones. Like most of the wise guys, Carmine the Snake had watched a lot of TV in his sorry life, but he was clearly not a fan of the Perry Mason school of courtroom drama. Whereas Mason delivered dramatic last-minute bombshells from his seat at the defense table, Carmine the Snake was a pacer, roaming the length and breadth of the courtroom like an aging bantam, waving his arms and muttering. During one such demonstration, the Snake paused dramatically and declaimed: "Without the Mafia, there wouldn't even be no case here!"

Persico didn't know it, but he was actually on to something. Just as the wise guys had been in the dark until lately about the mechanics of RICO, the defendants in the commission case could not figure out how the hell we could prosecute them simply for being members of the Mafia. Chertoff wasn't too concerned about setting the wise guys straight on that point, but he wanted to make damned sure the jury was satisfied.

"Ladies and gentlemen," Chertoff said toward the end of his closing remarks in the trial, "it has been said that without the Mafia, there would not be a case here." Mike paused, cast a funny look at Carmine Persico, then continued, essentially conceding Persico's point but drawing precisely the opposite conclusion to what Persico had attempted to urge on the jury. "Without the power of the Mafia," Chertoff said, his voice gathering power, "these defendants could not have taken control of an industry like New York's cement industry, they could not have authorized the murder of Carmine Galante, could not have engaged in a loan-sharking conspiracy, could not have taken over and dominated labor unions, could not have committed the crimes you have heard about during the course of this case. They could not have done any of these things you have heard about, ladies and gentlemen of the jury, without the Mafia. So that is why there is a Mafia in this case. That is what this case is all about!"

On November 19, the jury was in its fifth day of deliberations when Jim Kossler came rushing into my office.

"They're back, this is it!"

For a moment, I felt as if my heart had stopped. We all believed in the theory and evidence on which the commission case had been built. But trials, as any two-bit lawyer can tell you, are a crapshoot, and Charlotte Lang had expressed the fears of all of us about the commission case after her first meeting with

Mike Chertoff, more than a year earlier. "One strange case," she had called it. It was strange, but only because the legal theory had never been applied before in a courtroom.

The question now was whether the jury would buy it. In representing himself, Carmine Persico had proven once again the truth of the adage that the person who represents himself in court has a fool for a client. Most of the other defendants in the commission case, however, had retained very able counsel, and each of the lawyers had spent hours attacking the legal underpinnings of the government's case.

Had they scored any points with the jury?

Within minutes after the news of a verdict came from the jury room, Chertoff rushed in from a neighboring courtroom where he had been killing time watching another case. The press was calling it "the Pizza Connection Case." It was the product of a massive narcotics investigation begun while I was still in Washington. The case had grown out of an effort that Joe Pistone and I had initiated back in 1982. The investigation would document the incestuous criminal relationship between the Italian Mafia and the American Cosa Nostra in the distribution of heroin through dozens of pizza parlors across the United States. The investigation had been run by one of my closest friends, FBI Special Agent Lou Schiliro. In the courtroom, the case was being prosecuted by another dear friend, Louie Freeh, formerly of the FBI, now an assistant U.S. Attorney in Rudy Giuliani's office. I would have plenty of time later to catch up with the day's events in the Pizza case; for the moment, though, I could think only of the jurors in the commission case. What conclusions had they come to over the past five days?

At the door of the courthouse, a crush of reporters and television cameras blocked the way; the newsies had the scent of blood. Win or lose, the commission verdicts would be the lead story on all newscasts that evening.

The knot in my stomach grew tighter.

At the head of the courthouse stairs, Romulo Immundi, New York's chief federal marshal, spied me and Kossler elbowing our way through the pack of reporters, and he cleared a path, waving me and Jimmy up the steps and through the courthouse metal detector. Romulo Immundi was another friend, one of my oldest. Before I dashed off, he hugged me.

"Good luck, my friend. This is your day."

"It's our day, Ronnie—all of ours."

Shit, I thought, I sure hope so, anyway.

Upstairs, I stepped into Judge Richard Owen's paneled courtroom and slid along the rear wall, locking eyes with Chertoff for just a second. Gray-faced, Mike nodded and sat down. Barbara Jones came in a second later and took a place along the wall next to me. "This is it, guy." Her hand gripped my arm tightly. At least I wasn't the only one with the jitters.

Judge Owen instructed the marshals to escort the jury into the courtroom, and I closed my eyes. The flashback to the Colombo case was inevitable, but the stakes here were much higher. Back in June we had had just the one family on the hook; here it was the Mafia's board of directors.

More important than that, though, I thought, listening as the jurors shuffled into the room, was the impact a loss would have here. We were rolling ahead with our investigation of Fat Tony and the Genovese family. We had the civil RICO case working on the Fulton Fish Market. Though Paul Castellano was no longer among the living, the Gambino family was still very much in business, with John Gotti as its new boss. Bruce Mouw and his squad in Queens were pushing hard on the Gambinos: It was just a matter of time before we brought that case.

For me there was a personal stake in all of this, too, and I had made it clear to every one of my agents and supervisors. Two days after Paul Castellano was murdered, New York's governor, Mario Cuomo, stated publicly and for the record that there was no such thing as an Italian Mafia. The *New York Times* had played the story prominently the following day: "Cuomo condemns use of 'Mafia' for describing organized crime." That morning, I had sat down as usual with all my squad supervisors. Dave Binney was there. So were Damon Taylor and Lynn DeVecchio—the whole crew. I walked into my conference room and threw the *Times* in the middle of the table. "Gentlemen," I said without prelude but with considerable heat, "we are going to make this dumb son-of-a-bitch governor eat his fucking words."

Not the most politic of statements for an FBI agent, you might say. Well, fair enough. I don't care much about politics one way or the other, and I had no beef at all with Cuomo; but this statement cut me to the quick. At some level, a lot of things come back to family, to the things that first impressed you as a kid. I will never lose the memories of working with my father in his little tailor shop in Newark, and especially of seeing how upset he got when the greaseball wise guys came around demanding money from him. I respect no man on earth more than my father, and though he had toughed it out and never paid the wise guys a dime, it hurt me still when I remembered how those slobs had tried to humiliate him. So when Mario Cuomo, the most widely respected Italian American of my generation, made his dumb-ass statement about there being no Mafia, I did take offense. And that morning in my conference room I ordered all of my supervisors to redouble their efforts to get Pat Marshall and Charlotte Lang every last goddamned piece of evidence we could use to build our case against the commission and nail it shut.

So that's what I had riding on it.

The consequences to our other cases notwithstanding, I honestly didn't know how I would handle a loss now.

"Ladies and gentlemen of the jury, have you reached a verdict?"

The jury foreperson was a handsome middle-aged lady, and the Colombo case flashed again before my eyes. I quashed the hope before it was born, closed my eyes tighter, and listened to the rest of the familiar colloquy between judge and jurors, Barbara Jones's grip arresting the blood flow in my left arm.

As usual, we had listed the RICO counts first in the indictment. And first among the defendants we had listed Fat Tony Salerno, the place of honor having been vacated by Paul

Castellano. I wondered briefly whether Fat Tony had a candy bar stuffed in his mouth but resisted the urge to look.

Judge Owen asked a brief procedural question. Then the jury forelady began reading the verdicts: "As to count one on Mr. Anthony Salerno"—I held my breath and listened—"guilty!"

Next to me, Barbara gripped my arm with both hands, and I thought she was going to let out a war whoop. I exhaled quietly, then took another deep breath, my eyes still closed. Somewhere in the courtroom I heard another "guilty," then a third.

The quiet of the courtroom was interrupted by a sharp crack, and I opened my eyes immediately. At the defense table, a wavy-haired attorney had broken a yellow number 2 pencil in half and muttered, loud enough so I could hear it all the way in the back, "Jesus, they're gonna nail 'em on everything!"

And so we did.

For the record, all of the defendants in the commission case except one would be sentenced to one hundred years in prison. That's one hundred years apiece—just, as I say, for the record. And the hundred years was on top of whatever time some of the wise guys were already looking at and on the bottom of whatever we would pile on top of the rest of them in cases we would bring next year or the year after that.

The one defendant who didn't get one hundred years was Bruno Indelicato, but that didn't bother me. For the murder of the homicidal maniac Carmine Galante, Bruno got forty years, and I figured that was enough. Bruno was a Bonanno, after all, and the Bonannos never really could keep up with the other wise guys.

The bottom line, anyway, was still the same as far as I was concerned. No Mafia, Governor Cuomo?

No Mafia, my ass.

38

WILLIE Boy Johnson was a man who had not been blessed with a great deal of luck in life, but he had borne his lot with a certain stoicism, and for that, I thought, he was to be respected, if not admired. Where Willie boy's luck finally ran out was with Diane Giacalone.

I have already rendered my verdict on Giacalone: tireless prosecutor, dedicated public servant, and embarked on a totally hopeless mission in her investigation of John Gotti.

End of story, right?

Except it was not the end at all.

While we had been indicting and bringing into court cases like those against the Colombo family and the Mafia Commission, Giacalone was going back and forth with her investigation of Gotti and the Bergen Fish and Hunt crew. Under Giacalone's stern tutelage, a federal grand jury in Brooklyn had indicted Gotti, Willie Boy Johnson, and eight other Gambino family hoods on a racketeering and conspiracy case in March 1985. As a case, you'd have to call this one pretty anemic. There were no real good witnesses, for one thing. And as to overt acts, the best Giacalone and her investigators had been able to come up with was a highly circumstantial murder. (There was plenty of circumstance, just no body—a problem.)

Paul Castellano's death in December 1985 had pushed the Giacalone investigation into overdrive, until it stalled again four months later. Anyone who knew anything about the Gambinos was giving odds that it was John Gotti or one of his undesirable sidekicks who had set up Castellano outside Sparks Steak House on East Forty-sixth Street; we had confirmed, in fact, that Gotti's number two, a forgettable mope named Frank DeCicco, had provided the three shooters in the trench coats with the exact time of Castellano's arrival outside the restaurant.

Payback, according to wise-guy rules of engagement, was a reasonably simple affair: Get Gotti, and if you can't get him, the guy next to him will do. John Gotti was a stupid man, but he *was* becoming more careful, and the wise guys interested in avenging Castellano's death either couldn't or wouldn't make a try for him. So they went after DeCicco instead. One fine spring morning in April, Frank DeCicco went out to start up his car; the ensuing orange fireball ensured that the wake and funeral would have to be closed-casket affairs, and that, as the wise guys liked to say, was that.

The timing of the DeCicco hit was pretty good.

In a federal courtroom in Brooklyn, Giacalone had begun presenting her evidence against Gotti, Willie Boy Johnson, and the other defendants just a few days before DeCicco's car erupted. DeCicco was not a defendant in the Giacalone case, but after he was murdered, the high-priced members of the New York defense bar who were representing Gotti and Company swung into action. In their $800 suits and starched French cuffs, the lawyers made earnest representations to the presiding judge, Eugene Nickerson. The defendants were in the middle of a wise-guy shooting war, the lawyers told Nickerson; at the very least, news-media coverage of the mob carnage on the city's streets would prejudice jurors weighing the fate of their clients. Nickerson debated the lawyers, then questioned Giacalone. Then he ordered a postponement. The Giacalone case was once again on hold.

This was where Willie Boy Johnson figured into things.

Willie Boy was half Italian and half Cherokee Indian, a fact of genealogy that would prevent him, no matter what he did for the wise guys, from ever becoming one of them. As a kid, Willie Boy had grown up with the Gotti brothers, in the same neighborhood as Diane Giacalone, in fact. Willie Boy Johnson was a tough guy. Just under six feet, he weighed in at about 250 pounds, at least when he was in shape. Gotti used him as an enforcer and collection agent.

Although they went way back, John Gotti and Willie Boy Johnson were not especially close. Gotti often ribbed Willie Boy about his Indian heritage; Willie Boy got back at Gotti by calling him what he was, a punk with a perpetual hard-on who frittered away his days and nights whoring, drinking, and bullshitting with losers.

It was the tension that existed between Willie Boy Johnson and John Gotti and the other members of the Bergen Fish and Hunt crew that enabled the FBI to develop Willie Boy as an informant. We had pinched Willie Boy in a gambling and extortion investigation years before, and the deal we had cut was for Willie Boy to provide us with information on extortion and illegal gambling rackets, particularly as they involved organized crime in general and the Gambino family in particular; on our side, the deal meant deep-sixing any extortion and gambling charges on Willie Boy as long as he kept providing the information we wanted.

Life is made up of theory and practice, the former hopefully coherent and well ordered, the latter usually more scrambled, if not downright messy. In Willie Boy Johnson's case, the downright messy description fit like a glove. We knew that for Willie Boy to give us useful information on illegal gambling and extortion activities, he would have to have a certain degree of involvement in those things. So on a gambling or extortion issue that came in where Willie Boy might have a problem, we cut him slack; outside of gambling and extortion, though, the law was the law, and Willie Boy was just like everybody else. Where things got messy for Willie Boy was when he got himself picked up on a drug bust out in Queens. No matter how you looked at it, the violation was not covered by Willie Boy's compact with the FBI. Willie Boy knew this, of course, so before the arresting officers slapped the cuffs on him and hauled him away, Willie Boy first tried to offer them a bribe; then, desperate because he had failed to find the police officers receptive, he identified himself as a government informant. Willie Boy Johnson had just entered the bad end of Trouble City.

Sometime before she indicted Willie Boy along with John Gotti and the other defendants, Diane Giacalone learned through her own sources of Willie Boy Johnson's ill-advised admission concerning his cozy relationship with the FBI. Willie Boy denied it, and we sure as hell weren't going to admit it, but the day the indictment was returned, Giacalone immediately began pressing for our informant files on Willie Boy. When we held out, Giacalone and her boss, Ray Dearie, pressed the Department of Justice in Washington, and we were ultimately ordered to make available our files on Willie Boy Johnson.

What was going on here was simple. With her highly circumstantial murder, Diane Giacalone had a lousy case, pure and simple. By indicting Willie Boy for that murder, however, she knew she could eventually force the FBI to give up its files on Willie Boy and admit his status as an informant. That, Giacalone assumed, would force Willie Boy to flip and agree to testify as a witness for the prosecution out of fear for his own safety.

There was only one problem with this: Diane Giacalone was an extraordinarily talented lawyer, but when it came to street smarts, even though she came from John Gotti's old neighborhood, she didn't have any—none. Standard prosecutorial theory says that if you want to flip a bad guy, you charge him first. In Willie Boy Johnson's case, however, you had to throw that theory right out the window, and the reason for that was, John Gotti and his pals were so violent that there was no way on earth Willie Boy would ever agree to testify against them. We warned Giacalone of that on numerous occasions. She refused to accept it.

So Diane Giacalone got her files, Willie Boy Johnson was identified as a government snitch, and he and John Gotti both wound up being confined to Unit Nine South, on the ninth floor of the Metropolitan Correctional Center, in Lower Manhattan.

Nine South, should you ever have the misfortune to find yourself there, is a place intended to remind its inhabitants of the perils of straying from the path of righteousness. Its decorative motif could best be described as institution grim, but what really strikes one about the place is how, because of the large number of genuine psychopaths who tend to be confined there at any given time, the air is periodically charged with high-powered bolts of random menace; Nine South was not a place designed to put its inhabitants at their ease.

For Willie Boy Johnson, Nine South was an especially cruel place. There is one portion of the detention area that is reserved for the most violent and high-risk offenders. The other portion —because the security on Nine South is the best available anywhere in New York—is reserved for prosecution witnesses whose testimony is required at trials in which a defendant is deemed to possess sufficient motivation, means, or just plain mean-spiritedness to try and deprive the government of the testimony of said witnesses.

On Nine South, a bulletproof glass partition separates the two areas, one for witnesses, the other for hardcase criminals. As a result of Diane Giacalone's insistence on putting the screws to Willie Boy Johnson, poor Willie Boy found himself in the confinement area of Nine South reserved for government witnesses. Willie Boy had not agreed to testify against Gotti or anybody else, mind you; sticking him in the witness pen was just another way of pressuring the guy to flip. As for John Gotti, he was given a bunk on the far side of the thick plate glass with the other animals in the defendants' pen.

The hours, as hours are wont to do for those in stir, passed slowly up on Nine South while John Gotti and Willie Boy Johnson maintained addresses there. But hardly a day went by that Gotti didn't manage to catch Willie Boy's eye through the bulletproof glass. Usually, Gotti just smiled enigmatically.

Every so often, though, he blew Willie Boy a big fat kiss.

"How do you want to handle this, Jules?"

We were sitting in Bruce Mouw's cramped office out on

Queens Boulevard, and I marveled, not for the first time, at the unflappable demeanor of my friend and colleague. Maybe it had to do with his having been a submariner, or maybe it's just something about guys who smoke pipes, I don't know. Whatever it was, Bruce had headaches like Carter had pills, yet he never grumbled to me, and he never had anything but a kind word of encouragement for the agents on his squad who were working the Gambino family investigation. Bruce and his team had seen Damon Taylor and his squad move on the Colombo family, they had seen Lynn DeVecchio and his squad jump on the commission case, and they knew that Dave Binney and his squad were getting close to bringing their case against Fat Tony and the Genovese family. The FBI is a pretty competitive place, and if Bruce were a guy who was less sure of himself or less disciplined, he might have let the successes of the other squads get to him.

That wasn't Bruce Mouw, though. He had been through a lot of the bullshit we had had to deal with over in the Eastern District of New York with the prosecutors there, the Giacalone indictment of Gotti had further complicated his investigation of the Gambino family, and last but not least, he had lost the principal target of his investigation when the three guys in the trench coats canceled Paul Castellano's dinner reservation at Sparks Steak House. Another guy might have moaned and complained that he was jinxed. Bruce simply redoubled his efforts, assigned two of his best agents to help Giacalone prepare her case against Gotti, and then devoted increasing amounts of time to picking off various and sundry members of the Gambinos while he worked on building the racketeering case that would take out the entire family.

Among the Gambino hoods Bruce and his squad had bagged were the Gambino family *consigliere*, Joe N. Gallo. This Joe Gallo, as I mentioned earlier, was no relation to the notorious "Crazy Joey" Gallo, who had died so infamously while dining at Umberto's Clam House, his face down in the marinara sauce; Joe N. Gallo was a damn good score in his own right, though.

Other Gambino capos Bruce and the squad had taken out were Joe "Butch" Corrao, Joe "Piney" Armone, Nino Gaggi, and a human killing machine named Roy DeMeo, a one-man reincarnation of the Cosa Nostra's legendary Murder, Inc. For DeMeo alone, Bruce and his guys should have been awarded a bunch of medals. Over a twelve-year period, through a variety of violent, unspeakable, and at times indescribable means, Roy DeMeo personally had disposed of more than two hundred people in the Canarsie section of Brooklyn.

That DeMeo and those other Gambino clowns were no longer walking around as free men was a tribute to the work of Bruce and his squad, but as fine as those cases were, Bruce, like the rest of us, had the vision of the big strategic case that would attack the Gambino family at its roots. That case was still in gestation.

The birth would not be an easy one.

One reason for that, and the basis for Bruce's question to me as I tried to inhale as little of his pipe smoke as possible, sitting in his small corner office, was the problems we kept encountering with Diane Giacalone's case against Gotti. The latest problem was a serious one indeed: One of Bruce's agents had gotten word from a high-level informant that a wise guy had apparently gotten to one of the jurors in Judge Nickerson's courtroom.

Whether the offense you're talking about is murder, securities fraud, or just a plain old traffic violation, there is no more serious allegation that can be raised in the context of America's legal system than jury tampering. Even the suggestion that a juror may have been threatened, bribed, or in some other way coerced to decide a case in favor of one party or another undermines the sanctity of the nation's legal system.

Sound like theory? Imagine, for a minute, if the defendants in the Colombo case had reached a single juror and paid him or her to come back with a "not guilty" verdict. As courageous as she was, the kindly grandmother who had served as the jury foreperson in the Colombo case would have been stymied along with ten other jurors, taking time away from their jobs and families to do their civic duty for seven months, only to have to return and tell the judge they had not been able to agree on a verdict. (A jury verdict in a criminal trial requires unanimity among the jurors; fail by just one vote and the result is a hung jury: The defendants walk free or are retried later on.)

So you better believe we took the allegation of jury tampering in the Giacalone case seriously. Bruce Mouw conferred with me and Jim Kossler about how we should proceed, and Kossler and I both decided that Bruce's squad should not pursue the lead. We had no specifics; we didn't know if the juror who had supposedly been reached by the Gambinos was male, female, white, or black. Kossler and I obviously had no idea where a jury-tampering investigation would lead, but to avoid any possibility of a conflict of interest—since Bruce's squad was supporting the Giacalone prosecution of Gotti—we assigned the jury-tampering case to one of our squads working white-collar crime.

There would be allegations afterward that the FBI had failed to alert Giacalone to the possibility that a juror had been corrupted, but that's so far from the truth as to be absurd. Kossler and I informed Giacalone's boss and her immediate supervisor of the allegation we had received from the informant as well as of the fact that we had assigned a separate squad to pursue the lead. U.S. Attorney Andrew Maloney and the chief of his criminal division, Bill Mueller, both decided to confer on the matter with the chief judge of the Eastern District of New York, Jack Weinstein. Together, Weinstein, Maloney, and Mueller decided that neither Giacalone nor Judge Nickerson would be informed of the jury-tampering tip until our white-collar-crime squad could determine the validity of the charge. This, I should point out, is standard operating procedure. By erecting a wall between the jury-tampering investigation and the prosecution as it moved forward in the courtroom, we allowed Nickerson and Giacalone to proceed without a lot of second-guessing about a juror who may or may not have been reached.

As it happened, despite more than a thousand man-hours invested on the jury-tampering investigation, we were never able to develop a shred of evidence that any of the defendants had made contact, either directly or through an emissary, with any one of the twelve jurors. (A high-level informant, Sammy Gravano, would confirm the allegation many years later. We believed Gravano then, but we had no source during the course of the Giacalone trial to help us confirm the allegation.)

On March 6, 1987, Judge Nickerson gave the jury his instructions on how to weigh and evaluate the evidence Diane Giacalone had presented to them over the preceding weeks and months. Exactly one week later, the jurors returned to Nickerson's courtroom and informed the judge that they had found, as to all the defendants—John Gotti, Willie Boy Johnson, and the eight others—that the government had failed to prove its case beyond a reasonable doubt. Pandemonium, backslapping among the defendants; at the prosecution table, heartbreak.

"Shame on them," Gotti said aloud, pointing to Diane Giacalone and her coprosecutor, a brilliant young lawyer named John Gleeson. "I'd like to see what the jury's verdict would be on those two."

With Gotti's parting shot out of the way, he, Willie Boy, and the other defendants strolled out of the courtroom, free men.

Bruce Mouw called me minutes later with the news. "Not guilty on all counts," he said. "Everybody."

I thanked him, and we chatted for a minute or two. "Let's talk tomorrow, okay, Bruce, and sort all this out?"

"Sure, Jules, whatever you say."

I hung up, feeling ill.

Sure, we had had our differences with Diane Giacalone and her team, but I felt and still do that on the merits we were right. The case against Gotti was a weak one. As crazy Frankie Ancona would have said, that baby should have been thrown out with the bathtub. As hard as we had worked it, we had never gotten to first base on the jury-tampering case; it looked like a red herring. What had been done to Willie Boy Johnson, finally, was the most shameful thing. By refusing to testify, Willie Boy might yet be able to work his way back into the wise guys' good graces. But with wise guys, you just never knew.

As to John Gotti, he was well on his way to becoming a media darling. Paul Castellano had died ignominiously in the street, and Neil Dellacroce had just succumbed to cancer: Gotti had assumed the mantle of leadership in the Gambino family.

Gotti was a punk, but with his acquittal in the Giacalone case, his star was suddenly ascendant. Coming as soon as it did after the convictions in the commission case, the acquittal made Gotti appear to some people as if he were larger than life. There is an old saying, something about the elevation at which one stands being measured by the lay of the land around it. This applies more to John Gotti than anyone I can think of. Say what you will about them—they were criminals and murderers—but Paul Castellano and his generation of Mafia bosses had maintained positions of leadership over long periods of time and against hosts of vicious adversaries. In John Gotti's case, what had happened? He had stepped into a vacuum, that's what. It was a classic case of being in the right place at the right time.

That, of course, is not how most people saw it.

The new Gambino family boss had captured the popular imagination. The don's suits, it was advertised, cost an easy $1,200 each, the shirts a few hundred a throw; ditto the ties. The TV cameras waited in ambush for guys like Mafia bosses on courthouse steps. Guys like Tony Ducks Corallo and Fat Tony Salerno had been powerful men, but they were gray figures, shunning the media spotlight, preferring dim haunts like the Palma Boy or some other dump with ripped Naugahyde seating.

Not so Gotti. While he hung out for hours in the Bergen Fish and Hunt Club in Brooklyn and at the Ravenite Social Club on Mulberry Street in Lower Manhattan, Paul Castellano's successor as the head of the Gambino family had a pronounced taste for the finer things in life. Sure, Castellano had differed from *his* predecessors in that he preferred the tonier uptown eateries like Sparks Steak House to the cozy pasta joints of Little Italy. But Paul Castellano could have no more imagined bantering with reporters the way Gotti did than strolling down Fifth Avenue at high noon buck naked.

For an ever-ravenous news media, John Gotti was red meat. With the stunning acquittals in the Giacalone case, seldom a day passed that one of the New York tabloids didn't have a new nugget of gossip or hype about the new Gambino family boss.

In his Queens office the day after the acquittals in the Giaca-lone case, Bruce Mouw and I sat down to talk business.

John Gotti was the only item on the agenda.

39

AFTER Gotti's acquittal, everybody wanted a piece of him, and we were no exception. Gotti may have been a punk, but now he was the boss of the Gambino family, and that meant he was ours. Only who were we?

In Brooklyn, Andrew Maloney had assumed the duties of U.S. Attorney just in time to be shoved in front of a bank of microphones and explain to the assembled media how and why his office had blown the Gotti investigation. A lot of the men and women named to serve as U.S. Attorneys around the country are prize peacocks, political hacks who know little about criminal law but are nominated to the job, anyway, by their senator friends. Once in the job, the typical appointee will collect a government salary for a few years before he or she returns to a cushy white-shoe firm, there to tack another hundred bucks or so onto the billable-hour rate.

Happily, Andy Maloney was not a typical U.S. Attorney, so when the bad news came in from Judge Nickerson's courtroom, Maloney stood up, answered all the questions anyone had to put to him, and then vowed silently that if any goddamned federal prosecutor was going to nail Gotti's expensively attired hide to the wall anytime soon, it was going to be him.

Maloney was a guy with a temper, and he had used it to good effect over the years. A graduate of West Point, where he had captained the boxing team, Maloney had been known to leave courtroom adversaries, underlings, and just about anyone else who happened to cross him at an inopportune moment with a very real, if fleeting, sense that he had somehow earned an awful drubbing.

Maloney was nobody's fool, and he knew that blowing one's stack can have a good effect as well as bad, so he let a few days go by after the Gotti verdict before he ventured across the Brooklyn Bridge to pay a visit to Rudy Giuliani in his office at 1 St. Andrew's Plaza. Despite the political prominence that he would go on to achieve as mayor of New York, Giuliani, like Maloney, was no political hack. As U.S. Attorney for the Southern District of New York, Giuliani was a lawman's lawman— aggressive, smart, and unwilling to bend the rules no matter what. I knew Giuliani when I was a young agent and he was a young federal prosecutor, and if I worked until midnight dealing with the bullshit for an arraignment of a couple of wise-guy wannabes, Rudy would be there just as late, dotting the *i*'s and crossing the *t*'s. The guy loved the job; he knew the work.

There was no bullshit about him.

In Rudy Giuliani and Andy Maloney, what you had, basically, was two enormously talented and driven men, two men of not inconsiderable ego, both of whom now very much wanted to be the one to bring the next federal prosecution of John Gotti. Fortunately for them, Maloney and Giuliani are gentlemen. Both are also men of great political acumen, which is to say that they knew they could agree on anything they wanted but in the end it was the FBI that would make the case against Gotti, if indeed one could be made. So Rudy heard Andy out with appropriate deference, and Maloney indicated that he wanted an agreement with Rudy up front, then and there, on how any future racketeering prosecution of Gotti would be handled.

What, precisely, did Maloney have in mind? Giuliani asked.

The Gotti business came down to a matter of honor for him, Maloney said, his ruddy Irish jowls flushing. It was his strong belief, he continued, that the Eastern District of New York— his district, Brooklyn—should handle any future racketeering prosecution of the new boss of the Gambino family.

Rudy nodded: no problem. Of course, he reminded Maloney, there was still the matter of Paul Castellano's murder; there could be no jurisdictional dispute on that, could there?

None, Maloney agreed. The boss of bosses had been killed in Manhattan, and that was clearly Southern District territory: Giuliani's people would automatically handle any federal charges arising from the Castellano matter, Maloney said. Brooklyn would keep only the RICO case.

Giuliani smiled like a gnome. He knew that Bob Morgenthau, the distinguished Manhattan district attorney for the state of New York, had already assigned a small army of investigators to an FBI-NYPD task force working the Castellano murder; if Morgenthau could tie Gotti to that, he, not Giuliani, might be the first to bring a case in court against Gotti.

Maloney knew that, too, of course, but he figured that was a tangle Giuliani and Morgenthau would have to sort out between themselves; he had come only to get Rudy's agreement on any future racketeering case on Gotti.

The references to the Castellano murder out of the way, the pas de deux between Maloney and Giuliani continued for another quarter of an hour. Then it ended as it had begun, amicably.

It took exactly one week before I—across St. Andrew's Plaza at 26 Federal—learned of the Maloney-Giuliani summit.

Bill Doran gave me the news. Doran was the new special agent in charge of the criminal division in the FBI's New York office, and he could fool you if you didn't watch him. White-haired, avuncular, abrupt in manner if he wasn't being phlegmatic and unreadable, Doran was a decorated chopper jockey in Vietnam, and during his long career in the FBI, he employed many of the same skills he had put to such good use in Southeast Asia. Whereas an infantryman can see only his particular patch of hell on the battlefield, a good helicopter pilot can survey a war zone from the treetops and make snap decisions about what's happening where and who needs what kind of help.

That's the way Doran went to work in New York. He blew into town and studied up on all the different programs we had going in the Criminal Investigative Division there. Then, having no particular pride of authorship in any one program, Bill simply allocated resources as and when they were needed. He was, in that sense, an ideal boss.

He would also become one of my dearest friends. We were still just getting to know each other, however, when Doran summoned me to his office to give me a fill on the Giuliani-Maloney conversation, and he spared me none of the particulars.

I nodded—appropriately, I hoped—at one point or another during the briefing; then Doran concluded, looked across his desk at me, and said, "Well, what do you think?"

No matter what line of work you might be in, New York is a hell of a tough place. The words of the Sinatra song *weren't* bullshit: If you could make it there, you *could* make it anywhere. For us in the FBI's New York office, what made the city so tough was the competing jurisdictions, the outsize egos, and frankly, the politics of the place. How to explain these to a new boss, someone smart and fair like Bill Doran but brand-new to the city?

I always thought blunt was best. "Hey, Bill?"

Doran inclined his white head, the signal, I assumed, to proceed.

"There's no way we're going to have two prosecutions here, okay?"

Doran leaned toward me across his desk. "What do you mean, Jules?"

In conversations as in life, sometimes you've got to either plunge ahead or fall backward; I plunged. Call it what you want —insubordination, lack of reverence for authority, being a general pain in the ass—Doran could have booked and fingerprinted me on any one or all three charges because the fact of the matter was, the FBI in the field worked for the U.S. Attorney. With the Gotti case now, what we had was not one but two U.S. Attorneys sitting down and deciding how things were going to shake out, and along I come, a mere assistant special agent in charge—several big rungs down the food chain, by the way—

and I tell my new boss, Uh, sorry, that's not the way it's going to be.

It was as if Doran ran the tape of our conversation back and replayed it, because the next thing I knew, I got the same "Whaddya mean, Jules" question again.

I hunched forward in my chair, my elbows on the knees of my suit pants. "Hey, Bill, look. Whatever happens with this prick Gotti, there's only going to be one prosecution here, that's it. That's what I'm telling you."

"Just the one?" Doran leaned back in his leather chair and folded his arms across his chest.

"That's right, Bill. And that's going to be the RICO case on the family, and that's going to be when Bruce and his squad are good and goddamned ready to bring it—and not before."

Doran paused, then asked, "What about Castellano?"

I explained briefly why I thought the investigation of Paul Castellano's murder was a dead end. The hit had been too swift, too clean. Now Frank DeCicco was dead—no help there: You can't flip a corpse. As for the three guys in the trench coats, sure, there had been plenty of people on the street who saw them, and if we had fifty eyewitnesses, we had probably sixty different descriptions of them. No way we would ever make an ID.

Doran nodded, then played his ace. "The lawyers want a meeting, you know. Giuliani and Maloney."

I didn't hesitate an instant. "So? Let's have a meeting."

Doran studied me like an entomologist examining some particularly unusual species of bug. After about thirty seconds or so, he appeared to have reached some conclusion. "Look, you know these people and this game up here, Jules. How do you think we should handle it?"

I was reminded for just a second of Sean McWeeney. Here's a guy heading into uncharted territory with a couple of eight-hundred-pound gorillas in Giuliani and Maloney and he's willing to take his lead from an underling, a guy he has not known a hell of long time at all—hard to beat that kind of trust, I thought. Then I laid out my game plan. I suggested that Doran invite all parties to our office. Giuliani, Maloney, and someone from Morgenthau's office—we get them all up in our conference room on the twenty-eighth floor.

"It's neutral ground for all of them, Bill, so no one feels threatened. And I guarantee you, it'll be a nice meeting, maybe a little tense. But in the end we'll all agree to the deal."

"I thought you said—"

"I did. But for the purpose of our little meeting, the deal's the deal: The murder case goes to Morgenthau or the Southern District, whoever can make it. Maloney gets any RICO case in the Eastern District. Then everybody's happy, right?"

"But the real plan—"

"The real plan is we prosecute John Gotti right where he was acquitted—right in his face. When Bruce and his squad are ready, the case goes to the Eastern District. And if somehow we get lucky and there's something to bring on the Castellano murder, then we throw that into the RICO case as an overt act —but it's all going to be one case, not two."

Doran nodded but said nothing.

"And Bill?" Doran's look was unreadable, and I knew I was pushing it now.

Doran nodded again.

"This has got to be our little secret, okay? Or I guarantee you, we'll both be reading about this in the goddamned papers the morning after the meeting."

Doran looked at me for a full minute this time, then shook his head. "You're a fucking piece of work, Bonavolonta, you know it? Everything they told me about you was right on the money."

After walking the tightrope on the Gotti deal, I turned my attention to somewhat gamier matters: On the afternoon of November 25, 1987, I asked my good friend and colleague Lou Schiliro to go out to Brooklyn and dig up a couple of stiffs.

Louie and I had been through a lot together. A few years back, Bruce Mouw's squad had been working an extortion case against a Lucchese family member named Big Tom DiDonato, and Louie and I got to be pretty close then. Big Tom was shaking down a number of pornography dealers, and he was operating out of a bar in Brooklyn called the 19th Hole. I don't know where they got the name because it wasn't the kind of place you'd expect to see a bunch of guys in loud pants quaffing beers after a round of golf; what you had basically in the 19th Hole was a bunch of Lucchese family hoods bullshitting each other all day long because they had nothing better to do.

Bruce's idea on Big Tom DiDonato was to yank his chain, then see how he reacted. So one day he sent two of his guys, George Hanna and Tony Nelson, into the 19th Hole with a message. George and Tony were big guys, and they came calling as knee breakers from a rival family. They informed Big Tom that if he was at all interested in his future health and well-being, he would stop breaking the chops of the pornography peddlers because the porno guys were under the protection of a wise guy named Johnny Conti. Big Tom, needless to say, was none too pleased at this piece of news.

Where Lou and I came in was a few nights later. I was running the organized-crime program for Neil Welch at the time, but Bruce Mouw asked me as a favor if I would go into the 19th Hole with Lou, and he was such a good friend that I couldn't turn him down. So I posed as John Conti, and Louie and I went into the 19th Hole. Lou was wearing a body recorder and transmitter so he could get Big Tom's words on tape and also send a signal to the twenty or so agents we had waiting in cars outside to come busting in if things inside got unpleasant.

Lou is a great guy. He is not a bruiser or a door kicker like Hanna and Nelson. He is a gentle man but an unstoppable investigator, a guy who will beat you with his smarts every time and at every turn. If they asked me for an epitaph for Lou Schiliro, I would say this: If you have done wrong and the evidence is such that he cannot get you quickly, you're going to wish he had, because the guy won't quit. So you're either going to get it in the throat fast, or you're going to die from gangrene slow, because Lou won't let go.

Dogged he was. But what Lou Schiliro was not was a guy who

was real comfortable in tight spots with a bunch of pissed-off wise guys coming at you in a foul mood.

This is pretty much the situation Lou and I had in the 19th Hole. Lou and I had come in and asked for Big Tom at the bar. We were sitting there drinking beer when Big Tom approached. I had already identified myself to the bartender as *the* Mr. Johnny Conti, so Big Tom knew what he was getting into; or so he thought, anyway. As Louie remembers it, Big Tom addressed me at least three times, employing the standard wise-guy rules of etiquette. What Big Tom said to me was "Hey!"

My mother had always emphasized to me as a young man the proper forms of social intercourse, and my feeling, with wise guys especially, was that if someone didn't want to act properly in my company, the hell with them. I would pretend that they just weren't there. That's what I did with Big Tom DiDonato.

Big Tom was on his third "Hey," each one getting louder and Big Tom moving closer while Louie was perspiring up a storm.

I finally looked up from my beer. "You talking to me?" I said it as evenly as possible, no edge.

"Yeah, you!"

Big Tom was really light in the manners department, I could see that. I said nothing, took another sip of my beer.

Big Tom looked confused for a second, then said: "Who you wit'?"

I bounced my beer glass off the top of the bar and sat up straight; it was showtime. "Who am I with? Who the fuck are you wit'?"

Big Tom had at least five or six inches on me, but he was clearly a guy who was not used to backtalk, and I guess my response unnerved him a little. It must have, because instead of trying to muscle me and Schiliro, who was busy sweating through his undershirt and worrying that the sudden tide of perspiration down his chest would short-circuit his tape recorder/transmitter, Big Tom walked back down to the other end of the bar and conferred with five other wise guys. That conversation lasted just a few seconds, and then Big Tom was moving back up the bar again in our direction, the phalanx of wise guys hard on his heels, puffing their chests.

Louie nudged me in the ribs. "What do we do now, boss?"

Big Tom and his pals were slobs, big, but fat and out of shape. We weren't there for a fight, me and Lou, but if it came to that, fuck it, I had handled worse odds. I told Lou to take the guy closest to him. I would handle the other five. Schiliro still laughs when he tells the story today. "That's when I knew we were in trouble; Jules was fucking *serious.*"

There was a bit of bumping and shoving after that, but Big Tom was so stupid that he started talking out loud about how his extortion of the pornographers was this and how it was that and how no fucking asshole named Johnny Conti was going to screw it up for him. Fortunately, Louie's body recorder had not shorted out from all that perspiration, and we got what we needed on tape. Since it had not been our intention to go in and bust up the 19th Hole, we made our excuses and left after a little while, and I'm sure Big Tom and his idiot friends called us wimps, losers, and worse after we left. Good for them, I thought: Not too long after Lou Schiliro and I left the 19th Hole, we indicted Tom DiDonato on the basis of the tape we had recorded in the place. I testified at the trial that put him away.

So much for loud-mouth wise guys.

Lou Schiliro and I had had a lot of fun together over the years, but never had I had occasion to ask him or any of my supervisors to go out and unearth a couple of stiffs. Especially not stiffs nearly ten or so years old.

But that was what we had to do.

The background here, believe it or not, had to do with the commission case. The Lucchese family had taken the biggest hit with the commission convictions, losing their boss, Tony Ducks Corallo; their underboss, Tom Mix Santoro; and their *consigliere*, Christie Tick Furnari. After the convictions, I had instructed all my organized-crime squads to start looking hard at what I called the second teams coming up now in the families. Even Bruce Mouw's squad got the order. No Gambino family members had been convicted in the commission case, but Paul Castellano was dead, and so was the underboss, Aniello Dellacroce. Like the other four families in New York, the Gambinos were looking at major leadership changes. The second teams climbing up behind the fallen bosses were pale ghosts compared with their predecessors, much less powerful. Still, we had to watch them closely.

In our look at the second team in the Lucchese family, we saw some real losers. The two biggest, who were naturally at the top of the Lucchese heap, were Vittorio "Vic" Amuso and a guy named Anthony Caso, whose mob nickname for some reason, God only knows why, was "Gaspipe."

Vic Amuso and Gaspipe Caso were both heavily into drugs, which didn't surprise us, but they were also way, way into Local 580 of the Architectural and Ornamental Ironworkers Union, and that did surprise us. We couldn't figure the connection out. Squad C-17 had the Lucchese case, and the supervisor was Bob Liberatore, the case agent Dick Rudolph. From where I sat, they had a real puzzler on their hands.

With the help of an informant run by a veteran FBI agent, a real pro named Hoyt Peavey, Dick Rudolph was able to go in and get court authorization for a Title III on Vic Amuso's home. Again, much of what we got was the usual wise-guy bullshit, and we would have plenty to use to go after Amuso later. But we wanted the bigger case, and Amuso's conversations with the Local 580 shop steward, a guy named Jim McCann, perplexed us. What the hell was the deal with the ironworkers union?

We decided to wait and see.

The deal, as Dick Rudolph began to piece it together, was sweet. Some of Dick's information came from New York Labor Department files, which documented a classic pattern of antitrust activity in New York's commercial window industry going back years. The scam was every bit as sinister as the "club" system that Ralph Scopo had manipulated for the Cosa Nostra in the ready-mix cement business. The more Rudolph learned, the worse it appeared. According to the Title III we had installed at Vic Amuso's house and according to what Hoyt Peavey was getting from his informant over in New Jersey, a guy named Pete Savino was hip-deep in the windows scam.

Savino, as it would turn out, would become the Ralph Scopo of the windows scam—only with a twist.

The deal was a doozy. Savino had a company called Arista Windows. Arista and a few other big window companies were running a bid-rigging operation on the New York City Housing Authority (NYCHA), a government agency that spent tens of millions of dollars a year trying to house the legions of New York City's poor and disadvantaged. In the course of trying to accomplish that mission, the NYCHA had occasion to buy and replace windows in the public and subsidized housing units located throughout the five boroughs of New York City.

We didn't have nearly enough to move on the bid-rigging case yet, which is to say we were nowhere near being ready or even close to indicting. So we kept watching, waiting, and digging deeper into the muck of the Lucchese family.

Then one day Lou Schiliro walked into my office.

Lou, as I mentioned, was the FBI supervisor on the Pizza Connection case, and before we were done, he would be our principal expert in the prosecution of John Gotti. For the moment, though, the reason Lou was in my office was that he had a lead on two dead men in Brooklyn, and as far as I could tell, they had nothing whatsoever to do with windows.

These were, as I said, two very old stiffs.

What happened was this: Lou's squad, C-13, was a drug task force comprised of ten FBI agents and about fifteen NYPD officers and detectives. The day before Lou came to see me, two of his guys, Detective Bill Mitzeliotis and FBI Special Agent Leo Farrell, had interviewed a pathetic screwball named Barclay Faranga. Barclay had big problems. Not only had we pinched him in a major drug case; we had also arrested his girlfriend, his girlfriend's sister, and his girlfriend's mother.

A real family affair.

You wouldn't know it to look at him, because he was your

basic dirtbag, but Barclay Faranga must have had a good heart, because he approached Mitzeliotis and Farrell and said he would be willing to cooperate with the FBI and the NYPD if we would cut a deal and release his girlfriend and her family.

The decision got kicked up to Schiliro.

Who kicked it up to me.

"What's he going to give us?" I asked, the usual question in such a case.

"Bodies," replied my good friend Lou.

Hmmm. Hard to turn down an offer like that, I thought. I asked for details.

The first body in question, Schiliro said, belonged to one Richard Scarcella, a Colombo family associate, deceased approximately ten years earlier; cause of death: multiple gunshot wounds to the head.

"Interesting. What else?"

Second on Barclay Faranga's tip sheet, Schiliro told me, was one Thomas "Shorty" Spero, slimeball drug dealer, also deceased of multiple gunshot wounds, the decedent having passed from this vale of tears some eight years earlier.

Two dead mopes, I thought. "Good, okay, let's do it."

Barclay Faranga didn't interest me, but the bodies did. We talked for a few minutes across my desktop; then Lou Schiliro nodded, said he understood perfectly, and went off to wherever it is one goes to requisition jackhammers, shovels, and the like. Then Lou, Lt. Willie Krebbs, his NYPD counterpart, and most of the rest of Lou's task force went off to collect our new friend Barclay Faranga. By rush hour they were all headed out to Brooklyn to unearth some old stiffs.

A strange business, ours.

Barclay Faranga directed Schiliro, Krebbs, and the team to an address on Scott Avenue way to hell and gone out in Brooklyn; the street number was 99. I was sitting at my desk when Louie called it in. It was the same address as Pete Savino's Arista Windows.

When these kinds of things happen, no little man pops out of the desk drawer to yell, "Bingo!" You just tend to sit there feeling kind of numb. Now we had Pete Savino, the Ralphie Scopo of the windows scam, with two dead wise guys buried beneath the concrete floor of his factory in Brooklyn.

This was beginning to get interesting. If it was true.

As Barclay Faranga explained it, Shorty Spero was buried under the Arista Windows loading dock, the head facing due south; say what you will, Faranga was a detail man. As for poor Richie Scarcella, for some reason they had buried him directly beneath the urinals in the men's room; I'll spare you the wise-guy jokes that were made about that particular burial plot.

It was dark by the time Schiliro and Krebbs and Company had collected all the necessary digging and excavating machinery they needed out at 99 Scott Avenue, and with the arc lights they had erected, a cordon of New York's finest ringing the plant, and a bunch of understandably curious neighbors looking on, we had a regular three-ring circus going out there.

One of the details Barclay Faranga told us about the bodies is worth mentioning, if only because it may give you some further indication about what sensitive souls these wise guys were. After they dumped the bodies of Shorty Spero and Richie Scarcella in their shallow graves in the foundation of the Arista Windows plant, the wise guys had thrown themselves a little party. They had some beer and barbecued chicken wings on hand, a nice little do. Now, here the wise guys have these two dead men staring up at them from the unfinished concrete floor of Pete Savino's factory, and the wise guys are downing beers and tucking into the wings—and when they're done they dump the empties and the greasy chicken bones in with Scarcella and Spero.

What a bunch of nice guys.

I was sitting at my desk plowing through paperwork when Lou Schiliro called in about at eight in the evening. "Jules, we're down to the dirt, and still we got nothing."

Shit, I thought, if this guy Faranga has been jerking us around, we're going to look like a bunch of prime jackasses. I told Lou to go get Barclay, jack him up against a wall, and tell him what would happen to him if he was telling stories.

Lou called back thirty minutes later. They had found bones,

he said; the digging had stopped. A medical examiner was studying the bones, and Louie would call as soon as they had news.

Fifteen minutes later, Louie called again.

"The M.E. says the fucking bones are chicken wings. You believe it?"

I laughed. "Keep digging, Lou. They're down there."

Another half hour: "Bingo, boss. We got the body and the head, and it was facing due south, just like Barclay said."

"Good job." That accounted for Mr. Shorty Spero. "What about the other one?"

"We're workin on it, but he's gotta be down there."

They untombed Richie Scarcella an hour later.

As grisly as this business was, it was important, for now we had powerful leverage with Pete Savino. Burying the bodies of anyone in your home or office, never mind a couple of wise guys with bullets in their heads, is not a minor offense no matter where you come from.

Lou Schiliro and his lead agent, Leo Farrell, got a warrant for Savino and went out to pick him up. He was a cool customer. The first thing he tells Lou and Leo is that before they start breaking his balls they should call his friend, FBI special agent Hoyt Peavey, over in the Newark office.

Amazing, Schiliro thought. The Pete Savino working with Peavey in New York is the same Pete Savino with the two dead wise guys in his Arista Windows factory.

Schiliro made a beeline for my office at 26 Federal.

"Boss?"

I looked up from my desk and the seemingly endless paperwork. "Yeah, Lou?" I was getting used to this by now.

"We got a problem, I think." Briefly, Schiliro explained the situation with Savino.

Jesus, I thought, nothing was ever simple. This thing with Savino, however, could be a real opportunity.

We knew from a variety of sources now that Spero and Scarcella had been murdered by an accomplished mob hit man named Jerry Pappa. But Pappa was dead now, and there was no percentage in merely charging Savino as an accomplice to two murders eight and ten years old, not if we could use him to infiltrate the bid-rigging scheme that was being run on the New York City Housing Authority. Use Savino that way, I thought, and we get the evidence we need to put those bastards away. So we decided to recommend a deal for Savino on the murders in exchange for his cooperation on the bid-rigging case.

Pete Savino was not a dumb guy; indeed, he would prove himself quite an acccomplished actor as he went about his business rigging bids and consorting with the other window manufacturers who were having a field day picking the pockets of the taxpayers of the city of New York. Before he was through, Pete Savino, working closely with Special Agent Dick Rudolph, would give us not just the mopes from the Lucchese family but members of the Genovese, Colombo, and Gambino families as well—not to mention several stalwart officials of Local 580 of the Architectural and Ornamental Ironworkers Union. As the indictment would explain when it was eventually returned by a federal grand jury in Brooklyn, the corrupt labor union, conspiring with the corrupt window manufacturers and installers, conspiring with four of the five New York organized-crime families, had arranged things in such a way that the four families collected two dollars on every window installed anywhere in the city of New York at the behest of the city's public housing authority.

Dick Rudolph did the math. Over the course of more than a decade, between the late 1970s and the late 1980s, the four Italian Mafia families had stolen more than $150 million dollars from the New York City Housing Authority. That's taxpayers' money we're talking about, all of it. As Barclay Faranga might have put it, that ain't just chicken wings, baby.

40

WHILE Dick Rudolph was wiring up Pete Savino and running the traps on the windows case, Bruce Mouw's squad was working overtime on John Gotti. Specifically, what Bruce needed was just enough evidence to go in and persuade a judge to allow us to install a Title III at the Ravenite Social Club on Mulberry Street in Little Italy.

The Ravenite was the key to getting Gotti.

After months of work, Bruce and his squad finally had enough physical surveillance, informant information, and assorted other evidence to take into court. This was the lasagna theory of evidence: A little of this, some more of that, you throw it against the wall, and some of it is bound to stick—eventually.

We got the okay to go into the Ravenite on February 1, 1988. The installation, naturally, fell to Jim Kallstrom's Special-Operations teams. Kallstrom gave the Ravenite assignment, naturally enough, to John Kravec.

"What do you think, John?" Kallstrom was inquiring about the evening's festivities Kravec had planned for the Ravenite. Kravec had assembled a team and would be launching his attack on the club within a few hours.

"It'll never work; we'll all be arrested."

"Right, John." Kallstrom laughed.

Kravec went out the door, muttering intimations of doom.

It was a bitterly cold night. Kravec had chosen four of his best agents for the Ravenite job: Kenny Reder, Patricia Colli, Dave Swanson, and Bill Williams. The team had studied the place carefully. As you face the building that houses the Ravenite, two doors let out to the sidewalk. One goes into the club; the other, into an adjacent hallway that leads to a flight of stairs up to apartments on the second and third floors.

The plan was for Pat Colli and one of the other agents to approach the Ravenite and work on making a new key for the lock to the door to the club. If anyone came along, Pat and the other agent would huddle together in the doorway, pretending to be a romantic young couple, taking shelter from the biting cold.

It was a good plan, but someone somewhere must have gotten suspicious, because the next thing we knew, an NYPD blue-and-white was cruising the length of Mulberry Street, giving Pat and the rest of Kravec's team the old fisheye.

Kravec called the proceedings off.

The next night the team went back, and the Gotti crew had evidently gotten word of the blue-and-white drive-by. There's no way they could have known what we were doing, since the cops hadn't even stopped to question Kravec and the team. Just to be on the safe side, though, the denizens of the Ravenite had changed all the locks on the building.

Kravec and Company had to start all over again.

That sort of set the theme for the Ravenite investigation. It took a few more attempts, but Kravec finally got the microphone inside the club. Once it was in, however, the thing was virtually worthless. Gotti and his boys played jazz and old show tunes on a radio—constantly. As had happened at Paul Castellano's mansion on Todt Hill, where we had Phil Rizzuto and the crowd noise from Yankee Stadium covering up conversations, we couldn't hear Gotti and his guys over the soundtrack from *Oklahoma!* and the swing music of the Benny Goodman Orchestra. If that wasn't bad enough, the guys in the Ravenite appeared also to have installed some kind of machine that emitted what Kravec called "white noise"; to me, it sounded like water running steadily out of a leaky tap. It drove all of us nuts.

Gotti seemed especially paranoid about FBI bugs. Every time he had some business to discuss with a visitor to the Ravenite, the new boss of the Gambino family seemed to disappear on what Bruce Mouw had taken to calling "walk-talks," strolling around the interior of the dumpy building. Things got so bad after a while that Bruce and I agreed to pull the Title III from the Ravenite and give the little microphone a rest. Getting Gotti was not going to be a cakewalk, I could see that.

On May 4, 1988, another federal jury walked into another federal courtroom in New York City and convicted the hierarchy of yet another of the city's Italian Mafia families. This time it was Fat Tony Salerno and the Genovese family.

The jury hammered them.

Fat Tony, like a lot of the wise guys, was not having a particularly good year. Not only had he been convicted in the commission case, but just three weeks earlier, on April 15, Fat Tony and twenty-three other wise guys we had named as defendants in a civil RICO complaint arising from the Fulton Fish Market investigation had entered into a consent judgment prohibiting any of them from further involvement in any business relating to the operation of the fish market or in activities of any kind relating to Local 359 of the United Seafood Workers Union.

Jim Kossler's civil RICO gambit had paid off, big-time.

It had taken Brian Taylor and his squad nearly three years since Kossler had assigned them to the fish-market investigation. By following Kossler's lead, however, by thinking creatively and generally working their butts off, Brian and his team had succeeded in depriving the Genovese family of control of one of its most lucrative business arrangements. As a result of the consent judgment, a federal judge had appointed a new, independent administrator for the Fulton Fish Market. Fat Tony and other Genovese family members were barred for life, by federal injunction, from even going near the place.

As to the criminal case and the jury verdicts returned on May 4, that made for even worse news for the wise guys in the Genovese family. The guts of the FBI's case against the Genovese had to do with its control over the election of officials of the

International Brotherhood of Teamsters and, separately, of New York City's ready-mix cement industry. The case was a classic racketeering case—RICO à la Blakey. The investigation had begun with Dave Binney and his squad. After Binney moved on to Headquarters, his case agent, Tom French, had taken over the squad and carried the case across the goal line.

In the courtroom, I stood near Tommy as the verdicts were read. With the RICO convictions and the other charges, Fat Tony and seven codefendants would be sentenced to a total of 186 years in federal custody. Fat Tony alone would be sentenced to seventy years, and that was on top of the hundred years he was already looking at from the commission-case convictions.

Fat Tony was right: He *was* going to die in the can.

There would be the inevitable appeals, of course, but they would do more to line the pockets of the wise guys' lawyers than to put Fat Tony and his buddies back on the street.

Those guys were history.

On one of the last days of August 1988, as most Americans prepared for the long Labor Day weekend and mothers got their children ready for another year of school, Bruce Mouw phoned from his office on Queens Boulevard.

"Bad news, Jules, I'm sorry to have to tell you."

Just what we needed, I thought. After the Giacalone case, the squabbling among the prosecutors over the next Gotti prosecution, and the unproductive Title III in the Ravenite, I wondered what else could go wrong. Poor Bruce.

"What's up, pal?"

"It's Willie Boy."

On my end of the line, I knew what Bruce Mouw was going to say before he said it. "Oh, no—son of a bitch!"

"He was hit this morning, Jules. Took nearly twenty rounds as he was walking to his car on his way to work."

I said nothing for a minute. What the hell was there to say? I swallowed hard, then thanked Bruce for the call.

"Sure, Jules, I knew you'd want to know."

Bruce hung up, and I knew he felt every bit as bad as I did. Sitting at my desk, I noticed that the office outside was quiet for once. Agents and supervisors had grabbed a few days of vacation to make up for all the nights, weekends, and holidays they had missed spending with their families the past year. A few days to compensate for all the missed birthdays, the school plays, the anniversaries.

Good for them, I thought; the time off was richly deserved.

I thought then of Willie Boy Johnson and what we could have done differently. We had tried, but we had failed to protect him. Through no fault of his own, Willie Boy had been backed into a corner. And when he had, he had reverted to the rules of the street. Yes, he had been an informant for the FBI, and no, he had not been a model citizen—not by a long shot. By his own lights, though, Willie Boy Johnson had been a stand-up guy to the end. Cornered, he had refused to testify against John Gotti. And when the "not guilty" verdicts had been returned in Judge Nickerson's courtroom, Willie Boy was sitting right there along-side Gotti. They had hooted and pounded each other's backs like pals in the high-ceilinged courtroom.

I could picture the scene, but the image that came back to me most clearly was the one of Willie Boy Johnson prowling the glassed-in detention area up on Unit Nine South in the months before the trial: There was Willie Boy, locked in like a caged animal; and on the other side of the bulletproof glass there was Gotti, blowing Willie Boy a big kiss.

The kiss of death, I thought.

I added that to my list of reasons to get John Gotti.

It would not be easy, though, not that anything ever was.

A few days after Christmas, on an unseasonably warm January day, the telephone rang in my office, and my secretary announced Barbara Jones on the other end.

I reached for the phone immediately.

Together with Joe Pistone, Jim Kallstrom, and a very few others, Barbara Jones had been one of the original pathfinders. She had been there in the beginning, working and planning with me and Pistone, building the Bonanno case with Louie Freeh, then coaching every green-gilled new prosecutor who wandered into the U.S. Attorney's office at 1 St. Andrew's Plaza on what an organized-crime prosecution was and how such things were built. It would be easy to say that Barbara was like a mother figure to the young men and women who came through that office. But it would be wrong, too. Barbara was a professional, through and through.

And the people in the office knew it. Leave it to Barbara to take a bright but relatively untried young prosecutor like Mike Chertoff, sit with him as he dug deeper and deeper into the bowels of the commission case, then work with him as he prepared the case for trial. Selfless, exacting, loyal, and tough—those are the words that come to mind as I think back over my years of friendship with this remarkable woman.

Of course, Barbara could also make me crazy, and that's just what she was about to do. We gossiped over the phone for a minute before she got down to business. A year earlier, Barbara had left the U.S. Attorney's office for the office of Bob Morgenthau, the New York district attorney for Manhattan. Barbara was Morgenthau's first assistant D.A., a position of immense influence. She was Morgenthau's point person on Gotti.

I put both elbows on my desk and listened attentively.

"Jules, could you and Bruce come over to my office tomorrow night? I'd like to discuss where we're going with this thing."

This thing—I didn't have to be told—was the Manhattan D.A.'s long-running investigation of the many aspects of John Gotti's multifaceted life in crime. I had trepidations, but I knew I could trust my friend. "For you, Barbara, anything."

We agreed to meet at 6:00 P.M. I told Barbara I would be bringing Jim Kossler along with Bruce.

The Gotti case Barbara laid out for the three of us the following evening had nothing to do with the murder of Paul

Castellano. Barbara would not try the case, she was explaining; as first assistant D.A., she would be overseeing things. Her prosecutor would be Mike Cherkasky, a tough pro with a long record of big wins.

When Barbara and Mike began explaining the nuts and bolts of their case against Gotti, I felt my insides go clammy.

The case they had in mind involved an attempted murder of a guy named John O'Connor; not even an actual murder, I thought, reminding myself to hold my tongue. John O'Connor was the business agent for a carpenters' union, and he had allegedly ordered a restaurant in Lower Manhattan busted up by a bunch of hoods because the restaurant owner had been foolish enough to do some extensive remodeling without having retained the services of union carpenters. The restaurant was called Bankers and Brokers, a typical Wall Street joint, and O'Connor's alleged fit of pique in having ordered the place torn up would have been no big deal except for one small thing: The Gambino family had a sizable financial stake in Bankers and Brokers.

O'Connor either did or did not know this; it was not clear. What was clear, though, is that within weeks of the mischief done to the new carpentry at Bankers and Brokers, a couple of men in dark suits opened up with semiautomatic weapons and shot John O'Connor several times in the torso and upper extremities.

O'Connor did not, as I mentioned, die.

He also was not, as Barbara Jones and Mike Cherkasky explained it, either willing or able to identify his assailants.

Great, I thought. Here we've got a case where the intended murder victim is not only not dead; he can't or won't say who might have wanted him dead or tried to kill him.

I knew Barbara knew what I was thinking.

I said nothing.

O'Connor's testimony would be problematic, Cherkasky conceded, but he explained that they had some real good Title III evidence linking Gotti with a gang of violent Gambino family enforcers known as the "Westies." That evidence clearly linked Gotti to some Westies who had discussed the assault on O'Connor, Cherkasky said.

I thought this was pretty thin gruel, and when my time finally came to talk, I said so. "This is not the case to bring against John Gotti, guys. It's too weak, too insubstantial."

Barbara disagreed. The case had problems, she said, but it could be tried and won. Gotti would be put away for a long time.

"I want him put away as much as you guys, Barb. But this isn't the case to bring, I'm telling you."

To someone other than Barbara Jones, my words, I'm sure, would have sounded self-serving. She knew how hard we had been working the Gambino family investigation. In one way or another, Bruce Mouw's squad had been on the case for going on five years. We had made cases against individual members of the family, but the main act was still to come, and Barbara knew it. Someone else listening to me in Barbara's office that evening could have simply said, "The goddamn FBI, they just don't want anyone screwing with their case."

That's not what Barbara said—then or ever.

After our little meeting broke up, I renewed the pledge I had made to her and Cherkasky to assign one of Bruce's agents to their investigation full-time. I also wished her luck.

"Anything you need, Barb . . ."

"I know. I'll call, Jules, thanks."

A few days after that, John Gotti was arrested and charged with aggravated assault on the person of Mr. John O'Connor. The media circus commenced almost immediately, with Gotti the master of ceremonies. After he was arraigned and released on bond, Gotti spared a few words for the throng of reporters assembled on the courthouse steps. "Three to one," Gotti said, "I beat the case."

Great, I thought. Now the asshole is giving odds.

A day after that, Jim Fox, who was Bill Doran's boss and the overall head of the FBI's New York office, called me in to chat. Fox had a big corner suite on the top floor of the Jacob K. Javits

Building on Lower Broadway, and it afforded its occupant a grand view of the financial district and New York harbor beyond. Fox had lunched the day before with Bob Morgenthau, he revealed, and the New York D.A. had unburdened his soul, at least with regard to the Gotti case. If we picked up the tiniest shred of evidence concerning jury tampering in the Gotti prosecution, Morgenthau told Fox, he expected to hear about it right away. "You have any problem with that, Jules?"

"Not at all, Jim."

The D.A.'s office had all the bases covered.

"What do you think, Bruce? The fucking guy can't be in there taking a shit for a full hour."

Like me, George Gabriel wasn't too particular about his use of profanity. It was one more cross poor Bruce Mouw had to bear.

"I think it's probably like your guy told you, George."

Bruce never swore, but he didn't blame Gabriel for indulging. Bruce had assigned George Gabriel as the lead agent on the Gotti investigation, and what with the Title III not performing in the Ravenite and Gotti disappearing into the can or on another of his walk-talks, it had been a tough go.

George was ready to spit nails.

A SWAT-team agent, six feet three, George Gabriel was partial to active investigations, cases that kept you moving and doing things. The Gotti case—watching the goddamned Ravenite and wondering whether the Gambino family boss was in the can or what—could make anyone nuts. Gabriel had an informant, however, and if the guy was right, we would know sooner than later just what the deal was with the disappearing John Gotti. The informant had told George that when Gotti vanished on his walk-talks with one of his wise-guy pals, he usually went out into the hallway adjacent to the club. The man was reluctant to say more, but Gabriel had leaned on him, and the man had dropped one more pearl: "Whenever John wants to discuss the real heavy stuff"—the man had emphasized the word "real," then continued rapidly—"he uses the apartment upstairs."

With those two helpful pieces of information, George Gabriel and Bruce Mouw went to see the two prosecutors Andy Maloney had assigned to our Gotti investigation. Lenny Michaels was Maloney's strike-force chief, and before that he had been deputy chief of the rackets bureau in the Brooklyn district attorney's office for eleven years; what Len didn't know about organized-crime prosecutions wasn't worth knowing. Laura Ward was the other lawyer on the case, a dynamite prosecutor who had a beguiling way with witnesses that made them seem to want to talk, to incriminate their friends, to tell everything; I often thought Laura could make the dead rise up and testify.

With Bruce and George, Len and Laura prepared a lengthy application for court authorization to install a Title III in the hallway adjacent to the Ravenite club—specifically, behind the club's rear door. Additionally, permission was requested for another Title III in the second-floor apartment above the Ravenite. Last but not least, we renewed our application for the Title III in the club itself. White noise or swing music or whatever, it was worth another shot.

A judge signed the orders without too much hassle.

Once again, it was time for John Kravec and his team to go to work. This time, Kravec led his agents through the back door of the Ravenite. In minutes, the tiny recording device with its transmitter was concealed in the ceiling of the hallway next door to the club. Kravec then led the team upstairs. In preparing the Title III application, George and Bruce and the two prosecutors had specified that they were requesting permission to install the Title III in the second-floor walk-up.

In Special Operations work, at least the way Jim Kallstrom taught his agents, the motto is "Assume as little as possible." We had double-checked the phone number of the second-floor apartment. George Gabriel's informant had said clearly that it was the place Gotti liked to use. Kravec took nothing for granted, however: Before he was going to slip any more locks, he had one of his guys, Ken Reder, dial the number to the apartment while two other agents posted themselves outside the apartment doors on both the second and third floors. Son of a gun if the telephone didn't ring in the apartment up on the third floor! Kravec's use of profanity on the way out of the Ravenite would have made even George Gabriel blush a pretty crimson.

We had to redo the Title III application for the Ravenite, but a few days later, John Kravec's prognostications of doom notwithstanding, a tiny recorder-transmitter was finally placed in the third-floor apartment of the Ravenite building.

At long last, we were in business.

And how Gotti and his pals liked to talk!

There was Gotti himself, of course, yakking up a storm out in the hallway and up in the third-floor apartment. Then there was Sammy "the Bull" Gravano, the Gambino family underboss, so named because of his squat physical presence and his rather considerable strength. Sammy the Bull could be heard talking frequently with Frankie Locascio, a.k.a. "Frankie Loc," the Gambino family *consigliere*. Also overhead on the Title III in the apartment was Tommy Gambino, son of Carlo, the now-deceased paterfamilias of the Gambino clan.

There were some problems on a construction deal Gotti and his pals had an interest in, for instance, and John used the discussion, as he usually did, to show what a tough guy he was.

"Let me tell you something, see. If I was there, I woulda told the guy, 'Listen, ya fuckin' bum, if you wanna have dinner tonight and don't wanna be dead, you fuckin' rat motherfucker, you see that [we get] the money for that fucking house. Who would do this kind of work? Not even the fuckin' niggers would buy it. . . . You cocksucker, you tell me your troubles? You ain't got no troubles. *We* got troubles here, okay?"

"Now, let's don't get excited."

"Yeah, we got serious things, Sam."

"I know."

"And not selfish things—*serious* things!"

"Serious."

Gotti had jail on the brain. There was the attempted-murder case on John O'Connor hanging over his head. And Gotti knew that the FBI and every other police agency in the city were gunning for him—and for the rest of the Gambino family. "If you and Frankie fall with me, Sam, I mean with no bail . . ."

"Oh, sure."

"Even with bail, they can always fuck youse around for three or four weeks. And you just see the stupid confusion in three or four weeks. You'll see . . . what the fuck are we gonna have, an acting captain? An acting guy?"

"John, after we're out on bail—if we all get out—whatever the fuck we do . . ."

"Yeah, yeah."

"We structure whatever the fuck they want."

"I already have that in mind. You think maybe I wanna go away for a hundred fuckin' years? Or two hundred years? I'm trying to think of what's good for the overall picture here, Sammy. And the first thing is this: With these fuckin' lawyers on all these cases—even for a bail application they gotta go in there and argue—we'll win, Sammy. We'll win these fuckin' cases. And we'll be out a year from now, somewhere—maybe a year and a half from now—laughing a little bit. We'll be laughing!"

This was typical wise-guy bluster—a roller coaster of tough-guy talk, predictions of doom and gloom, and, finally, a ballsy statement of stupid defiance.

It was all talk, though. Just talk, nothing more.

41

ON February 9, 1990, John Gotti was acquitted of all charges arising from the attempted assault of John O'Connor.

It was not a good day.

New York's raucous tabloids immediately christened the Gambino family boss "the Teflon Don," and my friends Barbara Jones and Mike Cherkasky were second-guessed endlessly on radio and TV—when they weren't being lampooned for fumblers and bumblers. Law enforcement generally suffered a big black eye.

Two days after the "not guilty" verdict came in, the circus was still in town, and Selwyn Raab of the *New York Times* called me for a quote to use in that day's Gotti story. I had already begun to wonder when the stories would die down and when the media would move on to something else.

It didn't look like it would be anytime soon.

Selwyn asked me about one or another aspect of the verdict and whether I thought Gotti was even prosecutable now.

"Listen," I said. "The FBI hasn't brought a case against Gotti yet. When we do, he can take all the bets he wants, because he's going away to prison for a long time."

Well.

To judge from the reaction, you might have thought I had defamed the pope, dishonored my country, and sworn the vilest oath to the devil—all three things together. In Brooklyn, many rumblings from the offices of Andy Maloney's prosecutors. In Manhattan, much, much more from Bob Morgenthau and Mike Cherkasky; Barbara just laughed—she knew me well enough.

To a lot of people, I suppose, it looked like I was rubbing

everyone's nose in the Gotti mess; that wasn't the point at all. The FBI's position—my position—had been clear on this guy all along. The Giacalone case had been ill conceived and poorly drawn. It shouldn't have been brought, and I said so. Ditto the assault case on John O'Connor.

On both cases, however, I had assigned agents to support the prosecutors, so this wasn't about bureaucratic turf. What this *was* about was keeping the record straight. After each of Gotti's two acquittals, the news media had talked endlessly about how Gotti had beaten "the government." In that context, I thought, any reference to the government translated immediately to the FBI, and to be perfectly blunt about it, I was getting goddamned sick and tired of being asked why "we" had lost to John Gotti not once but twice. But the FBI had not lost to Gotti. We had supported the first two prosecutions of John Gotti, but we sure as hell had not brought our own case against him. When we did, it would be a whole different ball game. As I said, I just wanted to keep the record straight.

Was it absolutely necessary for me to go out and say what I did? No, but I'd probably do it again. Sure, I had offended some people, but those who knew me saw no reason to take offense. So my big mouth got me in trouble once again; what else was new?

The implied criticisms of the FBI on the Gotti acquittals were bad enough, but I would get madder still a few months later when Bob Morgenthau and Mike Cherkasky would go public with accusations that we had sat on evidence of jury tampering in the Gotti trial for the assault of John O'Connor. Jim Fox had promised Morgenthau that he would be told immediately about any evidence we had that Gotti or one of his pals had tried to reach a juror. We had a Title III in the Ravenite, and it was true that we had Gotti on tape talking about trying to get to one of the jurors in his case.

That was light-years from succeeding, however.

Bruce Mouw, George Gabriel, and I had gone over the tape from the Ravenite endlessly, but the only way you could interpret what Gotti was saying on the tape was that the wise guys should *try* to figure a way to get to a juror. I told Bruce to monitor this situation closely, and he and his squad did just that. But as hard as we looked, at no time did we develop the first shred of hard evidence that the wise guys had actually gotten to a juror.

The evidence just wasn't there.

Not telling Morgenthau's office was my decision and mine alone. I wasn't about to compromise our investigation of the boss of the Gambino family simply to provide the prosecution in the O'Connor trial with an excuse for losing a case that never should have been brought. When Morgenthau and Cherkasky went public, however, I decided to keep my mouth shut. As it turned out, I would be vindicated more than a year later when John Gotti's underboss, Sammy Gravano, agreed to cooperate with the FBI and testify as a witness for the prosecution against his old boss. One of the first questions Bruce Mouw and George Gabriel asked Sammy the Bull was about bribing a juror in the second Gotti case. Sammy the Bull said that the wise guys had bribed a juror in the Giacalone case and in another trial of a Gambino family capo. But they had never gotten to any juror in the trial where John Gotti was acquitted of the assault on John O'Connor. Of that, Sammy the Bull said, he was certain.

As for John Gotti, I didn't know what he thought about my quote in the *Times* predicting his future incarceration, and I didn't care. That guy's days were numbered.

My own days were numbered, too, at least as far as the FBI was concerned. In some strange way, the Gotti investigation had begun to make me think about retirement. I was reasonably young and in good health, so those things had nothing to do with the decision. I had been in the Bureau more than twenty-two years, but the length of service had very little to do with it, either.

As I have tried to explain, I had neither fondness nor respect for the old-time mob bosses, guys like Paul Castellano and Fat Tony Salerno. They were scum. But somehow the Gottis coming up behind them were even scummier. Even that, however, had little to do with my decision to leave.

What it was, I think, was that the internal battles within the FBI were over. Oh, the genius inspectors still came around, sure. Looking for trouble, snooping into things, causing a lot of headaches. I had bounced a couple of them out of my office just a few months earlier. They had made the mistake of asking some stupid questions about what Squad C-16 was up to. C-16 was Bruce Mouw's squad. It was made up of agents like George Gabriel, people who had been breaking their picks on the rock of the Gambino family for more than five years. That was no answer for an inspector, of course. Those guys wanted to know things like why the Ravenite investigation was taking so long, what its precise objectives were. And so on and so forth. I had those two clowns from the Inspection Division on the shuttle back to Washington before they knew what time it was.

So we still had those kinds of things, frustrating things. But they were annoyances now, that's all. They weren't the kind of thing that could stop a dedicated special agent anymore. Because the FBI had changed.

The good guys had won.

One consequence of that fact, however, was that the challenges of the job were no longer there for me the way they once were. We had new challenges all the time, of course—in dealing with the Asian organized-crime gangs that had begun deluging New York and other parts of the country with illegal drugs. With the blessings of Bill Doran and Jim Fox, I had established several squads in our organized-crime section to target the Asian gangs. But seeing that program through the way we had tackled the Italian Mafia would take years. It was a job for the next generation. For the Brian Taylors, the Lou Schiliros, the George Gabriels, the Dick Rudolphs.

My time was beginning to pass, and it is one of the many blessings of my life that I saw that fact clearly and without regret. Looking back, I had accomplished more than I had ever thought possible. but I had also paid a price for the way I had gone about the job. My "New York first, fuck you" attitude had definitely not gone down well at Headquarters. I loved the FBI, but the truth was, my ways were often not the FBI's ways. They had not sat well with the brass, and I was already being advised by Washington that I was going to be promoted. That would mean leaving New York and the work still to be done there. Promotions—that's the way the bureaucracy handled things when they wanted to get someone out of the way.

So it was time to go.

I talked it over with Linda. Then I had a few conversations with the appropriate people at Headquarters and put in my papers. I would be out in a few months.

I had a few more months to get Gotti.

The more I heard from Gotti's own mouth, the less I liked the guy. Not that there was much to like to begin with.

There was the Gotti who tried to tamper with witnesses and jurors, for instance, and who tried to spy on our grand-jury proceedings. That we definitely didn't like.

We had Gotti in one conversation with one of his lawyers, a sleazeball named Mike Coiro who would later do some heavy jail time of his own. Coiro had a source Gotti was very interested in because the guy had a line into a number of criminal investigations, and Gotti was expecting to be arrested once again.

Gotti summoned Coiro to the Ravenite, and the two repaired immediately to the apartment upstairs.

Gotti wasted no time telling Coiro what was on his mind.

"Mike, I've been told by a source that a pinch is coming down. A joint pinch, state and federal. . . . Now what you gotta do is you gotta grab this guy of yours, and you gotta tell him, 'Look, give us the motherfuckin' names.' You know, Mike, we've been good to this guy in the past. And we're gonna be good to him in the future. Just give us the names. I never asked you once who this guy is. Did I ever ask you once?"

"Never."

"Give us the fuckin' names, and I won't. I give you my word. . . . Just give us the names."

"You got it."

"I'm not going nowhere, okay? I'm not sayin' nobody else is going nowhere. But *I'm* not going nowhere. . . . Because you know why, Mike? Because if I'm away—if we're *all* away . . ."

"Then we're all in trouble."

"Listen!"

"I'll go see him tomorrow, you got it, John."

Legally, what this was known as was infiltration of federal law enforcement, a variety of obstruction of justice. We didn't take kindly to any varieties of that particular charge.

Then there was the John Gotti that was just plain greedy. We got another conversation from the Ravenite, Gotti pouring his heart out to his dear friend Frankie Locascio.

"You know, Frankie, I don't like you; I love you. And I don't like Sammy; I love him. As far as this life, no one knows it better than me. But if a guy offends me, I'll break him, and that's the fuckin' end of it. It's not for me, though; it's for this thing of ours —the Cosa Nostra. But it's gotten to be a circus, and I'm not goin' to leave a circus when I go to jail."

Frankie Loc grunted.

"But with Sammy, every time I turn around there's a new company popping up." Sammy the Bull was a big source of *agita* for Gotti. Sammy was getting rich, Gotti complained, while *he* had to carry the weight of the entire family on his back.

Frankie Loc grunted again.

"Every time we got a partner that don't agree with us, [Sammy says,] 'Kill 'em!' So he goes to the boss [Gotti], the boss says okay, and he kills them. He okays it. Says it's all right, good. But where are we going here, Frankie? Who the fuck are we? What do I get out of this here? Better not become a clown—but where am I going? What do I do with the rest of the family—throw 'em in the fuckin' street? The rest of the family! What am I gonna do with this family, huh? We got twenty-two *capodecinas*—twenty-two capos; I got *twenty-five* coming to beef to me. So what do I do here, Frankie? I got guys beefin' at me every fuckin' hour every day. What do I get outta this fuckin' shit? . . . This is bull-shit."

Frankie Loc grunted a third time.

The Teflon Don sighed. "Where are we going here, Frankie? Where are we going?"

Gotti was a killer, too. We knew that, but it was nice having the evidence from his own mouth, on our tape recorders. Sammy the Bull had told Gotti one day that a Gambino family member named Louie Melito had gone "subversive." If you consult Denis Maduro's wise-guy dictionary, "going subversive" was wise guy–speak for talking about someone else in the family—particularly the boss—behind his back. On Sammy the Bull's word alone, Gotti ordered Louie Melito murdered. "[Louie] didn't rob noth-ing," Gotti said. "He died because he refused to come in when I called. He didn't do nothing else wrong."

Killing for Gotti was all in a day's work. A few months earlier, a New Jersey wise guy named Corky Vastola was convicted on racketeering-conspiracy charges arising from his operation of a lucrative narcotics business. That was too bad for Corky, but after he was sentenced to eighty years of hard federal time, Gotti and a few other wise guys were convinced Corky was going to start singing to the FBI and elaborating on the hundreds of hours of Title III recordings they had made—recordings that potentially could implicate not just the five Mafia families in New York, but families all over the country.

Conclusion: Poor Corky had to go.

Once again, we recorded the conversation in the upstairs apartment of the Ravenite. Gotti was there, along with Sammy Gravano and Frankie Loc. John D'Amato, the boss of New Jer-sey's Decavalcante organized-crime family arrived mintutes later.

Gotti got right down to business.

"Johnny, I tell ya, this cocksucker, he deserves to go."

D'Amato agreed, reluctantly. "He says he can't do ten days; he can't do ten seconds."

"Not only that, Johnny. But if you think the guy is weak, that he's a rat, you're jeopardizing a whole *borgata*—a whole family, a whole Cosa Nostra for this guy. . . . If I know a guy's weak and I let him go running around on the street and he gets *you* locked up, I'm a fucking rat, too. And let me tell you, I was in the can with this guy. You're asking how he does time? I'll tell you: The worst I ever saw in my life."

"Definitely, definitely."

"Well, listen, I don't know if he's a rat now. But is he gonna be a rat someday? Yeah, he is."

"Yeah, that's the way I feel about him. That's the way I feel about him, John, so who should I go see?"

"You came here, okay, you know what I'm saying? If we cut a deal, well, we'll do it, and that's the end of it, ya know?"

"That's the way I am."

"That's why we gotta do things like this." Gotti paused. "And then we'll never hear those motherfucking tapes again!"

What a nice man.

One month after John Gotti was acquitted of the attempted murder of John O'Connor, I was summoned to a meeting in Bill Doran's office on the twenty-eighth floor of the Javits Building. It was another turf meeting. The subject—surprise—was Gotti.

Present and accounted for along either side of Doran's polished conference table were Andy Maloney and Otto Obermaier. Otto had taken Rudy Giuliani's place when Rudy decided to make his first try for the New York mayor's job. I respected Obermaier, but I felt that some of the esprit de corps that had animated the prosecutors in the office when Rudy was there had somehow dissipated under his successor.

The other two people already seated at the table were among my closest friends in this life. First was Barbara Jones; enough said. Sitting across from her was Louie Freeh. Louie's star had risen amazingly fast, from FBI special agent to Assistant U.S. Attorney. Louie was now chief of the organized-crime unit in the U.S. Attorney's Office for the Southern District of New York. Even that, though, was just a way station to a much higher road for Louie: Within just a few years, Louie Freeh would go on to become a U.S. District Court judge in Manhattan and, eventually, the director of the entire FBI—perhaps the best FBI director the Bureau has ever had.

But to the business at hand: For the past few weeks, Bruce Mouw and George Gabriel had been busy reviewing all the Title III evidence we had been taking out of the Ravenite club hallway and the third-floor apartment over the many months our little recorders had been in there. With Carmine Russo, another superb and dedicated agent on the squad, Bruce and George had been working with prosecutors Len Michaels and Laura Ward to tie the whole case together in a nice pretty package. The meeting in Doran's office was to decide who got to open the damned thing.

Believe it or not, Gotti had gotten so big in the minds of his pursuers that it was clear we would never decide the details of his prosecution at my level, or even at Bill Doran's; the thing would have to get kicked down to Washington. Which is precisely what happened. Eventually, Washington sent the case to Brooklyn, to Andy Maloney's Eastern District.

By the last week of November 1990, we had finished presenting all of our evidence on the Gambino family of the Cosa Nostra, John Gotti as boss. The grand jury had already voted to indict, and the indictment itself had been printed. We were ready to go.

The only thing was, Sammy "the Bull" Gravano had disappeared, and we had Gotti on tape talking about how Sammy—despite Gotti's constant complaining about him—would run the family for Gotti if and when he were jailed again.

We obviously didn't want that to happen. This was precisely the point of a strategic investigation, of doing it right. Bruce and his guys hadn't worked all those years just to put a thug like

Gotti in jail, only to have another thug like Sammy the Bull take his place. The point was to cripple the family, and that meant taking the entire leadership out, preferably in one fell swoop. So we would wait to indict and arrest until we could find and collar Sammy the Bull.

At least that's what I thought.

My retirement from the FBI was scheduled to take effect on November 30. Already, I had begun to savor the chance to spend more time with Linda and the kids. Ask any parent worth his salt if it's a cliché that childhoods fly by like strange birds on gossamer wings. You'll get a look, I guarantee you, like you're some kind of nut: Sure they do! Maria and Joe were nearly grown now; I wanted the chance to spend time with them before they were gone and completely out on their own.

Against these kinds of considerations, the timing of the arrest of a John Gotti, whether it came before or after I was gone from the Bureau, just didn't matter. And that's exactly what I told Bruce Mouw when he called me as I was packing up the odds and ends in my desk and dumping them into boxes.

"I just spoke to Fox and Doran, Jules, and they want to indict now so we can make the arrest before you leave."

I couldn't believe it. It was a touching thing, really, especially coming from guys as tough and unsentimental as Fox and Doran. For Bruce Mouw, though, whose life for the past five years had been consumed by the Gambino family investigation, it was a supremely generous gesture.

I wasn't buying it, though. "Listen, pal."

"Yeah, boss?" On the other end of the line, Bruce already was starting to chuckle quietly.

"Listen, I didn't put in all this fucking time just so we could do this thing half-assed right here at the end."

Bruce was laughing out loud now, but I kept on.

"What the hell's the difference if I'm here or not, Bruce? Goddammit, what's important, man, is that we do the right thing the right way. So let's just wait until we've got Sammy the Bull and can bring him in, okay?"

"Sure, Jules, whatever you say."

"Okay. Now what's so goddamned funny?"

"Nothing, it's just that I knew that's exactly what you were going to say before you said it."

It was my turn to laugh. "Well, let's just not screw it up at the end now, huh? Let's just wait."

"Right, boss. Good luck. And thanks."

On December 11, 1990, the entire hierarchy of the Gambino family of the Cosa Nostra was indicted and arrested. Among others, the arrestees included John Gotti, Sammy "the Bull" Gravano, Frankie Locascio, and Tommy Gambino. I was in the eleventh day of my retirement from the FBI at the time the arrests took place. The arrests dominated the evening newscasts.

I watched on my TV set at home.

Epilogue

THERE is little, it seems, that lasts. These days especially one has that sense.

And yet as I look both back and forward now—back at nearly a quarter century I spent in the FBI, forward to the challenges awaiting America and American law enforcement in the next century—it is hard not to be heartened.

Optimism is not fashionable these days, I know. But the heart grasps for hope, and I am inclined to indulge it. Everyone ponders the world from his own perch, and I suppose that's the best one can do. From my perch today, narrow though it may be, I think things look pretty good. Yes, crime is a terrible problem. And drugs still ruin too many lives.

Those are facts. But the facts have little to do with America's currently overheated debate about crime and criminals. Crime —a matter of fact—is down these past few years. Granted, Americans are too victimized by crime and violence—no question. But how to think about solutions?

In its own way, this book is about crime and criminals. But it is more, I hope, about solutions, which is why I am inclined to indulge my heart in its heady lurch toward hope. There was a time, as I have written, when I nearly left the FBI; luck, along with family and friends, prevented that leaving.

Friends—not luck or family—impel me now.

We were, as I look back on it, a band of revolutionaries in a place where revolution was regarded as a high crime. We were few in number and angry in spirit. Neither numbers nor spirit explained why we prevailed, however; perhaps it was that the old organization was tired.

The Hoover system had seen its day.

I think it was a lot of things; that's the way the world works. Whatever it was, though, the old days are past. As I write this, my friend Louie Freeh is sitting in the director's chair at our ugly Headquarters building on Pennsylvania Avenue. The scrawny little kid from Newark who wanted one thing and one thing only in life—to be a G-man—is today responsible for directing the world's preeminent law-enforcement agency and for guiding it into the next century.

Ask why I am hopeful? Louie Freeh is my short answer.

In Louie, America has a public servant of the type that has for too long seemed more storybook than real. Louie Freeh is plainspoken, hard driving, honest—I could pile up the adjectives, but I will leave it at this: Louie is a good cop. A tough cop. A very smart cop.

America is in very good hands.

Want the long answer about why I am hopeful?

Look below Louie. Directing the FBI's New York field office today, sitting in Neil Welch's old chair, is Jim Kallstrom, oldest and dearest of friends. With his emphasis on smart new technologies, his intolerance of anything less than perfection, his fierce loyalty to the men and women who do the FBI's hard and dangerous work in the field, Kallstrom represents the very best of the new FBI. It is because of people like Kallstrom that I have confidence the FBI wil meet and beat the many daunting challenges facing its agents today and in the years to come.

And he's not alone. Below Kallstrom, running the Criminal Investigative Division in New York, is Lou Schiliro. Tough and unflappable, Lou will still wade into a wise-guy hangout like Big Tom DiDonato's, if that's what it takes. But the way he really makes life tough for the criminals preying on the people of New York is with his smarts. Lou will outthink them, outwait them, outfox them. He did it to Gotti. He's doing it now to the new bad guys out there trying to fill Gotti's shoes. The Kallstroms and Schiliros, they're the soul of the new FBI. They are the future of American law enforcement.

And they are not alone.

What started way back as an insurrection is today an accomplished fact. But no one is standing still. Years ago a few of us sought to plant a seed. The strategic approach toward fighting the world's most well organized criminals found hard ground in the soil of the old FBI. Eventually, however, it flourished. Today it flourishes not just in the FBI but in virtually every federal law enforcement agency in this country. U.S. Customs Service, the Drug Enforcement Administration—they have embraced the strategic approach once shunned by the FBI.

In his job as director of the FBI, and in a new role created for him by Attorney General Janet Reno, Louie Freeh today helps direct the investigative work not just of the Bureau but of several federal police agencies as well. In that capacity, Louie is seeing to it that those agencies, like the FBI, not be content with the status quo, that they not rest on past laurels.

But that's not all. Louie has already been to Russia and to Eastern Europe. There he has opened FBI offices in places once impossible to imagine. It is easy to talk about the post–Cold War world but more difficult to fathom.

Our people are already working there. The problems they confront there are real, they are large, and they will not go away. Neither will our people.

Thinking about these things, I am reminded so often and so vividly of Vietnam. There we were ill led, underprepared, assigned a mission with neither definition nor clear objective.

As a young special agent of the FBI, I was scared half to death by the parallels between the Bureau and my time in Southeast Asia; it seems a long time ago now.

Today, in a far different context, our leadership in American law enforcement is without parallel, our mission in no doubt. There are questions, to be sure, and no easy answers. But as I look to the future, I indulge my heart. Chekhov says it is at the beginnings and endings of stories that we are tempted most to lie. We have lied nowhere in this account, not in the beginning, middle, or end. What is told here is true.

It is the reason I have hope.